Truth and Storytelling

Truth and Storytelling

Scripting the Visual Narrative

Emily Edwards

Anthem Press
An imprint of Wimbledon Publishing Company
www.anthempress.com

This edition first published in UK and USA 2022
by ANTHEM PRESS
75–76 Blackfriars Road, London SE1 8HA, UK
or PO Box 9779, London SW19 7ZG, UK
and
244 Madison Ave #116, New York, NY 10016, USA

Copyright © Emily Edwards 2022

The author asserts the moral right to be identified as the author of this work.

Illustrations by Kaliyah Landrum

All rights reserved. Without limiting the rights under copyright reserved above,
no part of this publication may be reproduced, stored or introduced into
a retrieval system, or transmitted, in any form or by any means
(electronic, mechanical, photocopying, recording or otherwise),
without the prior written permission of both the copyright
owner and the above publisher of this book.

British Library Cataloguing-in-Publication Data
A catalogue record for this book is available from the British Library.

Library of Congress Control Number: 2021953408

ISBN-13: 978-1-78527-307-0 (Hbk)
ISBN-10: 1-78527-307-8 (Hbk)
ISBN-13: 978-1-78527-310-0 (Pbk)
ISBN-10: 1-78527-310-8 (Pbk)

Cover image: Illustrated by Kaliyah Landrum

This title is also available as an e-book.

CONTENTS

List of Illustrations   vii

1. Truth and the Search for Story   1
2. Creating Authentic Characters   29
3. The Shapes of Visual Narrative   59
4. The Structures of Time and Perspective   77
5. Outlines and the Spines of Stories   101
6. The Truths of Style and Format   121
7. Guarded Dialogue and Candid Silence   149
8. The Scene and the Story   175
9. Honest Revisions   197

Index   221

ILLUSTRATIONS

Figures

1.1a–1.1d	Ellen and the gator in convenience store	14
1.2a–1.2d	Ellen and the rotag in the retail utility	17
2.1a–2.1d	Introduction of Jaz	49
4.1	A nonlinear hero's journey	81
5.1	Hot mess	115
6.1a–6.1c	Police are in the hall	139

Tables

1.1	Classic Stories with New Genre and Setting	11
4.1	News Story Structure	79
4.2	Structure of a Television Episode: *The Big Bang Theory*	84
4.3	A Nonlinear Multi-Story Structure: Pulp Fiction	88

Chapter 1

TRUTH AND THE SEARCH FOR STORY

Fiction is obliged to stick to possibilities. Truth isn't.

—Mark Twain
The Story and the Lie

When I was a small child, I could go outside to play, but I was not allowed to leave the yard without permission. One day I did. My boredom with the tedious familiarity of my own backyard lured me into the noisier yard of neighbors who had a little boy about my age. Wade was an imaginative child with heroic ambitions. We tended to lead each other astray. On that particular day, the warm air of late spring made us both restless. We quickly tired of his yard and wandered into the carefully terraced and landscaped yard of an older, childless neighbor. This neighbor had superb gardens, where he cultivated vegetables and flowers in careful beds labeled with quaint wooden markers. Here was the marvel of butterflies on the hunt, the ripe smells of recently mowed grass, and the spectacle of pollen floating in the afternoon sunlight like fairy dust. Wade and I learned that if we pulled out our neighbor's garden markers, the end that had been stuck in the ground was pointed, like a sword or a wizard's wand. We proceeded to trample about in our neighbor's garden, pulling up markers and having sword fights or wizards' duels, and a fair number of other fantastical adventures. As the day crept closer to dusk, I realized we should probably go home, but the charms of the game made us linger. The decision was settled for us when we heard our neighbor's car, returning from wherever he'd been all afternoon. We fled the scene of our destruction to our respective houses. When I got home, my mother confronted me.

"Did you leave the yard without permission?"
"No."
"Are you telling me a story?"
"No."

My first response was a flat-out lie, but my mother never accused me of lying. Instead, she would accuse me of telling a "story," which was her euphemism for a lie. But I had not actually shared a story with my mother, so there was some truth in declaring that I hadn't told one. A story in which mischievous fairies had tricked me into our neighbor's yard would have been closer to truth than the one word lie I told her in a hope of escaping punishment. If I had told her a story, it would have had an explosive beginning, a furious middle with challenges and magical setbacks, and a gloriously triumphant ending, as Wade and I escaped this enchantment and found our way back to the safety of home. That would have been a story. My mother would have recognized it as a story, though one tainted with the underlying effort to distract her from the facts of my disobedience and the destruction of our neighbor's garden. Mischievous fairies didn't haunt our neighborhood or hold ill-behaved children captive. The reason such a story would have been closer to the truth than my simple one-word denial is that a story would have more closely revealed our glorious emotional and imaginary circumstances when Wade and I journeyed into our elderly neighbor's yard looking for magical adventure.

Story is not synonymous with lie, which is a deliberate departure from fact in the effort to mislead. Stories are human creations that might guide us to a better understanding of events and motivations, inching us closer to a truth. Awkwardly composed and inauthentic stories make the world more confusing as do narratives that purposefully manipulate, distort, or hide human motivations. Because people must choose how to explain the world they experience, all the narratives people tell are fabrications. Some are more authentic than others.

Authenticity is what individual writers bring to original work when they encounter and react to life, observing, absorbing, and reflecting from an inward journey to bring that new story into being. That is the goal of creating authentic narratives, offering an audience the gift of a story that will engage, inform, and inspire. In this effort, there is nothing more practical for a writer than knowing who you are, what you believe, and the ideas you respect. Understanding the motivations for storytelling is as important as the substance and form a story takes.

Several years ago, the Academy of Television Arts and Sciences invited me to a faculty seminar, where the Academy actively promoted their internship program. These highly sought-after internships included many opportunities for writers. I remember asking one of the professional hosts what he personally looked for in the student scripts submitted to him. This was a person actively involved with the evaluation of scripted program ideas, purchase of literary material, the selection of writers, and the oversight of script development for professional production. His answer was rather smug.

"Authenticity," he told me. "I am always looking for authenticity."

He wasn't forthcoming about how he defined his ideas about authenticity. He just knew what that was when he saw it. He also knew he wanted something that was different, not "cookie cutter."

Our discussion in this book deals with the creation of "authentic fictions." Fiction is a form of story created at least in part from imagination. Sometimes the places, characters, and events in fiction seem realistic. The situations seem possible. Characters behave the way we expect real people to behave. While real people and events can inspire a fictional story, authors will use imagination and their own perspectives to fill in the gaps between facts to make those facts come alive with emotion and purposeful action, weeding out facts that may be true but are less relevant, distracting, dull, or unnecessary to the story's purpose. But fiction need not be realistic to be authentic.

Other fiction may seem completely outlandish. It is a fact that Dr. Seuss was a real man named Theodor Seuss Geisel, but the children's books Geisel wrote were bizarre rhyming fictions accompanied by wildly colorful illustrations. Dr. Seuss's fictions take place in imaginary worlds exploding with impossible characters and events. The character of *The Cat in the Hat* (1957) is the title character from one of Dr. Seuss's more well-known stories. It is certainly not a fact that a talking cat wearing a tall red and white striped hat and a red bow tie will appear to bored children. Yet, underneath that fictional story and its flamboyant characters is an elemental truth about the restlessness of unsupervised children yearning for adventure but stuck inside the house on a cold, rainy day. It is a truth that anyone who has experienced boredom can understand. It was a truth Wade and I experienced on our visit to our neighbor's garden. Unlike Geisel's children, Wade and I didn't have a moralizing pet goldfish nagging us to behave or a miraculous machine that would clean up after us, setting our neighbor's tangled garden right again and hiding our disobedience from our mothers. However, when I finally encountered *The Cat in the Hat* as part of my first-grade reading, I immediately recognized the truth about boredom in the story, even if my younger self didn't catch the minstrel show references or racist suggestions (Sawchuck, 2017).

The emphasis of this book is on crafting fictional scripts for a screen. Many elements of the moving image story are shared with other narrative forms such as graphic novels, dramatic plays, and narratives written as text like novels and short stories. Most types of fictional storytelling have similar ideas about characters, conflict, and action. People create fictions to entertain themselves and other people. Like games of pretend, fictions are fun. Our imaginations get swept away in the creativity of other people as well as our own innovations. But audiences also look to stories to help them create meaning, to reveal at least some part of the truth about the events, feelings, and characters they encounter in life. Fiction lets us understand what it might be like to live in another time or place or what it might feel like to be a different person from the one we are. Fiction helps us to develop empathy. It permits us to dream. Fiction allows us to imaginatively experience the multiverse.

This is a book about finding story, discovering protagonists, shaping stories, scripting stories, the discoveries of revision, and fully connecting to each part of that process. This book will not reveal insider tips for breaking into Hollywood inner circles or a secret formula guaranteed for commercial success. It would be inauthentic and wrong to make such a promise. Neither can this book promise to bestow upon writers the discipline it takes to develop ideas into a professional piece of writing. That discipline comes from within an individual dedicated to the work. What this book will do is help those dedicated writers develop fictional stories into scripts intended for the screen.

The Relevance of Fiction

When the coronavirus pandemic began to close businesses across the globe early in 2020 and sent citizens everywhere to shelter at home, we wondered how our creative culture would survive the isolation. Traditional commercial media industries like those labeled 'Hollywood' are big, powerful infrastructures that include manufacturing and hospitality. As with other manufacturing industries, the virus disrupted the entire line of work on narrative products, from proposal to production to distribution. Producers weren't listening to pitches. Studios halted productions. Directors, cinematographers, actors, entire crews went home. Like bars and restaurants in the hospitality industry, local movie theaters closed, and more than forty thousand employees went on furlough (Chappell, 2020). In the spring of 2020, I was teaching a writing class when my university closed its physical spaces and put classes online. Students left the dorms for their parents' homes or scrambled to find other places to live. A few were temporarily homeless. When I finally reconnected with my students in a virtual classroom, the ones who were able to join me in the digital workshop seemed grateful to be there. The lockdown was lonely. The online space was a place to talk, and table read each other's scripts. We joked that we were like the storytellers in Giovanni Boccaccio's *Decameron* (1353), escaping our twenty-first-century version of the plague by reading aloud original screenplays.

One student observed that multiple cable channels were binge-programming fantasy or action-adventure series and she noticed that she felt compelled to watch these movies even though she had seen them already. She decided that she was drawn to watch these stories over and over again because it was comforting to escape into fantastical worlds where good characters would ultimately triumph over powerful but frightened leaders who wanted to crush any opposition or difference with the formidable power of authoritarian magic. The films provided an escape, but they also seemed relevant to what she was feeling. While in lockdown, many of us were binging on television and streaming videos, reading books, and playing video games. Story had become vitally important. When the larger social environment is stressed with war, domestic terrorism, or a pandemic, those entertainments that divert, inspire, and fortify audiences become crucial. The virus showed us how vulnerable some storytelling systems are and how these systems needed to adapt to survive. Production companies would need to find ways to keep a cast and crew protected before they could go back to work. Some theaters across the county closed permanently, but those that didn't needed to find ways to operate safely so they could reopen and endure as a vital part of the cultural landscape. Audiences will always need narrative escapes, excitement, nurture, and awakening, even if it means writers must adapt to different technologies, new production methods, and perhaps different delivery systems for sharing those stories.

I encountered some writers who wondered if their voices and experiences could have any meaning in a global crisis. How could their poems, novels, screenplays, or games possibly contribute anything substantial when the entire world was suffering? It was one thing to write a rollicking adventure story when the world was less chaotic, but when schools, bars, and businesses closed, when sick people overcrowded hospital emergency rooms and the death toll rose at an alarming rate, some considered it to be trivial if not irresponsible to imagine a protagonist on a thrilling quest.

"It's ridiculous to even think about," one young writer lamented. "We can't even travel outside the country; it's foolish to write about a hero who can. Soderbergh already put out a movie about a pandemic. *Contagion* back in 2011. What else is there now?"

It's worth noting that the fourteenth-century storytellers attempting to hide from the Black Death weren't telling each other stories about contagion but stories dealing with human failings, romance, and ambition. These were stories about the human condition that would still be relevant when the plague was over. Rather than eliminate stories or making them irrelevant, the virus added new tensions to narrative. The coronavirus pandemic uncovered much about human nature some of us were oblivious to before we scrambled into quarantine. Writers examining these truths do not need to set them inside a pandemic or any other disaster for the stories to have relevance. The human need to understand human problems makes our stories relevant. Stories are vital to the human spirit especially when it feels threatened. The relevance of writing is making a cultural contribution through a narrative that connects people dealing with the ordinary struggles of life as well as its extraordinary challenges.

The impulse to tell a story begins inside an individual with preverbal tensions, the internal pressures to connect culturally (Johnson, 1975). The source of this tension may be intrapersonal, or what happens inside the mind of an individual, or the tension may come from external pressure such as the demands of a job or a creative partner. What the story will be about, the shape it will take, and what the story will mean may not even be clear at this stage. To usher a preverbal tension toward the beginnings of visual narrative, writers will look for a concept that can inspire their stories and allow their voices to grow.

Finding Concepts: The Logline

Every project begins with finding and committing to a concept. Some writers begin by developing a conceptual premise as a logline that describes the potential script. A logline is a short, one or two sentence description of the story's essence. Because it reveals the protagonist and basic dilemma, a logline can provide direction for writers, helping to keep the crucial elements of a story central to the writing process. Internet "logline generators" essentially spin a protagonist with a situation and a conflict to create a sentence that might inspire story potential. The generator might also ask authors to fill in fields for an antagonist, a theme, and a genre.

The logline is both a useful device for writers to think about the essentials behind a developing story as well as the hook that will eventually lure producers to consider the production of a finished script. In a character-driven story, the focus of a logline is often on the leading characters and their relationships. In a plot-driven story, the focus is on the circumstances or events that drive characters into action. For example, one logline that describes the story of both the 1998 Disney animated version of the film *Mulan* and the 2020 live action adaptation emphasizes the protagonist and her situation: "When the Emperor drafts a man from every family to serve as a soldier in his army, a young Chinese maiden becomes a warrior to substitute for her ailing father." The logline for *Mulan* tells us that the protagonist is a young woman in a culture where women are not warriors; however, the protagonist has no option but to pretend to be a man and become a soldier to spare her aging father from battle. *Mulan* is based on an ancient Chinese poem about a legendary young woman who disguises herself as a man to replace her frail father when he is once again conscripted to serve in the army. Mulan has no brothers and the emperor's decree is that one man from each family must serve. People interested in learning the details of Mulan's struggle and whether she is successful in her deception would be drawn to this story. Loglines are useful at the front end of script creation to motivate story possibilities with a clear direction.

Loglines are also important to advertisers for creating the promotional campaigns that will tempt audiences to the finished film. The advertising *tags* or *taglines* for *Mulan* are less specific than the logline. "The flower that blooms in adversity is the most rare and beautiful of all," or "This time the princess saves the prince." Because these taglines don't reveal a protagonist and a clearly defined struggle, they are less useful as a guide for the initial writing of a script.

During the writing process it is possible that characters and conflicts might develop in unanticipated directions, so a logline originally created as a writing guide may not be the same one ultimately sent to potential producers. Sometimes developments or conflicts emerge that seem better than those in the original idea. However, using the original logline as a reference, a writer can decide if a shift in direction is a better route to a more compelling story. This ability to see the essence of stories at the beginning of a project can serve writers whether they are crafting a script, a videogame, or even a novel. For a screenplay or television series, the premise of the story should be so clear in the descriptive logline that potential producers will be intrigued to read the script and perhaps invest in its production.

The Influence of Genre on Story

One way to think about story is to consider genre or recognizable patterns in story elements such as plots, atmospheres, and characters. Genres operate under cultural consensus. The word "genre" means category. Genre is a way of assigning order to narrative by style, form, or subject matter. A story's genre includes those patterns audiences recognize and use to make predictions about the direction, contents, and tone of a narrative. A genre can indicate a visual style of production (such as a *film noir*), a type of production technique (such as animation), an expectation of setting (such as the American Western), or the plot expectations for stories of romance, horror, action-adventure, or science fiction. Deciding to write a story in the classic action-adventure genre suggests a story involving a heroic protagonist in a courageous struggle that involves high energy and intense physical exploits to reach some important goal. Such a story is less about a character's inner motivations and more about the character's measurable accomplishments toward that goal.

The 1998 version of *Mulan* is an animation combining elements of the action-adventure with the musical. Cartoon characters include a talking dragon, a cricket, and an anthropomorphic horse who help the animated Mulan in her mission to become a warrior. In its musical elements, the lyrics of songs move the plot forward or reveal the moods of characters. The song, "I'll Make A Man Out of You" reveals both Captain Li Shang's belief that "real men" are tough, capable fighters as well as his determination to turn incompetent recruits or "boys" into skilled soldiers. The visuals accompanying the song advance the plot, showing how Mulan survives her bootcamp training, fools her fellow recruits into thinking she is a man, and proves to be the best of them even though audiences know she is a young girl.

Categorizing by genre is a way to predict certain story elements. Considering audience expectations for classic stories with a fresh approach and unexpected genre is one way to inspire new stories. Dangers of using genre this way come with clinging too closely to the pattern or playing with form and audience expectations in gimmicky ways.

Reimagining Classics, Myths, Epic Poems, and Fairytales

Some writing professionals recommend borrowing ideas from classic stories, myths, fairytales, and folklore and then reworking the narratives to give them new life. The work of Gregory Maguire's novel, *Wicked: The Life and Times of the Wicked Witch* (1996) draws inspiration from the classic work of L. Frank Baum's children's novel *The Wonderful Wizard of Oz* (1900), which also inspired a musical fantasy film *The Wizard of Oz* (1939) directed by Victor Fleming. Baum's children's fantasy additionally inspired a Broadway musical *The Wiz* (1975), which was adapted into a movie in 1977, starring Michael Jackson, Diana Ross, Nipsey Russell, and Lena Horne. Additional remakes or adaptations include *Return to Oz* (1985), *The Muppet's Wizard of Oz* (2005), *Dorothy and the Witches of Oz* (2012), *Oz the Great and Powerful* (2013), and *Ozland* (2014), among others. The point here is that rich ideas, like fertile soil, produce much fruit. Creative people can use older themes and ideas to generate original works of art, taking story ideas from the classics and putting them in a new genre with a different protagonist, and another setting to reveal fresh tensions or concerns that were not part of the original story.

In a textbook on crafting the short script, Pat Cooper and Ken Dancyger recommend adapting fairy tales into screenplays for exercising the creative muscle (2005). I'm going to suggest a similar creative exercise that uses well-known stories more for general inspiration than a strict adaptation. The columns in Table 1.1 list a classic story, myth, fairy tale, or epic poem in the first column, a genre in the next column, and a situation or setting in the third. Applying a new genre and situation to a classic story can help writers think about an old story and familiar protagonists in new ways. A shuffle of these elements can help to create original loglines. For example, "The Tortoise and the Hare" might become a "Romance" set in a "Mental Hospital." Keep or remove elements from the original story or myth as you like. Be inventive. In a remix of "The Tortoise and the Hare," the two lovers who discover each other might be a patient in a recovery program for amphetamine or speed addiction (the hare) and another patient, who has been involuntarily admitted for crippling depression (the tortoise). The original folklore suggests that the tortoise and hare are in competition. The hare assumes he will win any race with the tortoise because he is so much faster, running circles around the plodding tortoise. The hare decides to take a little nap, while the tortoise persists with the race in a slow and steady fashion and ultimately wins. Changing the genre to a romance could make the tortoise and hare lovers but does not prevent them from also being competitors. In many romantic comedies, lovers begin the story as competitors, at odds, or at least distrustful of each other. In our tortoise and hare inspiration, the tension might be increased if a family member or a person on the hospital staff manipulates the recovering addict and the love affair for nefarious reasons, such as helping certain family members keep the depressed patient institutionalized until after some financial decision is settled. A logline for such a story might be, "After a lonely patient finally discovers love in the psychiatric ward, the race is on to get discharged before her fortune is stolen."

Examine the myths or classic stories for the underlying "truth" the original narrative wants to tell. Maybe you disagree with the original moral of the story or see something unique or overlooked in the traditional version. Maybe the "truth" in the traditional version of a story is disappointing or wrong. Historical versions of *Snow White* show us a powerful Queen who uses her political clout and magical talent in a self-imposed beauty contest to protect her vanity and her title as the "fairest in all the land." Audiences never learn if the Queen has ambitions for her country and its people. Her only concern seems narrowly focused and paranoid. It is interesting that in the Disney adaptation, *Snow White and the Seven Dwarfs* (1937), the Queen uses her powerful magic to hide beneath a disguise of those things she hates and fears most: wizened old age and wretched poverty. In this more traditional version of the story, the Queen learns nothing from her self-inflicted experience with hardship and hideousness. She will be struck by lightning on a cliff and plunge to her death, no lesson learned. With the Queen reimagined as the protagonist with a difficult lesson to learn about goals and happiness, the story could have a different energy. The point of this exercise is to reinterpret a classical story from your own perspective of what is important. Ask the "what if" questions that could spin a familiar and perhaps disappointing story in a new direction. Once you've decided the important essence of the original story and what you want to change or emphasize, add the story to a genre and situation or setting to inspire other ways the story can have new life. Table 1.1 lists examples of classic stories, genres, and situations that can be combined and rearranged for inspiration.

"Adam and Eve" from column one, combined with the genre "Crime" from column two, and "Corporate Treachery" from column three, might result in the following title and logline.

Title: *Urgent Business*

Logline: Caught sharing corporate knowledge, a company insider is fired and publicly shamed but secretly vows to get revenge on all who tempted her, to expose and punish the real snake who stole her job.

Notice that the miraculous elements from the Biblical story are gone in this logline. It suggests a contemporary, realistic drama about corporate intrigue. Unlike Robert Crumb's graphic novel, *The Book of Genesis Illustrated by R. Crumb* (2009), which attempts to be a faithful, literal illustration of the stories in Genesis, *Urgent Business* suggests a radically different story from its biblical inspiration.

The difference between inspiration and adaptation is the difference between using an old story to motivate an original one and revising an old story but keeping the major elements of the story in place and recognizable. Crumb's work was a literal adaptation of the Biblical text into the visual form of sequential art. Crumb did not change a word (2009). In contrast, the corporate drama proposed in *Urgent Business* would focus on such things as insider trading, non-disclosure agreements, whistleblowing, blackmail, shareholders, the risks of an office romance, or other concerns of modern industry, instead of an exclusive garden, obedience to God, and a talking snake. If the logline was ever scripted and produced as a film, audiences for *Urgent Business* might not even recognize Genesis as the source of the story idea. In a similar way, the Polish television series, *Dekalog* (1989–90) is a modern exploration of the Ten Commandments. In each episode, characters living in a bleak housing project must face moral challenges loosely corresponding to the Ten Commandments.

In another example, the myth of Orpheus and Eurydice has inspired several screen adaptations such as *Orphée* (1950), *The Lyre of Orpheus* (2004), and *Orpheus* (2005). The mythical story is about a musician so skilled that his music could charm animals and make the trees dance. When a viper bites his wife Eurydice and she dies, Orpheus goes to the Underworld to find her, hoping to bring her home. He charms the god Hades with his music and Hades agrees to let Orpheus return with his wife to the world of the living. However, Orpheus was not allowed to look back at Eurydice until they had left the Underworld

Table 1.1 Classic Stories with New Genre and Setting

Classic Tale/myth	Genre	Setting/Situation
Tortoise and the Hare	Disaster	Corporate treachery
Little Red Riding Hood	Satire	Stem cell research
Theseus and the Minotaur	Urban fantasy	School dormitory
Little Lame Prince	Dark comedy	Child custody battle
Hansel and Gretel	Dystopia	National talent competition
The Boy Who Cried Wolf	Thriller	Border crossing
Town Mouse and Country Mouse	Science fiction	Mining camp
Orpheus and Eurydice	Gangster	Vacation cruise
The Story of Tam and Cam (Vietnamese fairy tale)	Buddy film	Deadly storm
Adam and Eve	Animation	Mountain climbing
Beowulf	Teen drama	Exotic rainforest
Peter Pan	Urban adventure	Extortion
The Fox and the Grapes	Murder mystery	Abandoned theme park
Pied Piper of Hamelin	Legal thriller	A new baby
Pegasus and Bellerophontes	Family drama	Animal shelter
Three Little Pigs	Crime	Funeral parlor
Ant and the Grasshopper	Steam punk	Music festival
Robin Hood	Tech noir	Evacuation
Othello	Comedy	Exclusive spa
Legend of Icraus	Magical realism	Marital infidelity
Rumpelstiltskin	Occult	College football
The Calabash Kids	Detective	Protest march
Epic of Sundiata	Musical	Arrested for possession
Beauty and the Beast	Horror	Contaminated water
Dr. Jekyll and Mr. Hyde	War	Mental hospital
The Ugly Duckling	Action	High school prom
Pygmalion and Galatea	Western	Deserted mall
Thumbelina	Romance	Vacation gone wrong
The Tinderbox	Fantasy	Suburban neighborhood
The Lion's Whisker	Court room drama	Mysterious tunnel
Hamlet	Children's comedy	Condemned house
The Little Red Hen	Futuristic drama	Struggling small town newspaper
Saat Bhai Champa	Science fantasy	Uncontrolled shapeshifting
The One-Handed Girl	Absurdist/surreal drama	Boot camp
The Bilko (African Myth)	Science fiction horror	Deer hunting
The Prince and the Pauper	Neo-noir	Political scandal
The Goose Girl	Bromantic comedy	Farmer's market
The Bremen Town Musicians	Social thriller	Extortion
Jack and the Bean Stalk	Kitchen sink realism	Housing project

and reached the surface. When Orpheus stepped through the opening of the cave that led to the Upper World, he could not resist the temptation to glance back and see if his beloved wife was following him. However, Eurydice had not yet set foot on the Upper World, so when Orpheus looked back at her, she vanished forever. *Black Orpheus* (1959) moves the story from Ancient Greece to Rio de Janeiro during a cornular street festival or Carnival but follows the plot of the Greek myth closely enough that the inspiration is obvious. It also helps that Marcel Camus used the original character names. A less obvious use of the myth might tell a futuristic, *Tech Noir* story about a popular beat musician performing at a large, international music festival, who discovers after his performance that his devoted backstage groupie has gone missing. The new story might look to the original for inspiration about characters and plot direction, but substitute imagined futuristic, high-tech experiences for mythological ones, layering the characters and their situations with different stresses and expectations. There are many myths, folklore, classic stories, situations, and genres that might be added to this list. Look for ones that speak to you. Examine the truth the original story wants to tell. Determine whether this original perspective fits comfortably with your thinking or rubs a blister. Explore how changing genre, situation, or protagonist might expand or enrich the story.

Ideas from Life Experience

Another way to generate ideas is to reconsider intense experiences from your own life. This might be a joyful event you would happily live over, a powerful incident that imprinted on your emotions, or perhaps a tragic occurrence that you would like to forget but can't. When did this happen? In what period of your life did this occur? What season? What time of day? Try to remember details about that day: where you were, who you were with, what you were doing, why you were doing it, what sensations you remember. What were other people doing? What were you thinking? What physical sensations (sounds, sights, smells, tastes, touch) did you experience? Write these down as you remember them: causes, effects, details. Personal experiences show us how people react to situations and what they say and do in moments of tension. These experiences bring authenticity to the development of stories. Everyone's experience has value, even moments we might dismiss as ordinary. Writers often become observers of their own lives, using personal experiences to inform their narratives. As with the use of fairy tales and classic stories, personal experiences do not have to be the verbatim account of an event applied to a script. Remembering how people react to a situation, your own motivations and responses will help predict what a fictional character might do.

Story Inspirations from News Accounts

Some writers look to real events or news stories for fictional ideas. Some events may not be enough material for crafting a full narrative but might offer useful ideas for revealing character or moving a larger plot forward. My personal collection of headlines from 2018 to 2019 includes stories about a man who brought an alligator into a convenience store while on a beer-run, a woman who knitted a skirt and jacket from plastic grocery bags, and a story about vandals breaking into a historic Dublin church and stealing the head of an 800-year-old mummy. Though these are all factual reports (some with videos or pictures), on their own they seem a bit thin. If I was going to write a larger story using the news item about the alligator in the convenience store, instead of making the inebriated man my protagonist, I might consider the gator in the convenience store a smaller incident in the life of another character. This protagonist might be a woman working in the Division of Law Enforcement at the Florida Fish and Wildlife Conservation Commission. I'll call her Ellen. Peculiar and funny stories involving alligators could be a recurring theme in Ellen's life, but not necessarily the main conflict. The smaller events contribute to the larger conflict between nature and humanity where my protagonist is caught in the middle. Because my parents and in-laws once lived in Florida, and because I have friends who currently live there, I have a healthy collection of bizarre alligator stories: six-foot gators on golf courses delaying the putt or stopping traffic as they lumber across a busy highway, pet dachshunds eaten, pools invaded, and swimmers chased from lakes during alligator mating season. I also have a decent understanding of the challenges, eccentricities, and frailties of a culture dependent on tourism, where livelihoods can be upended with a storm, an infestation, or a pandemic. Idiosyncratic events involving alligators might be the threads that connect the larger fabric of Ellen's story as a character who deeply loves the natural resources of her state, including its dangerous alligators. A guiding logline for developing this story might be: "A Florida Fish and Wildlife officer who dares to do her job might be punished if she succeeds."

Visualizing a Story Idea

The storyboard is a style of scripting in the form of illustrations that allow creators to better visualize a film, animation, commercial, or interactive media sequence. Though the storyboard is not a widespread conceptual tool for writers, I include the panels below in Figures 1.1a–1.1d to imagine a sequence where the protagonist goes inside a convenience store to confront a drunk man who is frightening other customers with an alligator.

Some film directors routinely have script sequences storyboarded prior to shooting. An animator like Hayao Miyazaki might use storyboarding instead

14   TRUTH AND STORYTELLING

EXT. CONVENIENCE STORE- NIGHT
An excited CUSTOMER runs from the convenience store as a car from the Florida's Fish and Wildlife Conservation Commission pulls into the parking lot.

CUSTOMER: There's a guy inside with a live alligator!
ELLEN: Stay here.

Figures 1.1a–1.1d Ellen and the gator in convenience store

TRUTH AND THE SEARCH FOR STORY   15

INT. CONVENIENCE STORE- NIGHT

ELLEN: What are you doing?

MAN: Me and Larry are on a beer run. This is Larry.

Figures 1.1a–1.1d (continued)

of a screenplay to visualize his entire film. Advertisers use storyboards to help their clients better understand the visual concept of their commercials. Unlike a comic, the sounds and dialogue are generally placed beside or underneath the image rather than in a balloon or speech bubble, unless the speech bubble is meant to literally appear on screen. Generally, the visuals of a storyboard won't be too cluttered with notes about sound effects or dialogue, but there are no hard or unbreakable rules about how a storyboard should look. If certain nonverbal aspects in the fame seem unclear, the storyboard may add additional verbal explanations outside the frame, arrows or other markings to suggest those movements and nonverbal elements.

Troubles with alligators might be a persistent theme in Ellen's life but red tide and algae blooms and the political battle over whether they are naturally occurring events or intensifying because of human pollution could inspire her larger story. Even though I have experience with South Florida and some of its issues, to authentically craft such a story, I would need to do more research to understand the larger truth, if that truth can be uncovered. Thinking about genre can help decide the direction and shape of this story. It might be an industrial crime drama with the protagonist as a reluctant detective caught between agricultural and tourist industries, or between scientists who want to better understand the dynamics of red tides and politicians who stop them from monitoring the water quality. If my research doesn't fully satisfy the story or there is too much about the situation that is still unknown, my story could shift to be more about Ellen's dilemmas as she is drawn into confrontations between Florida's people and its wilderness. The story could take the form of a troubled romance, *film noir*, or even a comedy. Choosing the genre would help to determine the tone of this story, but I would still want to do my research.

If I decided to depart from realism and take my story into the realm of science fiction or fantasy, I would likely strip the story of its recognizable South Florida culture, perhaps relocating it to a colonized planet in a future time. Alligators would become an imagined species native to this fictional planet, perhaps a species that colonists have attempted to eliminate because it is troublesome and dangerous. In a science fiction version, Ellen might have a similar job protecting the planet's natural resources from encroaching homesteaders, tourism, and aggressive agricultural industries. The tensions and truths might be the same ones I originally started with, but dressed in the conventions of science fiction, the ideological conflicts might be more acceptable and entertaining for audiences who need a distance between the facts of their lives and the truths in their stories. Research on red tides and algae blooms could still be useful, though I'd likely call the phenomena something else and give them new characteristics unique to my fictional planet. The storyboard below, Figures 1.2a–1.2d, reimagines the sequence as science fiction.

EXT. CONVENIENCE STORE- NIGHT
An excited CUSTOMER runs out of the store as a vehicle from the planet's conservation commission enters into the parking lot.
CUSTOMER: There's a guy inside with a live rotag!

A uniformed officer, ELLEN, exits the vehicle.
ELLEN: Stay here.

Figures 1.2a–1.2d Ellen and the rotag in the retail utility

INT. CONVENIENCE STORE- NIGHT
ELLEN enters the store. Customers are upset.
ELLEN: What are you doing?

A drunk man holds the rotag with his mouth taped shut.
MAN: Me and Larry are enjoying altered cognitive states. This is Larry.

Figures 1.2a–1.2d (continued)

Though storyboards are rarely a conceptual tool for writers, I do know writers who will use drawings and photographs to inspire their writing. Photographs of a desert can stimulate the imagination for a story set in a desert location.

Ideas from Historical Accounts

Like borrowing ideas from news, a writer might consider using events or personalities from history as a basis for narrative fiction. One question to consider carefully is whether the historical event will simply be an inspiration or if the narrative will attempt to stay as close to the historical facts as possible. Writers might place completely fictional narratives within a specific, historically accurate time period, imagining what an entirely fictional character might have endured under the reign of King John of England (1166–1216), during the Han Dynasty in China (206 BC–AD 220), or some other historical era. Even though the protagonist of such a story is invented, real historical elements would shape the character's life and how the character reacts. To be authentic, the writer would want to research the era to understand how historical events would influence protagonists, their choices, and viewpoints. Writers might also attempt the biography of a significant individual, staying close to what the research tells them about a historical personality. Examples of such biopic movies include films such as *Rocket Man* (2019), *Bohemian Rhapsody* (2018), *Vice* (2018), *The King's Speech* (2010), *Walk the Line* (2005), and *The United States vs. Billie Holiday* (2021). History is full of lesser-known stories that could make for captivating scripts. Maybe these deserve to be researched and revealed. If you intend to use history as a basis for your story, ask yourself what it is about this historical character, this period, and its events that fascinate you. Are you already an expert? If not, would you be excited by the idea of doing the research?

If rather than adaptation you wanted to use a news story or historical account as inspiration, you might examine the event for the truth you believe it tells, then combine the story with a genre and perhaps a new setting as in the exercise with fairy tales and myths. Consider keeping a file or a journal of headlines, ideas, incidents, settings, pictures, drawings, notes, and accounts of your own life's confrontations and discoveries to motivate your creativity.

Questions for Authentic Fiction

Story ideas are certainly not limited to these exercises and suggestions. Stories are found anywhere a writer looks or listens for them. They swim beneath the lyrics and melodies of ancient ballads and modern music, under a coworker's off-color joke, behind a child's heartfelt prayer, within the profane slogan of a protester's sign. Creativity is the ability to associate ideas that are not necessarily conceptual siblings, to be able to transcend the traditional for the innovative, and to have the capacity to consider unfamiliar alternatives for solving story problems. Like pouring old wine into new bottles, the classic story is decanted and allowed to "breathe," made appetizing to contemporary tastes or more relevant to current concerns. A creative idea is surprising or at least not obvious, yet it works.

There have been debates about whether creativity can be taught or whether it is the instinctive condition of a privileged cult of geniuses born with the exclusive creativity to entertain the rest of us (Tomasulo, 2019). I believe creativity is a human characteristic. Like the cardiac muscle, everyone is born with it. It may be innately healthier in some than others, but like any muscle, creativity develops with use, growing stronger with exercise. The skill in using creativity comes with knowing how far to go beyond commonly recognized boundaries without trespassing into the generally unacceptable or the incomprehensively absurd. This means forming a personal aesthetic that understands conventions well enough to disrupt them but does so with ingenuity, insight, and even respect. The most outrageous fiction must be true to the world it creates with elements in it that an audience can recognize.

Because my professional training was as a journalist, I tend to ask myself questions about a story idea that are like the questions reporters are taught to ask in gathering facts for a news story: who, what, when, where, why, how, and how much. You might ask similar questions for a fictional story. *Who* is the protagonist? *What* is this story about? *When* did this happen? *Where* did this happen? *Why* did this happen? *How* does this happen? *How much* is the cost (literally and emotionally)? And a few more important question in the "what" category: *What* does the protagonist want? *What* prevents the protagonist from getting it? *What* the Hell is going on?" *What* is the essential truth in this story and *what* does it mean? Knowing the answers to these questions for a fictional story is helpful to writers, even if the writer chooses not to fully reveal all the answers in the final script. Not knowing the answers to these questions can create blocks to writing. It is helpful to stay flexible if new answers develop in the writing process that seem more plausible, more interesting, or more authentic than ones initially imagined.

Language and Lies

The commercial concern for writers doesn't appear to relate to authenticity but instead seems focused on finding the formula, the insider trick, or the global solution to the problem of *story selling* not necessarily story telling. Industry standards infused with the principles of capitalism, where the value of a thing is equivalent to how much attention it gets and how much money it earns, can confuse the reasons why people are driven to create stories and the restless hunger of audiences to experience them. The books and websites for writers reflect a professional mood settled deeply in cultural pessimism. Something has value only if someone else is willing to pay for it. The idea of grabbing attention and exploiting it doesn't seem to be much reconciled with authenticity. Instead, the advice is to do what the professional code demands, which the authors proceed to interpret in terms of popular formulas and current preferences in formatting.

So why does authenticity matter?

There is a genuine hunger for authenticity, for stories rooted in human experience. The last few decades have revealed a general shift toward fact-based entertainment with the popularity of documentaries rising steadily along with attention for fictional stories based on real events. It's not surprising that audiences feeling bewildered and insecure about their world actively look for answers or for something meaningful in the media they consume. A problem with authenticity is that it is difficult to generate with a formula. Authenticity derives from what a person knows, experiences, feels, and observes. It finds its roots in lived experience.

A fact is something we can confirm or prove. A fact might be experienced directly with the senses. We can see it with our own eyes, hear it with our own ears. The usual test for a statement of fact is verifiability—that is, whether something can be shown, recorded, or proved. Science determines facts with careful observation, measurements, or experiments that are repeated with the same results. This also works with math. It is a fact that if you add two rocks to four rocks you will have six rocks. No matter how many times you do this, two rocks added to four rocks will result in a collection of six rocks. This is a reason why so many people like math. You can literally count on the facts in math, except perhaps in a post-truth era. Babak Anvari's short film *Two & Two* (2011) shows how a brutal authority forces young students into ignoring the facts they know, instead repeating "two plus two equals five."

The very nature of truth and belief is fertile ground for fictional exploration. Based on the 1981 award-winning novel by Paul Theroux, the 1986 film *Mosquito Coast* tells the disturbing journey of a disgruntled inventor who believes he can build a utopia based on the lies he tells his family and himself. The film wasn't a commercial success, possibly because it is disappointing to watch characters flounder in the heat of conflicting delusions. It may also be that audiences in 1986 were unaccustomed to seeing a brilliant and idealistic protagonist become so flawed with conceit that he willingly threatens the well-being of his family. It's interesting to see that the concept reappears in 2021 as a streaming television series (*Mosquito Coast*, 2021).

It is a fact that tree seeds were brought to the moon during the National Aeronautics and Space Administration's 1971 Apollo 14 mission in an experiment to see if the seeds that had been on the moon would grow on Earth. The seeds were planted in 1976 and are now full-grown trees still growing in places across the United States, though only some were planted with commemorative plaques (Weise, 2011). How do we know that it is a fact that some trees growing across America were once taken to the moon as seeds? When a fact is beyond personal ability to check, people rely on experts to explain or help in the search for facts. We have historically relied on professionals, specialists, and trusted references. In the case of the "Moon Trees," we must rely on NASA to explain that the seeds really did go to the moon and are now really growing as trees on Earth. One of the hazards of living in a post-truth era is a lack of faith in experts. No one is trusted: not scientists, not reporters, not mathematicians, not research. It is an environment that feeds hoaxes. The earth is flat. The Apollo moon landing was a trick. Doctors and vaccinations are not to be trusted. Incidents of mass murders are really a government ruse to take away citizens' guns. A danger of living in a post-truth world is that verifiable facts are no longer a guaranteed rebuttal for an outrageously false claim (Slier, 2018). A fact is something we can confirm or prove, but to be understood, the truth of a situation needs all the facts revealed.

An exaggeration is not a lie but a fact that is made to seem worse or better than it is. People also call this "stretching the truth," though it is more accurately, "stretching a fact." Exaggeration can be important to storytelling, particularly important for comedy. In the *Comic Toolbox*, John Vorhaus explains that in addition to truth and pain, comedy is about exaggeration (1994). Humor arises from relatable, recognized, authentic experiences, and exaggeration becomes the exclamation point on that truth and pain. Hyperbole can even make a truth more apparent. Audiences who don't "get" a joke, or become offended, might react that way because they don't understand or accept the "truth" the joke represents. On the other hand, jokes based on lies just aren't funny. Their intentions are to insult, demean, belittle, and inflict pain without revealing a truth. Even a false statement told for comic effect works best with an understanding of the sincere and painful truth underneath the situation. For example, when concerned friends come crowding into the hospital room bringing balloons and flowers, the heart patient recovering from his second stroke might jest, "No worries, guys. I only come here for the food." The truths in this situation are a serious heart condition and regretful hospital cuisine. His anxious friends know this. The patient's ability to laugh at his own painful truth eases the tension in the room. In a similar way sarcasm uses irony to criticize something or someone with statements that appear to be flattering, but tone and delivery suggest otherwise.

Mistakes happen when someone is careless, or forgetful, or just doesn't understand a situation. A mistake is not a lie but an accident. For example, the screenwriter who wants to craft a police drama but has no personal experience as a police officer and doesn't do the research to better understand how a police department works, is likely to make mistakes leading to creation of an inauthentic story that misleads audiences. The writer's distortions may not be intentional or political but simply be the result of laziness and a lack of appreciation for the rules, procedures, challenges, and frustrations of police work that a bit of research would have provided. The carefully crafted police drama will come from understanding the hard realities of police routines and how police departments function, even if some characters in the story might behave in deceitful, self-serving ways and certain police practices or policies are harmful.

But I Just Want to Entertain

I've encountered young writers who complained that nothing important ever happened to them. Their lives had been sheltered. They can't remember any time when their emotions or their sense of ego or self was badly bruised. They claim that sifting through personal memories, there is nothing there to inspire a story. They don't pay attention to the news. They don't like folklore or the classics. They believe history is boring. However, these young writers do have favorite movies and video games. These writers want to be commercially successful. If a movie they liked also made money at the box office, that would be reason enough to meticulously imitate it. The favorite movie is not the inspiration for something new with personal insight brought to it, but a carefully copied pattern with predictable details and cardboard characters. The writer won't engage the story pattern with unique encounters, personal insight, and unexpected choices. No surprises or new awareness is added, no vibrations of a lived experience anywhere. I had one aspiring screenwriter tell me bluntly, "I don't have any philosophy, ideology, or big truth to uncover. I just want to entertain an audience. That's the reason why people tune in or buy tickets. People don't go to the movies to find truth. I just want my audiences to have fun."

This becomes an excuse for the derivative tale.

Whether my aspiring screenwriter believed it or not, he did have an operating ideology that influenced his devotion to the derivative story. His belief that the production of a film should create a giddy rollercoaster ride of entertainment without any ideological underpinning suggests that he was unaware of the ideology that supported his derivative story. For my aspiring screenwriter, a story needed the excitement of nonstop violence interrupted only with the hero's wanton, heterosexual exploits. He wanted a story to demonstrate that a natural sovereignty belonged to a powerful man with the skill and nerve to exert violence and humiliate enemies. His protagonist would be a hero because of his strength to eliminate the inferior and evil people who got in his way. His hero would not need much help to achieve these goals. The hero's buddies existed to respect the hero and provide comic relief. The story should also emphasize that beautiful women will inevitably admire those fearless and forceful men. However, the hero will remain free from romantic or family commitments because a hero cannot be tied down. This young screenwriter could not see anything ideological in his substantially derivative work. It was "just fun." If anything, he thought his attachment to violent adventure labeled him a true Hollywood liberal, because the traditional conservatives in his family would not openly endorse daring, vigilante bloodshed or sexual abandon.

People who develop entertainments for public consumption do not craft these stories in isolation from their political, economic, aesthetic, and cultural environments. Even a rollercoaster relies on foundational rails. It is practical and essential for writers to understand their own views about the world. A writer's ideology reflects personal ideas about people, nature, purposes of life, and the values the writer regards as important. In an examination of how ideology shapes journalistic practice, J. Herbert Altschull observed that the less conscious an individual is of personal ideology, the more intensely it is protected (1990). The emotional scaffolding of an ideology helps it recede beneath awareness, but ideology supports what a person admires and surfaces in what a person writes. Whether they are journalists, screenwriters, game developers, advertisers, or novelists, it is useful for writers to know themselves. Altschull offers a list of basic, disconcerting, and contentious questions as a way for journalists to organize and think about their own ideas and values (1990, p. 29). I've adapted some of Atschull's questions here for the consideration of fiction writers. As you read these, consider your own answers. These answers are clues to why you admire certain stories and what ideas provide the scaffolding for the stories you write. My goal here is not to tell you how to answer these questions, or what to admire, but to be aware of who you are.

What Is the Nature of Humanity?

Are people generally good, striving, and diligent, or are most people fundamentally flawed creatures, weak, lazy, greedy, and depraved? Do people need a strong authority to protect them from their own evil nature? Are most people reasonable? Can they be trusted to make competent, respectable decisions on their own? Do most people have a natural sense of respect, courtesy, and compassion? Are good people easily corrupted? Do people inherently care about each other or will they narcissistically put themselves first? Are some individuals innately more deserving of privilege? Will naturally gifted people inevitably surface, rising above the inferior crowd? Can degenerate individuals change their basic nature? When it is obvious that all people are not born with the same identical abilities or talents, is it wise to declare a self-evident truth that they are all equal?

What Is the Relationship between the Individual and Society?

Which is better, a culture that cherishes individual freedom or one that respects the mutual interests of the group? What is the nature of authority in society? Where does power originate? Who has the right to exercise it? Are some people inherently gifted for leadership? Can leadership be accidental or is it divinely bestowed upon someone righteously deserving to have power? What are the limits of authority? Are all people capable of making contributions to society? How should a person's contributions be recognized or rewarded? Does allowing a culture to change in fundamental ways insult the honor of those traditions a culture worked hard to create? When, if ever, should precedent be disregarded, and rules be broken?

What Is a Just Society?

How does society adjudicate competing claims over resources, over wealth and power? Who can society trust to make those judgments? Do all people deserve the resources and opportunities to improve their situation or maintain a comfortable lifestyle? Does society have any responsibility to people whose life events prevent them from getting those resources? Does charity make people dependent, removing the motivation for self-sufficiency and making some people a burden on society? What duties or obligations do people have to each other? To the social group? Does mercy have limitations? Are social institutions like law, science, education, religion, and media too corruptible to be trusted? What sources or institutions can be trusted?

What Is Happiness?

Is happiness measured quantitatively by amounts of money and the number of retweets? Does everyone deserve to be happy? How much money does it take to be happy? What should happen when one person's happiness interferes with that of another? Is truth necessary for happiness or can a person be happier living a lie?

What Is Truth?

How important is truth to the overall functioning of social life or individual well-being? Who decides what is true? On what basis? Who is privileged to find the truth and give it expression? Should facts or a truth that hampers an important objective be rejected or hidden? When is it justified to hide the truth? Does an objective truth even exist? Is the truth essential for social progress? Can truth exist without pain?

What Is the Proper Role of the Storyteller?

What is the value of storytelling to the functioning of society? To the development of individuals? Who gets to decide whether or not a story is good? How should a story's value be measured?

Authenticity is what individual writers bring to original work when they encounter and react to life: observing, absorbing, and reflecting from an inward journey to bring something new into being. Creating the authentic narrative means understanding the truth of your own perspective and from that perspective, shaping and then offering an audience the gift of a story that will engage, inform, and inspire. Authenticity is not preaching but recognizing that a writer's perspective shows in a character's choices.

Like it or not, our stories do scrape up against the great mysteries: love, death, the insanity of war, the purpose of human existence, human grief, human yearning, the manifest indifference of the tangible universe to injustice and human suffering, the excessive jest of human dignity, and the enigmatic twist and wring that natural beauty has on the human heart. When our stories authentically reflect our humanity, they will always have relevance.

In 1963, in an address at Amherst College, President John F. Kennedy declared that art should be the artist's expression of truth. He believed the great duty of writers is to remain true to themselves and suggested that by serving the public their vision of truth, a writer nourishes the very roots of culture. Fiction and art take up considerable space in our lives and are important to who we are and who we become. These products of imagination help us create the world in which we live and give it meaning.

Before I leave this chapter on searching for our truth and our stories to consider the mysteries of diversity and authenticity in characters, I have one more observation inspired by my play dates with my young neighbor Wade. On several occasions when Wade and I were so heavily engrossed in games of pretend that he didn't want to stop playing to pee, Wade delegated this biological necessity to his younger brother. After his younger brother dutifully went off to take care of business, Wade was good to keep on playing for another half hour or more. Today I wonder how he managed this feat of magic. As children, it seemed completely logical that a younger brother could be appointed to take care of boring physical necessities so Wade could keep on with the excitement of make-believe games uninterrupted. Biological processes can't really be appointed to a gullible surrogate, but this is what Wade did. I have come to believe that reality may be tough and unyielding stuff, but the human imagination is impressively stubborn.

References

Altschull, J. H. (1990). *From Milton to Mcluhan : The Ideas behind American Journalism*. New York: Longman.
Chappell, B. (2020). "Regal Movie Chain Will Close All 536 U.S. Theaters on Thursday." NPR. October 5, 2020, 1:38 p.m. ET.
Crumb, R. (2009). *The Book of Genesis Illustrated by R. Crumb*. New York: W. W. Norton.
Epstein, R., and Friedman, J. (Directors) (1995). *Celluloid Closet* [documentary]. United States: HBO.
Johnson, W. (1975). "The Communication Process and General Semantics Principles." In W. Schramm, ed., *Mass Communication* (2nd ed.), pp. 301–15. Urbana: University of Illinois Press.
Sawchuck, S. (2017). "Is 'The Cat in the Hat' Racist?" *Education Week*. October 4.
Slier, G. (2018). "The Post-Truth World." *International Affairs* 64(1): pp. 132–40.
Tomasulo, F. (2019). "Teaching Creativity: A Practical Guide for Training Filmmakers, Screenwriters, and Cinema Studies Students." *Journal of Film and Video* 71(1): pp. 51–62.
Vorhaus, J. (1994). *The Comic Toolbox: How to Be Funny Even if You're Not*. Los Angeles, CA: Silman-James.
Weise, E. (2011). "NASA Launches Search for Moon Trees." *USA Today*. February 17, A.3.

Chapter 2

CREATING AUTHENTIC CHARACTERS

> Reputation is what men and women think of us; character is what God and the Angels know of us.
> —Thomas Paine (1737–1809)

In news and documentaries, characters are not created but revealed. Listening to an interview or watching how individuals behave on camera, how they look, and what they say tells audiences something about those individuals and their personalities. In fiction, writers create characters but in an essential way these characters should also be revealed. Fictional characters show us who they are through:

- their actions, behaviors, and choices,
- their needs, drives, and goals,
- their attitudes and their perspectives,
- the things that they say, forget to say, can't say, or refuse to say,
- their quirks and idiosyncrasies,
- their demographics and physical appearance.

Most of these are things an audience can observe. Even deliberately withheld elements may be obvious when other characters or circumstances uncover what a character wants to hide. What characters do, where and how they live, what they like, the choices they make, habitual mannerisms, the work they do for a paycheck, the things they do for fun, and how other characters react to them are all things that help to show who that character is, how that character thinks, and the character's capacity for change.

Protagonists, Antagonists, Heroes, Antiheroes, and Villains

Protagonists are those characters who are central to a story. This is the character who makes the key decisions that move the plot forward and the character who usually faces the most complications and conflicts. An *antagonist* is not necessarily the villain of the narrative but a character who prevents the protagonist from achieving some major goal. In the case of a child or teenage protagonist, the antagonist might be the character's parent. This antagonistic character loves the protagonist, but creates obstacles such as curfews, rules, prohibitions, and uselessly small allowances that prevent the protagonists from their ambitions. In the case of an antihero, an antagonist may actually be a force for good, working in the best interest of the community or even the best interests of the protagonist when protagonist's goals are self-destructive. Sometimes the antagonist is a competitor, a character who wants the same the protagonist wants, such as the opponent in a chess game.

Heroic protagonists might use wit to challenge conventions and escape sticky situations. They might be committed to simplicity, self-sufficiency, self-control; have an indifference to hardship; and are able to physically accomplish things that would exhaust or overwhelm ordinary people. These protagonists are less vulnerable to the seduction of material comforts and their illusions. They assert their independence. They are better at adapting to or confronting difficult circumstances. They have a supple courage that enables them to deal with grim conditions and tough challenges. Actions of heroic protagonists are generally consistent with their values in spite of the pressures of external forces, stresses, and the influence of others. Heroic protagonists are usually balanced.

A *balanced character* is one whose behaviors follow from recognizing deeply held personal values and ethical ideals. Balanced characters acknowledge the material world with some awareness and are better able to deal with its burdens and demands. They have learned to stabilize external pressures with their inner goals. They have a personal code but are willing to listen to others. They are generally trustworthy. It is possible for other characters and external forces to pressure a balanced character into acting in ways that deny those inner values, distracting, confusing, or causing the character to act in dishonest ways that will be regrettable for the character but perhaps important to the authenticity of the story. Many things can inspire unbalanced behavior: fear, pain, urgency, greed, jealousy, and pride, to name a few. If conflicts in a story challenge the hero to a point where they cause balanced heroes to change, heroic characters can become disoriented. They may ignore their own heroic qualities and disregard their inner values. The story must then decide if the change is permanent for the heroic protagonist or if the protagonist can recover, perhaps becoming even stronger for this personal encounter with weakness.

The heroic protagonist is a character that audiences can admire. But to seem authentic, the heroic character should also have the quirks, failings, and vulnerabilities that make the character feel human, traits that make the character seem like a real person. Consider the character of Peter Parker in the

Sam Raimi *Spider-Man* trilogy (2002, 2004, 2007) or in more recent versions such as *Spider-Man: Homecoming* (2017) and *Spider-Man: Far from Home* (2019). As played by Toby McGuire and Tom Holland, Peter Parker is a vulnerable young man even though he has superpowers. His feelings can be bruised, his ego insulted, and his self-doubt might render him temporarily incapable of heroic action. He can misinterpret events and what they mean. He makes mistakes. These peculiar traits of his humanity allow audiences to better connect to the superhero, making him more relevant. Human qualities, emotions, and failings make any character more relatable, even if that character is not a human but an alien (*ET*, 1982), a toy (*Toy Story*, 1995), a ghost (*Casper*, 1995), a robot (*WALL-E*, 2008), a horse (*War Horse*, 2011), or an abstract emotion like Sadness (*Inside Out*, 2015).

An *antihero* is a protagonist whose flaws are prevalent and obvious, even exaggerated. The character may be an outcast, a cynic, a character who is indifferent to anything but money and power, or perhaps even a sociopath who enjoys the physical and emotional pain of others. An antihero may be so flawed that it can be difficult to separate this protagonist from a villain. If writers decide to develop an antihero as the protagonist, this character needs some traits that will arouse audience empathy, helping audiences care about what happens to this obviously flawed character. For example, in the television series *Breaking Bad* (2008–13), Walter White is a high school chemistry teacher with cancer who is an antihero and a change character. Walter White has many characteristics an audience can admire. He is smart, funny, courageous, has mad chemistry skills, and is a committed family man. Once he learns that he is in the advanced stages of lung cancer, Walter White wants to provide for his family's financial security. His high-school teacher's salary won't finance the expensive healthcare he needs much less support his family's well-being after he dies. Audiences might empathize with a character who has serious health problems and deep financial worries. Audiences might also understand the pressures that cause Walter White to turn to crime, becoming a drug lord and using his chemistry skills to make and sell crystal meth. As the series progresses, Walter White's actions become more and more morally ambiguous. He goes from being the protector of his family to putting his family in danger, from being a mild-mannered teacher to a murderous criminal. It becomes a mission of arrogant vanity to stockpile a criminal wealth that is more than his family would ever need for basic comfort and security. This is money his family will never be able to spend without arousing suspicion. Yet, at the end of the series, Walter White remains committed to his family even as he is estranged from them. While Walter White's character progresses in villainy and his perspective changes from that of a law-abiding man into a lawless one, his love for his family, his intellect, and respect for chemistry are elements that remain steadfast, helping audiences continue their interest in what happens in Walter White's story, even if concern may have shifted to the other characters White endangers.

Some antiheroes may never have developed or fully tested their personal values. Some may ignore their personal ethical and aesthetic objections to an action or event and behave according to external pressures, acting on harmful directions or coercion from friends, parents, or preachers. They may never listen to good advice if listening is inconvenient or uncomfortable. These characters may act in defensive and judgmental ways, deceiving themselves and others. They may not learn from mistakes. They are paragons of hypocrisy.

Adapted from the novel *You* (Kepnes, 2014) and *Hidden Bodies* (Kepnes, 2014, the television series *You* (2018–) features a protagonist, Joe Goldberg, who manages a bookstore and restores rare books. When Joe meets an aspiring writer, Guinevere Beck, he becomes obsessed with her, which leads to stalking and violence. His aggressive, predatory behavior continues in the second season, when Goldberg meets a woman named Love. The harmful things Joe Goldberg does he rationalizes as necessary actions he undertakes for the benefit of others. Though Goldberg appears to be mild mannered, thoughtful, loving, resourceful, and highly educated, his obsessions and twisted reasoning render him a danger to his community and the people he loves. Yet audiences may root for the stalker even as they condemn him. The bookish nerd charms as the creepy felon simultaneously disgusts.

A *villain* has many of the flawed characteristics of the antihero with the big difference being that villainous characters are less likely to have audience sympathy, though the boundary between villainy and antiheroic action can be a thin and leaky membrane. Villains choose to be on the wrong side of justice or decency. They are the hateful adversaries that keep the story's protagonist from important goals and threaten anyone in their way. The professional hitman, Anton Chigurh, from the film *No Country for Old Men* (2007) is an obvious villain. Ruthless and goal-driven, Chigurh will keep a promise to commit a murder even though it does not advance his cause, as if his word on this vow to commit murder had some moral value. He will also honor the outcome of a coin toss even if he lost the toss. Yet the boundary marking Chigurh as a villain is resolute. Chigurh is cold, violent, and disconnected from his humanity and any typical human sense of morality.

In the television series *Turn: Washington's Spies* (2014–17), the sadistic British officer John Graves Simcoe stabs, shoots, hangs, poisons, and tortures his victims through four seasons of the historical revolutionary war drama. He is an obvious villain, ruthless and bloodthirsty, yet Simcoe was also a complex villain, capable of kindness and even love. He practiced courteous manners, had a sense of human dignity, and the Colonial practice of slavery offended him. He cares about the men under his command. As the series comes to an end, the boundary around Simcoe's villainy becomes more porous. Though the American television series largely treats Simcoe as a villain, Canadian history remembers him as a hero. There is a town, streets, parks, and buildings named for him, and a statue in Queen's Park, Toronto, erected in his honor.

Some villains are exaggerated versions of humanity's worst faults.

Inspired by the character of King Claudius from Shakespeare's *Hamlet* (1599–1601), the character of Scar in the two Disney animated versions of *The Lion King* (1994, 2019) is cowardly, manipulative, and treasonous. Eaten up with jealousy, Scar conspires with hyenas to kill his brother, King Mufasa. Scar convinces his nephew and the story's protagonist, Simba, that the young lion's recklessness is to blame for his father's death. Burdened with that guilt, Simba goes into exile, leaving Scar to usurp the power of the throne. Scar is undoubtedly a villain, though the envy that drives him is an understandable human emotion. He tells his nephew how unfair life is. Life indulges some and deprives others. Scar feels that he has been robbed of the beauty, wisdom, power, and admiration that had been too abundantly bestowed on his older brother.

Heroes and villains are on opposite ends of a complex spectrum of character types. Most characters, like most people, will fall somewhere between these extremes. Like people, authentic characters are not perfect. They have weaknesses and negative qualities. They can be stingy, stubborn, careless, grumpy, weak, forgetful, and selfish. But for audiences to care about characters, they should also have traits an audience can admire, such as compassion, loyalty, tolerance, mercy, energy, generosity, intelligence, skill, or sincerity. Exaggerations of a villain's nasty traits that also allow for human complexity can create interesting, compelling characters.

Characters and Perspectives

In a discussion about how people become confused about the meaning of social justice, a second-grade teacher lamented that social justice is an extremely difficult concept to teach 7-year-olds. In the school's social studies unit, the teacher had compared justice with fairness. The teacher told her students that school rules were similar to American laws; their purpose was to protect people and keep them safe and explained that these rules applied to every student, regardless of race, gender, or the wealth of the student's family. If school policies were wrong or unfairly disadvantaged some students, it was the job of teachers and students to speak out. Similarly, it was the duty of citizens or their representatives to speak up when laws or rules were unfair, when policies or common practices put some citizens in danger. The class discussed Martin Luther King Junior and his declaration that "injustice anywhere is a threat to justice everywhere. […] Whatever affects one directly, affects all indirectly." Children nodded their heads approvingly. They knew that Martin Luther King is a hero of history. Still, a few students never seemed to grasp the idea of justice, even though they thought they did. As an example of her challenge in teaching this concept, the teacher shared the story of one of her students (I'll call him Darrel) who eagerly raised his hand, wanting to tell the class about his personal experience with injustice. When she called on him, Darrel stood up and told the other students about a day his mother offered to take Darrel and his siblings to see *Spider-Man: Into the Spider-Verse* (2018), a movie they had all been eagerly anticipating. When they arrived at their local theater, the family was disappointed to learn that the movie wasn't showing there. No one would be able to see the movie that day. "It was so unfair," Darrel whined, "We didn't see the movie and we didn't get popcorn."

Young Darrel could not understand injustice as a policy that favored one group over another but only as something that kept him from getting whatever he wanted. Darrel's perception of fairness didn't serve equal buckets of happiness or disappointment to everyone. Something was fair only if Darrel was personally happy about it. If the school cafeteria was not serving his favorite chicken nuggets that day, it was "unfair." If his teacher assigned homework to the whole class over the weekend, it was "unfair." If rain canceled the school's field day event, it was "unfair." However, when his teacher in the same social studies unit mentioned that women in 2018 still earned less than men working the same job, Darrel celebrated with gleeful hooting and a triumphant, "boys are better" declaration. In his view, the inequity was "fair" because he believed boys are inherently superior to girls and he also belonged to that privileged group. From Darrel's perspective, his future adult self would be deserving to make more money than some "dumb girl."

A character's *perspective* is the way that character understands the world. Recognizing a character's perspective helps writers predict how the character will react to situations in the plot. Religious beliefs, personal values, experiences, culture, ideology, community, and other individuals can all influence a character's perspective. If Darrel was a character that we were developing for a story instead of a child we observed in a class, his personal understanding of injustice would be a fundamental part of his perspective, or the way Darrel believes the world naturally works. This perspective might adjust as Darrel gets older and perhaps develops a broader, more experienced understanding about life. However, it is also possible that Darrel's views on injustice might remain firmly anchored to his own personal advantage.

It's possible that Darrel as an adult businessman maintained and even embellished his selfish childhood perspective. Injustice would be tied to his personal disappointment, fairness benefitted his bottom-line, and it would be perfectly fine to discriminate against "inferior" people. His "truth" is tied to his perspective. He might decide that his female employees don't merit equal pay because, "they go crazy stupid once a month," or they will eventually, "get pregnant and quit work anyway." He may not make a public announcement of his feelings, though his policies secretly reflect them. In the company of supportive, like-minded friends, he might privately complain: "In this lunatic, P-C universe, a businessman can't say the truth out loud, because courts will get involved. You certainly can't be truthful with H-R." As an adult character, Darrel's perspective is that an effective businessman will do whatever it takes to win financially. If his female employees file a lawsuit, Darrel will consider such a lawsuit "unfair." An investigation of his business practices will distract from the financial growth of his company. Darrel might indignantly add that it is "unfair" to his other employees, "who rely on me for their salaries." It would be "unfair" of a judge to make him pay a fine and force him to compensate his former employees with money Darrel doesn't believe they deserve. An exaggeration of Darrel's perspective might even consider some forms of criminality to be "justified."

This perspective of our fictional Darrel embraces the common flaw of hubris found in some heroes of ancient Greek tragedies, when those characters believed they were superior to others, above the law, and even more noble than the gods. Sometimes when main characters exhibit this flaw, events in their stories will offer them a very tough lesson in humility.

Knowing that a young woman's perspective is that "life should always be comfortable and casual" and "formality is restrictive and unpleasant" makes it easier for a writer to predict that character's choices. A character with this perspective might refuse to wear anything that must be ironed or hung up in a closet. If she can't toss it in a drawer, forget it. She is not a fashionista. She has two pairs of shoes: tennis shoes and flip flops. She consistently chews gum because "every moment should have flavor." She might not bathe every day because she'd rather lounge in bed than get up and shower, rationalizing that "too much cleanliness is a waste of water." This character will show up for a job interview, unshowered, wearing jeans and a tee shirt, and chewing her Wrigley's because "it makes sense to be relaxed and comfortable in a stressful situation." Continual nagging from friends and family telling her not to act like a slob may not easily change this character's behavior, even if her behavior threatens job prospects and romantic possibilities. From the character's perspective, this is not sloth but practicality. Her perspective considers things such as style, decorum, and etiquette as pretentious and unnecessary. She will always choose a path with the least amount of effort and discomfort unless something extremely significant compels her to do otherwise.

Perspective and Experience

Perspective is also closely tied to experience and what characters know or think they know about the world. An old parable about "Six Blind Men and an Elephant" makes an important point about characters and perspective. In one version of the story, the blind men have never had any experience with an elephant and when an elephant comes to their town, out of curiosity, they each touch the animal to discover what an elephant is and to understand the "truth" about the elephant. One man touches the ear and announces that the elephant is like a fan. Another pats the leg and says the elephant is like a tree. Another feels the trunk and proclaims that the elephant is like a snake. The fourth blind man strokes the elephant's side and declares the animal is more like a wall. The fifth touches the tail and states that the elephant is like a rope. The last blind man feels the tusk and claims all the others are wrong: the elephant is like a spear. Soon the men begin fighting, each accusing the others of being liars. It is useful for writers to know that while one character's subjective experience may be accurate, it may be limited, not having the totality that is necessary for truth. Characters can become fooled or confused by the things they experience and deny what they don't know or can't understand. While characters may be blindly feeling their way around the many facts of a larger truth, it is the writer who needs to fully understand the elephant in the room.

Every authentic character in a story needs a consistent pattern of behavior, a consistent voice unique to that particular personality with a distinctive way of looking at and understanding the world. Contentious questions screenwriters ask of themselves about how they view the world can also inform the world view of the characters a writer develops. Consider how your character might answer the pesky ideological questions from Chapter 1. (What is the nature of humanity? What should be the relationship between the individual and society? Who is a hero? What is a just society? What is truth?) It is important to understand how your character sees the world, how that view might be blocked or limited, and if that perspective will change as the story unfolds and events reveal the larger shape of the elephant. The answers to these questions are like research; they help build the story and the writer's understanding. Even if these answers aren't actively incorporated into the plot, they are part of a character's biography and an important guide to what that character will do in a situation.

Change and Character Arcs

A *change character* is one whose ideas will shift over the course of the story, often in dramatic ways. This character's perspective will adjust, modifying as events in the plot teach that character to consider an alternate viewpoint. Some screenwriting professors refer to this change in perspective as the character arc, an inner transformation of the character as the story progresses. This change can be substantial, causing the character to be very different by the end of the story. But to seem authentic, the change in a character's perspective should happen as events, experiences, newly revealed facts, or other characters cause a shift in the worldview. Real people tend to be deeply tied to their perspectives. Only consistent events and compelling facts might cause them to let go of long-held beliefs and begin to see the world differently. It rarely happens overnight. People have been known to cling to a worldview even when that perspective is personally harmful. For example, physician Jonathan Metzel describes the case of a man suffering with a painful illness because he cannot afford the medical treatment he urgently needs, yet this man is adamantly opposed to universal healthcare even though it would directly benefit him (2019). The sick man's opposition is rooted in the notion that universal healthcare would also cover the medical expenses of undeserving immigrants or lazy minorities and he would rather die from his illness than have his hard-earned tax dollars support such people.

When it comes to changing a character's perspective, carefully consider what would convince a character to change. Authentic characters don't suddenly alter their perspectives simply because the change would be convenient for a plot.

Changes can happen in various directions; the character's viewpoint might deepen with experience, become more generous, or go in the other direction, becoming more restrictive or self-serving. People who are usually dependable can be temporarily derailed to have dramatically painful moments that could be instructive in fiction but traumatic in social life. Traumatic events, deceptions, or other malevolent characters can negatively impact the way that protagonist views the world and other people, affecting the choices the protagonist will make and perhaps moving the plot in a tragic direction. In one classic example in the movie based on the Shakespearean play *Othello* (1995), the jealous character of Iago manipulates others with deception and trickery, ensnaring them in a complex and destructive trap of lies. He spreads slander about Othello's wife, finally persuading Othello that Desdemona is unfaithful to him, goading Othello into murdering the woman he loves. Othello begins his story as a balanced character, a respected general in the Venetian army, but Othello's passions and Iago's lies destabilize and conquer him.

If our character of Darrel as a child had matured into a man with an understanding of justice and a perspective that considered justice to be important to the type of world in which he wants to live, the altered perspective would make Darrel a changed character. He had learned to look beyond himself to a wider world and fully understood that injustice can have sad consequences. Alternately, if life events forced Darrel to live in a deprived environment where violent crime was prevalent and police either consistently ignored the crime or perhaps arrested and even brutalized the wrong people, these experiences might constrict Darrel's perspective, shaping and hardening the character's attitudes toward other people. If Darrel is mugged one night, badly beaten, and his wallet and watch are stolen, he may decide that people in general are "no damn good" and his personal experience "proves" it. Like the blind man who touches only the elephant's tusk, Darrel's experience shows him that part of the world where the truth is hard and dangerous. Thugs get away with murder and innocent people are shot, robbed, or put in jail. Under these circumstances, Darrel might come to reject the idea of justice, considering justice to be a fairytale taught in school. He might consider Martin Luther King's justice to be a cultural myth like Santa Claus. His childlike selfishness becomes further layered with adult cynicism, solidified in a belief that the world is relentlessly cruel. He might decide it is important to make others afraid as a matter of self-preservation. This perspective can also include a belief that respect is not something people earn through hard work and talent. Respect is tied to fear. If Darrel walks with a swagger, carries a gun, and other characters are afraid of him and what he might do, then Darrel believes they "respect" him. Even the slightest hint of an insult would be reason for violent retaliation in order for Darrel to maintain the fear and the "respect" of other characters. If our deprived Darrel consistently comes across people and events that contradict his perspective that a person must be tough to live in a brutal world, Darrel may ultimately be persuaded to change his thinking and embrace an ideal of justice he believes is worth hard work and self-sacrifice to achieve. Such a change won't be instantaneous.

The character of Christopher or "Rio" from the NBC television series *Good Girls* (2018-) is the ruthless boss of a criminal money laundering business, whose perspective seems to be that only money and power have value and a crime boss does whatever is necessary to get the money and maintain the power. What makes Rio interesting are those instances where he violates that tough perspective. He takes his young son to play in the park and his advice to the boy reveals that the crime boss seems to honor an ethical center. Rio's undeniable soft spot for Elizabeth, a housewife and mother of four, develops into a complex chemistry when they become partners in crime. Elizabeth, her sister Anne, and her best friend Ruby all experience devastating financial woes, and the women decide that robbing a grocery store is the solution to their troubles. Rio violates his criminal code when he mentors Elizabeth, guiding her from an amateur dabbling in crime to a crime boss, performing profitable felonies on his behalf. The criminal shenanigans in episode plots might need an audience member's devoted suspension of disbelief, but unswerving frontal attacks on the values of the core characters helped create a devoted audience for the series (Li, 2019). The ordeals Rio puts these women through continually test whether Elizabeth, Anne, and Ruby really are the "Good Girls" the series title suggests they are.

A *steadfast character* is one who will stubbornly hang on to a viewpoint no matter what evidence the character encounters that contradicts that perspective. The character of our adult businessman who clings to a selfish concept of "fairness" is a steadfast character in a negative sense, unless the story's overall perspective (the writer's perspective) defends selfishness (or pragmatic self-interest) as an asset. In a story about a superhero dedicated to protecting the world from evil, the heroic protagonist usually remains steadfast, his virtue remaining intact throughout his righteous battle, no matter how arduous or hurtful his challenges become or what temptations try to lure him away.

One example of a steadfast protagonist is the title character in the 1993 political comedy film *Dave*. Dave Kovic holds the Jeffersonian perspective that the American government exists to serve its people and that elected officials should be dedicated guardians, concerned about the needs of all their constituents. The movie's situational concept is that citizen Dave could be the identical twin of the president of the United States, Bill Mitchell. Though the two men look exactly alike, they are polar opposites in their perspectives on the role of government. Dave is humbly working in local government to improve the lives of citizens, while Bill Mitchell holds the bridle of power. The president is greedy and opportunistic, colluding with his White House Chief of Staff, Bob Alexander, on schemes that enable his philandering and Alexander's manipulation and greed. When President Mitchell suffers a stroke and falls into a coma during an extramarital tryst, rather than allow the honorable Vice President to take the reins of government, Bob Alexander recruits Dave to impersonate the president. Alexander convinces Dave that this deception is a matter of national security and because of his deep patriotism Dave agrees to Alexander's scheme. While he is acting the part of the president, Dave learns that power and privilege are seductive drugs for the politicians around him, who play dangerous games with the well-being of the American people. Yet, to the end of the story, Dave remains steadfast in his belief that government can and should work to benefit its citizens. The movie's optimistic perspective also suggests that if people in power only behaved with Dave's gracious brand of sincerity, goodwill, and determination, many of our national problems could be solved. Dave is an example of both a steadfast and a balanced character.

The situational concept in *Dave* does have similarities to Mark Twain's 1881 classic, *The Prince and the Pauper* (Mark Twain Project, 1983). In both the 2000 British action adventure film as well as Mark Twain's original story of *The Prince and the Pauper*, two identical boys are born on the same day, but one is an adored prince surrounded with luxury while the other is an unwanted son delivered to squalor and crime. When the two boys trade places, their exchange allows the future king Edward to have experiences that give him the broader understanding of the world that a wise leader needs. Tom's experiences in court better prepare him for the official appointment Edward will bestow. As with any rich concept, the story of the *Prince and the Pauper* has been adapted into multiple film and television movies (1937, 1963, 1977). However, the experiences of the characters in *The Prince and the Pauper* cause them to change and develop broader perspectives, while the character Dave remains essentially steadfast in the face of the corruption he uncovers and becomes even more devoted to his ideals.

Characters and Stereotypes

Stereotyping happens when media portrayals of characters rely on commonly held beliefs or assumptions about a group, which may be completely wrong. These beliefs may not reflect all or even the majority of the members of that group, but may instead reflect the ignorance, bias, or laziness of those relying on the stereotype. Not only does stereotyping create inauthentic characters, but this type of categorical thinking can also lead to serious problems in real life, particularly if media stories help to exacerbate the tendency for some people to consider others who are different in a negative way.

Categorical thinking encourages people to ignore unique individual characteristics and instead judge people as one homogenous group. For example, because many of the National Basketball Association's best players are African American and some of the most celebrated football players and track stars are also African American, categorical thinking expects African Americans to be naturally gifted athletes. The categorical thinking that suggest the primary or only path to success for young men of color is through athletic prowess becomes dangerous when those young men neglect other important talents or abilities in a desperate pursuit of athletic abilities they may not possess. The categorical thinking that suggests African American men naturally have violent and criminal tendencies is dangerous when police encounter an African American man on a routine traffic stop and prejudicial stereotypes make them jittery and quick to feel threatened. Finally, finding a real-life example of the stereotype does not prove the stereotype true. The observation that a fair number of people of color are gifted athletes doesn't mean every person of color naturally has these abilities.

Authentic characters don't develop from stereotypes. However, it is possible for authentic characters in a fictional story to engage in categorical thinking, acting in prejudiced ways toward certain groups just as real people too often do. Our character of businessman Darrel engages in categorical thinking when he claims women do not deserve to be paid the same as men working the same job because "all women go crazy dumb once a month" or "eventually get pregnant and a pregnant woman is overly emotional and useless to business."

While writers want to avoid categorical thinking, the practice of *counter-storytelling* to flip stereotypical expectations can make for interesting characters. The Cohen brothers' dark crime comedy *Fargo* (1996) is an example of writing against stereotype. In this movie, the police chief in Brainerd, Minnesota, is Marge Gunderson, a woman who capably solves the crimes of murder, kidnap, and extortion even though she is seven months pregnant and waddles her way through the movie's most violent action. Chief Gunderson illustrates how a woman might actually remain logical, resourceful, smart, and competent even while pregnant. Other stories might intentionally use prejudice as a theme. Once they manage to remove a boss who exploits and sexually harasses their coworkers, three women in the comedy film *9 to 5* (1980) are capable of increasing a company's productivity and introducing initiatives that foster employee satisfaction and company profits. The French film *Potiche* (2010) shows how a trophy wife becomes an effective leader when her husband's heart attack forces her to take over the family business. *Hidden Figures* (2016) works against negative stereotypes, showing how three Black women contributed their mathematical prowess to help NASA launch its first trip to space. It is important to note that the heroines of *Hidden Figures* were drawn from historical women and not simply a writer's imaginative determination to subvert stereotypes.

It is not a surprise that gender, age, racial, and ableist stereotyping benefit the group of the person maintaining the stereotype. It's likely that members of every group have been guilty of stereotyping the members of other groups. However, it is also possible for people to practice categorical thinking about themselves, believing popular stereotypes about their own race, gender, age group, ethnicity, or handicap. In the documentary *Celluloid Closet* (1995), American writer and producer Susie Bright comments on the self-loathing of the lesbian character, Martha, in *The Children's Hour* (1961). Martha's self-disgust over the homosexual feelings she has for her business partner will ultimately drive this character to commit suicide. Bright acknowledges that the old movie "still makes me cry. [...] Why does this still get to me? This is just a silly old movie, and you know, people don't feel that way anymore. But I don't think that's true. I think people feel that way today, still [...] there's part of me that's like, how could I be this way?" Stereotypes and categorical thinking can fester and turn inward, damaging both people and characters.

Sometimes people are unaware that they engage in categorical thinking. As you begin developing the characters for your story, consider the unique traits your characters have that distinguish them as the individuals they should be. Be aware of the idea of representation. Who are the heroes of your story? Who are the villains? Respect your characters as multidimensional personalities living complex lives. Beware of prejudices your character might have and how these threaten the character's choices, the result of those choices, and what the character and the audiences watching will learn from those experiences.

Archetypes and the Collective Unconscious

Stereotypes are conceptually different from archetypes. *Archetypes* also deal with types, but these types are considered to be patterns within humanity's collective unconscious, not the result of categorical thinking. Swiss psychologist Carl Jung explained the concept of the archetype as contemporary remnants of archaic memory (1964; Jung and Campbell, 1971). According to Jung, the human psyche has distinct parts:

- the *individual consciousness*, which is personal thinking while awake and aware;
- the *individual memory*, which is where personal recollections and knowledge are stored and easily retrieved to personal consciousness;
- the *personal unconscious*, which is where forgotten or repressed memories and knowledge are stored; contents of the personal unconscious are more difficult for an individual to retrieve to consciousness;
- and *the collective unconscious*, which contains the archaic memories and visceral drives of all our mutual ancestors.

Jung considered the collective unconscious to be universal, impersonal, and identical in all of humanity. Some believe these archetypes are imbedded in the human brain or encoded in our DNA (Williams, 2012). The thinking is that every person inherits the collective unconscious like instinct. The archetypes that supposedly exist in our collective unconscious are reoccurring forms that may surface from the deepest layers of this archaic memory to make appearances in dreams, myths, and storytelling. Jung considered that through the pathway of our dreams, these ancestral archetypes influence the substance and direction of our stories and the cultural myths those stories become. However, because they exist in the deepest structure of the human psyche, archetypes of the collective unconscious are not easy for a conscious individual to effortlessly retrieve and control.

American mythologist Joseph Campbell noticed that cultures around the world tell similar stories and that these can be distilled into one single mythic pattern that is told and retold with varying details, a similar hero on a similar journey but with a thousand different faces (1949). This pattern found in the myths and stories of widely separated cultures seemed to reinforce Jung's idea of a universally shared, collective unconscious populated with the shadowy memories of archaic experience. These myths were stories about primordial beginnings, supernatural beings, and marvelous heroes dedicated to protecting their loved ones, families, and communities. Campbell's recognition that the heroes from vastly different cultures take comparable journeys has inspired screenwriters to deliberately apply Campbell's theory of the hero's journey to the writing of new scripts in hopes of capturing the power of that mythic story (Indick, 2004, pp. 143–64). We will examine the hero's journey in more detail as a structural device in the next chapter. In our present concern about developing character, there have also been suggestions that Jung's archetypes and the archetypes of character that appear in a hero's journey can be useful for writers.

Some Internet resources suggest that to create successful characters, all a writer needs to do is retrieve and manipulate these archetypes that swim in the depths of the collective unconscious. Some writers' resources additionally provide templates of various archetypes for writers to use, such as the warrior, the amazon, the mentor, the trickster, the magician, the monarch, the rebel, the seductress, the mother, and the father, among other types. Each archetype comes with a description of the character's role in a story. For example, the job of the warrior archetype would be to defend a monarch or government against its enemies. The implication is that because the human psyche will recognize the archaic pattern, this ancient familiarity will have profound resonance for audiences, who will be helplessly drawn to characters based on those archetypal traits.

I'm not convinced that an individual human consciousness can deliberately maneuver through the deepest recesses of the collective unconscious for personal creative advantage. According to Jung, the influence of an archetype is involuntary, not something the conscious mind can influence. Archetypes enter an artist's individual consciousness through dreams and meditative thinking. These preconscious mental energies might drift upward into a writer's consciousness to activate individual creativity. Artists then transform the archetype, giving it expression within their own traditions and the flesh and bone of their own experiences. Any conscious attempts at manipulating the collective unconscious will likely result in stock or trite characters and may additionally invite stereotypes. The fundamental motif or pattern of an archetype, particularly the brief descriptions readily available on the Internet, might not inspire the distinctive perspectives, unique histories, or the idiosyncrasies of the extraordinary individuals that genuine characters should be. They can feel like formulas, not authentic personalities. If archetypal features organically emerge in the development of a character without conscious attempts to control the collective unconscious and if the character is additionally layered with perspective, unique traits, flaws, and idiosyncrasies, then the character is less prone to becoming an Internet cliché.

Archetypes of the Personal Unconscious

More related to an individual's personal unconscious than the collective unconscious, and more useful for writers, are the archetypes of the anima, animus, and shadow. The *anima* is the female principle in a man, which he will repress if he views his female aspect as culturally improper. Similarly, the *animus* is the male principle in a woman, which are those human characteristics she may repress because her culture regards these traits as unsuitable for women. In the human psyche, the *shadow* has the same gender identity as the person whose unconscious stores it, but the shadow also consists of suppressed traits. The shadow is composed of those things individuals don't like about themselves or that their culture disparages as inappropriate or unworthy regardless of the individual's gender. The shadow, anima, and animus hide in the personal unconscious beneath the *persona*, or that *mask* made of traits the culture accepts as proper and admirable. The persona is the face individuals are willing to show the world. This face, or mask, may genuinely reflect some qualities of the person behind it, but the persona may also be a disguise displayed for the sake of social approval.

Knowing that real people suppress parts of themselves that their social world might insult, stigmatize, or condemn can be useful for writers.

Some critics of Jung's ideas have raised concerns that his definitions of masculine and feminine are restricted and outdated. Jung's concepts do not tell us much about nonbinary gender, though character archetypes such as the trickster have expressed gender fluidity (Edwards, 2019). What is useful for contemporary writers is understanding how people (and characters) might suppress parts of who they are because of social pressure to conform to cultural norms. The anima and animus might be interpreted as an individual's repression of natural human traits and gender fluidity because of cultural insistence on exclusive gender distinctions. Heterosexual characters may maintain personal, internal gender closets for an anima or animus they are ashamed to show the world.

Fictional stories can take advantage of these concepts when characters allow their suppressed traits to come forward. In the comedy film *Mrs. Doubtfire* (1993), a divorced woman considers her unemployed ex-husband too unreliable to have shared custody of their children. The unemployed actor pretends to be an elderly woman so that his ex-wife will hire him as a babysitter. She does, unintentionally allowing the father to have access and quality time with his children. In the role of Mrs. Doubtfire, the father reconnects to his anima, permitting those repressed feminine characteristics to surface and improve his relationships with his children and ex-wife. Similarly, in the comedy *Tootsie* (1980), an out-of-work actor disguises himself as a woman to get a part in a soap opera. The movie suggests that connecting with his anima broadens the actor's smug, self-centered perspective and ultimately makes him a better man. The young boy in the British drama *Billy Elliot* (2000) suppresses his creativity, love of ballet, and ability to dance because in the English mining town where he lives, such things are inappropriate for men. In the episode "Profit and Lace" (1998) from the television science fiction series *Star Trek: Deep Space Nine* (1993–99), the selfish Quark decides against sexual harassment of an employee after he has spent time as a woman. Reconnected to his anima, Quark understands that there is real profit potential in female equality. If a character has suppressed some talents or useful traits because of fears about how the social world will react, releasing the anima or animus and allowing those traits freedom of expression may create interesting story tensions.

In mythical stories, the persona and shadow are often represented as separate characters with the persona embodied as the heroic protagonist and the shadow as the hero's villainous enemy. Modern writers may prefer to think of the persona and shadow operating in a single character in the same way they operate in individuals. In stories where there is a negative character change, like Walter White from *Breaking Bad*, the suppressed shadow self is permitted to emerge. The argument is that the good father, dedicated husband, and caring teacher always had the qualities of a ruthless drug lord but suppressed those qualities because of cultural expectations and because White did not admire those violent qualities in himself. When his cancer and accompanying financial distress open the door for his shadow, White shows he is willing to watch someone die, endanger a child, and flood his community with illegal drugs and the accompanying crime if it benefits his personal ambitions.

Allowing the shadow to surface can turn a protagonist into a villain. In the original *Star Wars* trilogy (1977, 1980, 1983), Darth Vader is the principal antagonist, hiding his virtuous qualities behind a literal mask. Vader was once

Anakin Skywalker, an earnest young Jedi knight who permits the ambitions of his shadow to emerge and betray the Jedi. In the sequels *Star Wars: The Force Awakens* (2015), *Star Wars: The Last Jedi* (2017), and *Star Wars: The Rise of Skywalker* (2019), the character of Kylo Ren is a similar shadow character. As the privileged son of the powerful and heroic Han Solo and Princess Leia, Ben Solo rejects his parents' faith in a democratic republic. Ben Solo feels his parents' commitment to the Resistance, the democratic New Republic, and "the light side of the force" caused them to neglect their son. He is sullen and bitter, allowing himself to be radicalized. He embraces his authoritarian shadow, "the dark side of the force," and becomes Kylo Ren, a petulant, spiteful, and formidable villain, who admires the ruthless vitality of his grandfather, Darth Vader, and the use of the force for aggression and personal power.

The shadow isn't always evil. Characters who have kept part of themselves hidden can feel inauthentic, like they are living a lie and damaging their psyches to fulfill the cultural demands or expectations of others. Characters who free their shadows may actually be liberating aspects that aren't negative traits but an inhibited part of themselves that needs expression. An artist who successfully suppresses his artistic abilities because his family demands that he join a profitable family business and "forget all that art foolishness" has created a shadow of his artistic nature.

Dramatic Goals and Dramatic Needs

A *goal* is something external a character wants. The character's willingness or drive to take the necessary risks to accomplish that goal will move the plot forward. What does your character want to win, gain, get, or achieve? What is the current central mission in your character's life? The goal may not necessarily come from the character's inner drive; the ambition might be related to some problem the external world has thrust upon the protagonist. An antagonist or some other external force pushes a protagonist out of the usual routine. The demands to recover whatever has been lost, broken, or disrupted then becomes the character's dramatic goal.

A character's *dramatic need* tends to be psychological, and characters may be unaware of their needs. A dramatic need is the personal flaw, missing quality, or limitation that pursuit of a goal might help the character rectify through the course of the story. As characters pursue their goals, they may realize unknown needs. and the character's internal needs must be addressed to fulfill the goal.

American psychologist Abraham Maslow developed a *hierarchy of needs*, which considers the different levels of human needs from basic biological requirements to stay alive to the higher dreams of personal ambition and accomplishment. Basic needs to breathe, eat, and sleep must be satisfied before a person can consider the objectives of safety, security, order, and stability. Characters who are homeless or food insecure have to find shelter and sustenance. Disaster and survival stories are based on goals at this basic level. After achieving food and shelter, people need safety as well as the security of employment and income. A villain attempting to undermine a protagonist's job or cheat an entire business community is a threat at this level. After achieving key resources, people look to realize goals of finding love and belonging. Many screenplays deal with the ambitions of characters actively looking for love or trying to fit in with a social group. The fourth level of Maslow's hierarchy concerns individuals who may have found love and acceptance but are now looking to become competent, to achieve a level of respect, and be recognized as a success. The highest level of Maslow's hierarchy is self-actualization, where individuals have realized profound goals and look to give back to their communities. However, one goal does not have to be completely satisfied before the next one emerges; the structure may be more fluid than a rigid hierarchy suggests (Maslow, 1982). Characters in a disaster story striving for the basics to survive may also be motivated by the goal to achieve the respect of others. In the 2006 film *Pursuit of Happyness*, a single father experiencing financial instability and homelessness has dreams of becoming a stockbroker, but he must also feed, clothe, and house his 5-year-old son.

A character's dramatic goals give the plot direction. For example, the character of young Olive Hoover from the Academy Award-winning screenplay *Little Miss Sunshine* (2006) learns that she has qualified for a beauty pageant. Her dramatic goal is to compete in the pageant. Each member of her family has goals that become entangled with Olive's desire to participate in the contest. Wanting to support their young daughter, Olive's parents and grandfather reinforce Olive's ambitions, taking the entire dysfunctional family on an 800-mile road trip, which will involve setbacks, complications, and revelations for each of them. Goals and needs are linked, so that as protagonists achieve goals, they can correct the deficiencies or dramatic needs that also drive them.

Finding Character in a Concept

Combining the situation of "National Talent Competition" from the list in Chapter 1 with the basic story ideas from the *Little Lame Prince* and the genre of "family drama" might suggest a plot and a young character like Olive Hoover, but the physical limitation of lameness suggested by the fairytale adds a different complication to the dramatic need to compete in a contest. The classic story of the *Little Lame Prince* (1875) is about a paralyzed boy exiled to a tower in a wasteland. He wants to see the world beyond his cold tower.

His fairy godmother gives him a magic cloak that lets him travel, secretly flying out of the tower window to have adventures and learn many things. When the prince is eventually rescued from his tower, he becomes a wise king. A rearrangement of this story might delete the magic and the monarchy. The prince could be a poor, 14-year-old, club-footed boy from Mississippi. (I'll call him Jaz, though his classmates call him "Gimp.") Jaz feels exiled in poverty, eager to see something of the world, and anxious to prove his ability to overcome what others view as his deficiency. Jaz has illogical dreams about competing and winning the grand prize in an international skateboarding contest. The goal to compete in the contest will propel his story forward. The skateboard becomes his metaphorical traveling cloak. There are plenty of obvious obstacles a poor, crippled boy from Mississippi would have to overcome to get to Rye, New Hampshire, and compete in an event that usually requires sure-footedness. The plot might become a series of struggles. Jaz must acquire a worthy skateboard, master the skills for impressive tricks that accommodate his deformed foot, raise the money necessary to participate in the competition, convince his disapproving father that this competition is a worthwhile goal, and overcome various rival antagonists who want to humiliate him. If our protagonist manages to get to New Hampshire and be entered into the competition, he must outperform all the other entrants to win the 20,000-dollar prize. Jaz should be passionate about his goal and committed to it. Though Jaz believes he wants to outperform everyone as a skateboarder, this goal masks what he truly needs: his father's recognition, appreciation, and love. If Jaz finally gets his father's admiration, he would have achieved his dramatic need even if he didn't win the big skateboarding prize in New Hampshire. The storyboard in Figures 2.1a–2.1d suggest how the character's dreams and challenges could be quickly revealed.

Psychological Drives and Character

Sigmund Freud's ideas about the human personality suggest that the development of a healthy personality means that the ego must learn to balance the demands of the id, the superego, and the external reality (2011). The id, ego, and superego are powerful drives that shape subconscious life and surface in individuals to influence their thinking and behaviors.

The *id* is the subconscious impulse that expresses biological needs and personal desires. When an infant is born that infant is pure id. A small child cries when she is hungry, demanding to be fed. She cannot delay gratification. She must be fed this minute. She cries out at discomforts; she will not tolerate them. She must have everything she wants and have it all immediately, even if those wants conflict. The id-driven child is irrational. If a pretty toy in the checkout lane of the grocery store excites her, the id-driven child demands

CREATING AUTHENTIC CHARACTERS

EXT. SKATEBOARD PARK-DAY
JAZZ enters the skateboard park.
SFX:laughing and shouting,wheels scraping across concrete, thuds, clapping.
MICHAEL (OS): Great job, Bentley!

JAZZ looks through the fence.
SFX. SKATEBOARD SOUNDS CONTINUE
BENTLEY: You there. You need proper footwear inside the park. No barefoot skateboarding.

Figures 2.1a–2.1d Introduction of Jaz

MICHAEL: That's the Gimp. His feet are too messed up for shoes. Go home, Gimp. You got no business here.

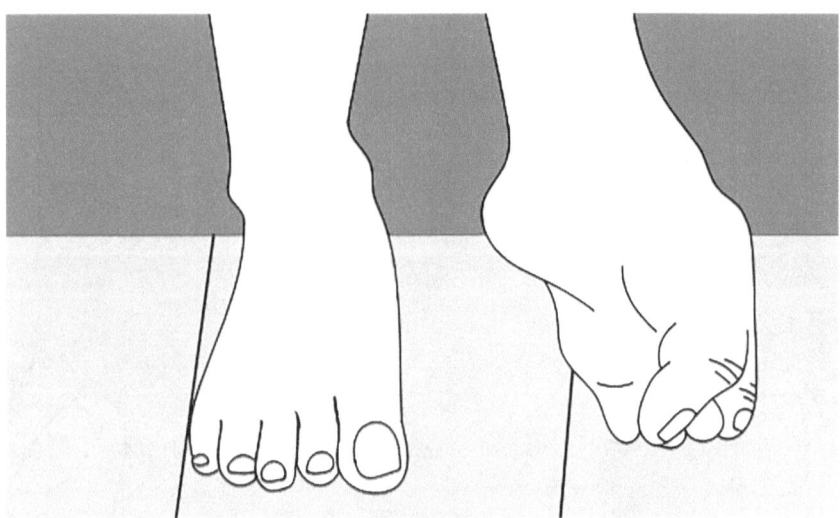

SFX. BOYS' LAUGHTER
JAZZ looks down at his feet. The left foot is a club foot.

Figures 2.1a–2.1d (continued)

that toy, even if she doesn't understand the toy and is too tired to play with it. If the child's mother says she can't have the toy, an id-driven child might have a grand melt-down in public, embarrassing the mother and annoying all the other shoppers. The id-driven child has not developed the ego to be able to delay gratification or deny any fleeting desire. Parents have shared instances where their children have succumbed to screaming fits because they can't pick up a toy they are sitting on, can't go inside their television set to hug a TV personality, are not allowed to eat the dog's food, or feel insulted because a bird flew away. The id can be impulsive, perverse, and foolish even as it is necessary.

Under Freud's definition, the *ego* is not necessarily vanity or development of individual identity as in the Jungian definition, but the development of the rational, practical portion of the unconscious. As the infant grows, she should acquire the ego that will control her id and help her better deal with the stresses and pressures of the external world. However, the id's energy will always remain a vibrant drive. A child learns to delay gratification, but the id's biological demands must ultimately be met. The child may be able to wait awhile for dinner, but she will eventually have to eat. The ego will not deny the id but will judge whether the id's demands are vital and how they can be balanced with the demands of the external world.

Freud's *superego* is internalized moral authority, those rules and limitations families, teachers, religious leaders, or civilization place on people and the guilt individuals might experience when they break those rules. It is the element of the subconscious that tells an individual what is right, what is wrong, and how to behave. The superego is that part of the individual unconscious that interrupts the budding rascal. An individual who obeys laws or rules only when an authority figure is watching and breaks the rules at any opportunity has an underdeveloped superego. The individual that lives with a consistent feeling of guilt and self-loathing because of perceived personal flaws and deficiencies has an overdeveloped superego. The superego can be a harsh internal critic. When the ego cannot balance the drives of the id, the rules of the superego, and the pressures of external reality, the individual becomes troubled. If she is unable to achieve balance, she may become a destabilizing force in her family and her community.

Media critics have used these Freudian concepts to describe and analyze fictional characters. Instead of an individual struggling to achieve a balanced ego that is able to control the id, steady the superego, and capably deal with the external world, a writer can treat these different aspects of an individual personality as entirely separate characters (Indick, 2004; Mahan, 1986). Applying Freudian ideas to fictional stories often associates the ego with the protagonist, who must cope with all those pressures the plot will bring. The crippled boy from Mississippi who wants to be a skateboarder could be an ego character, trying to stabilize the demands of his own desires with the stress of external pressures and his physical limitations. Other characters in the story might represent the forces that the ego must attempt to balance in the journey to achieve a goal.

Id-driven characters are those who cannot control their desires or refuse to accept the constraints of external authority or society. Id-driven characters have a limited sense of guilt and need an outside authority to restrict their harmful behavior. Bullies, villains, and criminals are frequently id-driven characters. But id-driven characters can also be sidekicks, good-hearted, madcap, impulsive characters who haven't learned how to delay gratifications. The id-driven character could be the best buddy of the protagonist and desperately want to help but instead the id-driven character's impulsive behavior creates more complications. For example, Jaz might have an id-driven friend, a sidekick, or deuteragonist who wants Jaz to succeed. So, this id-driven friend spontaneously steals the money Jaz needs for the competition's entry fee. This would create new problems for Jaz when his superego-driven father discovers the stolen money in Jaz's room. A character representing the superego might be harsh and punitive, distrusting the ability of the protagonist to do the right things.

Protagonists might begin their story as id-driven or superego dominated characters, but change. Their character arc is involved in developing ego and finding more balance as their story progresses. One example of an id-driven protagonist is the character of Randle McMurphy from the film *One Flew Over the Cuckoo's Nest* (1975) based on the Ken Kesey novel (*One Flew Over the Cuckoo's Nest*, 1962). Because he is an id-driven character, McMurphy needs the external moral authority of prison; he has no self-control. He is a repeat offender, driven by self-gratification. When the film begins, McMurphy is serving a jail sentence for statutory rape. McMurphy pretends to be mentally ill to be moved from prison to the more comfortable environment of a mental institution, where he can avoid any hard labor. His perspective is that life must be his party, fully enjoyed right now, in this moment, no matter what the future consequences might be. McMurphy's personal party consists of events such as games of poker, watching sports, drinking, smoking, casual sex, and basketball games played with friends. McMurphy rebels against the tyrannical Nurse Ratched, who runs the ward at the mental institution and interrupts his party. Nurse Ratched represents a negative superego. She has a love of rules and power, but no honest concern or love for her patients. For a negative superego like Nurse Ratched, rules do not exist to protect people; people exist to uphold the rules. McMurphy has not internalized any superego. For McMurphy, the delight of a rule is found in breaking or circumventing it. As he develops concern for other patients, helping them to enjoy the party he wants life to be, McMurphy becomes a bit more balanced, more representative of Freud's ego. He maintains his perspective that life is his personal jamboree, but he won't selfishly abandon his friends and will sacrifice himself to defend them against the destructive influence of the harmful superego, the manipulative Nurse Ratched.

Physical Attributes

Physical descriptions of characters in a screenplay tend to be limited, allowing the director some freedom in casting. The character's name, age, gender, and socioeconomic level might be included in a quick introduction. Unusual physical traits, physical abilities, and handicaps are also important for developing character and can help inform the direction of a story. Age or a character's stage in the human life cycle is significant. The perspectives, traits, and habits that are important for developing character are less necessary in this initial character description, since they will be continually revealed in the character's dialogue and actions throughout the script. It is better to omit too much detail in initial physical descriptions. It isn't necessary to itemize specific details about hair styles, wardrobe, or jewelry unless these are important to the character or the plot.

Sometimes physical characteristics are critical to the story. For example, the movies *The Elephant Man* (1980), *Mask* (1985), and *Wonder* (2017) are all films about protagonists with severe physical deformities, which will determine how other characters treat them. The physical trait of a deformed foot is important to our penniless, 14-year-old boy from Mississippi. Still, he might be very simply described as: JAZ "THE GIMP" BENNETT, a club-footed teen dressed in clothes pulled from a charity bin. The ways that Jaz is clever and talented will be revealed as the story unfolds. Unless his race is also critical to the story, the screenwriter can leave that detail to a casting director.

Physical traits can determine character choices. The television crime series *In the Dark* (2018–) features an attractive female protagonist in her 20s who is promiscuous, a heavy drinker, and dedicated to solving the mysterious murder of her friend. Murphy Mason is also blind. She is literally and figuratively "in the dark" as she navigates deceptions, cover-ups, and her own poor choices. Murphy's blindness is as central to the situational concept of story as it is to her character. If a character's humpback, bald head, muscular body, extraordinary beauty, or mismatched eyes are important to the story, these physical traits should be mentioned when the character is first introduced.

Quirks, Hobbies, and Passions

In addition to a character's physical traits, perspective, psychological drives, and humanity or lack of it, characters' quirks, hobbies, habits, and idiosyncrasies also make them memorable. Quirks are those odd traits that make a character unique. Individuals we know in our social lives have distinctive habits and mannerisms, and so should characters in fiction. A character might have a tendency toward pessimism, always pointing out the extreme worst that could happen in any situation. Another character might be a word junkie, enthusiastic about the game *Scrabble,* crossword puzzles, and abysmal puns. The word junkie might have a perspective that "actions talk, but words explain." The word junkie may also cling to debate so that other characters in the story must push the word junkie into action. There are any number of things characters might do that mark them as unique personalities. An avid golfer might express the events of his life in ridiculously exaggerated golf metaphors, referring to his second and third marriages as "Mulligans" or his infant son as his "hole-in-one."

Hobbies and habits are sometimes connected to a character's perspective. Drawing on the news clip mentioned in Chapter 1, a character who is a knitting enthusiast might not go anywhere without a bag of needles and unusual materials such as plastic garbage bags to knit into the strange clothing she wears. If this knitting enthusiast is a dedicated environmentalist, her hobby is an extension of her commitment to recycling.

Perhaps a nervous character always carries river rocks in her pocket, taking them out to fiddle with when stressed. Another character might be obsessed with adult coloring books. Another character might have quirkier obsessions, hoarding odd objects that other people discard. For example, a character might collect used cigarette butts with lipstick imprints, which he identifies by cigarette brand and lipstick hue before pinning to mounting boards for display as if these finds were rare insects. The nice thing about giving a character a persistent or unusual habit or hobby is that the actor will have business for scenes that may not have much action otherwise. An actor's *business* consists of those smaller tasks or actions that make a scene feel natural and add believability. Business also gives an actor a way to subtly communicate the character's mood. The knitting enthusiast can clank her needles angrily, nervously drop stitches, or happily cast on her recycled yarn, depending on her mood in the scene.

Location as Character

A location can take on such distinctive properties that it can seem to have as much force in the story as another character. In the 1980 film version of the Stephen King horror story *The Shining*, the Overlook Hotel is as much a character as Jack Torrance, his wife Wendy, and son Danny. The historic hotel is a luxury vacation spot for wealthy tourists at a beautifully remote location high in the Colorado Rockies. During winter months, snowy weather and mountainous terrain isolate the hotel from nearby communities, so the owners shut it down, leaving it to the winter caretaker who will live with his family in the hotel all winter. As a character, the Overlook is malevolent and haunted with tragic memories. Built in 1907 on sacred Indian grounds, the hotel has a sad reputation. The former winter caretaker developed cabin fever while secluded with his family at the Overlook and killed his wife and young daughters. Though some critics watching the movie might interpret Jack Torrance as his own worst enemy, succumbing to madness in the cold, winter isolation, critics can also interpret the Overlook Hotel as the film's antagonist. The Overlook toys with Jack's emotional stability, preventing him from doing any successful writing and seducing him to violence with suspicions about his family. The hotel seems to have the goal to destabilize and destroy those characters vulnerable to its influence. It is not unusual for the haunted places in ghost stories to seem like distinctive personalities.

The sprawling castle and grounds of Hogwarts School of Witchcraft and Wizardry from the *Harry Potter* series is not only a medieval stronghold with dungeons, tunnels, turrets, moving staircases, talking portraits, a whomping willow, rooms of requirement, and other wondrous spaces, Hogwarts is also a character. The school gives help when a student asks for it or when the student needs and deserves that help.

In the science fiction film *The Martian* (2015), the planet Mars with its desolate, lonely environment is both an ominous and spectacularly beautiful antagonist for the astronaut stranded there. *Guardians of the Galaxy II* (2017) creates a character that is literally a planet, a god-like being that formed matter around its consciousness to create both a planet and a humanoid form. Similar to ancient Greek and Roman gods, the character falls in love with a human woman and impregnates her. Interestingly, the character's name is Ego, though not in the Freudian sense of achieving balance but in the Jungian sense of a creature that has established himself as an individual, separated from the whole of the universe to manifest as an independent male personality.

The personality of a location is also a key lure for interactive stories, offering players the ability to inspect, linger, and imaginatively live in an extraordinary space.

Characters in Games and Interactive Stories

Avatars are the protagonists of interactive stories and games. Avatars represent the character a player wants to be. Because the term "avatar" also designates images individuals use as representations on social media, other digital forums, and in non-game contexts, the game player's representative character is often more specifically referred to as a player character or playable character or P-C (or PC, not to be confused with the older acronym for personal computer). Writers and game developers provide the choices the P-Cs can make, but the personalities of people playing the game make those choices, however perverse they may be. The amount and kinds of choices writers provide along with their consequences help players develop their characters.

Non-player characters (N-P-Cs or NPCs) are the characters controlled by the writer and programmer. Like the characters in movies and television, these characters have fixed dialogue, predetermined actions, and responses. N-P-Cs serve specific roles in interactive media, but there is no rule that says these characters can't be as interesting, complex, quirky, and layered as characters in other screen media. N-P-Cs may be most fully realized in cutscenes, which pause the game play for film-like sequences that provide the player with the background to understand the game's situation, help to clarify choices, recap player actions, suggest choices for the future, or reward the P-C for a well-played game, among other potential tasks to support the game's story. Unlike screenplays where physical descriptions are brief, the development of N-P-Cs for interactive stories might require detailed physical reports to help guide the designers creating the conceptual graphics for the character.

Character Biographies

Many seasoned writers recommend developing biographies for all significant characters in a story. These biographies include the character's name, demographics, physical characteristics, psychographics, and perspective, as well as notations about significant events in the character's life. This is one way to really understand your characters and how they will serve the story. When, where, and why does this character appear? If you are creating an id-driven character, you know your character is defiant with a slippery sense of logic. Knowing that the character is id-driven makes it easier to predict this character's choices and how the character will behave toward authority. Knowing that a character is superego-driven means understanding the character's obsession with rules and power. Knowing that a character is shadow-driven means providing that opportunity for the shadow to emerge. Consider if the character has an anima or animus longing for expression. Will this character remain steadfast, holding tight to an ideology or will the character experience a transformation of perspective? What is the character's perspective? Is the character trustworthy? If there has been a destabilizing force, how will the character rediscover balance if balance is possible? Understanding a character's biography and drives helps writers predict what that character will do or say in any event that will appear in the plot.

Every character in a story should have unique perspectives, drives, hobbies, and habits. Certainly the *deuteragonist*, who is a buddy to the protagonist and occupies nearly as much screen time as the protagonist does, and *tritagonist*, who is also important to the protagonist, helping or hindering the journey, should be layered personalities. Even *tertiary characters*, whose screen time may be limited but whose contributions to the story are significant should be developed as individuals with independent perspectives and goals. It is helpful to a story's authenticity if all characters are respected as individuals. There is really no good reason to have an amorphous MAN #1 and MAN #2 in pivotal dialogue with the protagonist. If a character has an important purpose in the story, that character should at least have a name and a hint of personality.

There are three primary ways that fictional characters can be authentic: to themselves, to other characters, and to the story. Like real people, characters in fiction can be insincere and untrustworthy, authentically reflecting the inauthentic people we sometimes encounter in life experience. In this way, a character who behaves in dishonest ways can be important to the credible story a writer needs to tell. A character's insincere behaviors toward others or herself might be intentional or accidental. Characters may cynically realize their duplicity and not care, pretending to have emotions they don't feel. To be accidentally insincere, characters may not fully understand their own needs and values. It may be necessary for them to learn from a story situation or other characters what those real needs and values are. Authentic characters will be more like real people than abstract types. Both the heroes and the villains in a story are believable when they are layered with recognizable perspectives, habits, drives, and idiosyncrasies. Even exaggerated personalities work best when they also exhibit a truth and pain audiences can understand. If your characters have strong perspectives, ambitions, passions, and foibles, at some point in your writing you may notice a peculiar magic happening. It can seem as if the characters have commandeered your story and are making their own decisions.

You are just along for the ride.

References

Edwards, E. D. (2019). "Moonshiners and the Media: The Twenty-First Century Trickster." In C. D. Lippard and B. E. Stewart, eds., *Modern Moonshine: The Revival of White Whiskey in the Twenty-First Century* (1st ed.), pp. 67–84. Morgantown: West Virginia University Press.

Freud, S. (2011). *The Ego and the Id*. LaVergne, TN: Pacific Publishing Studio.

Gibran, K. (1926). *Sand and Foam: A Book of Aphorisms*. A. A. Knopf.

Jung, C. G. (1964). *Man and His Symbols*. Garden City, NY: Doubleday.

Jung, C. G., and Campbell, J. (1971). *The Portable Jung*. New York: Viking Press.

Kepnes, S. (2014). *You*. New York: Atria/Emily Bestler Books.

Li, S. (2019). Why *Good Girls* Is Such a Rewarding Show. *Atlantic*. May 24.

Mahan, J. H. (1986). "A Freudian Analysis of the Private Detective Tale." In S. M. Kaminsky and J. H. Mahan, eds., *American Television Genres*, pp. 145–60. Chicago: Nelson-Hall.

Maslow, A. H. (1982). *Toward a psychology of being* (Second, Ser. Van nostrand insight books, 5). Van Nostrand Reinhold.

Metzl, J. (2019). *Dying of Whiteness: How the Politics of Racial Resentment Is Killing America's Heartland*. New York: Basic Books.

Twain, M., and Bancroft Library. Mark Twain Project. (1983). *The Prince and the Pauper: A Tale for Young People of All Ages*. V. Fischer and M. B. Frank, eds. Ser. The Mark Twain Library. Published in cooperation with the University of Iowa by University of California Press.

You. (2018–19). Television series. G. Berlanti and S. Gamble, developers. Lifetime and Warner Bros. Television.

Williams, D. (2012) *The Trickster Brain: Neuroscience, Evolution, and Narrative*. Lantham: Lexington Books.

Chapter 3

THE SHAPES OF VISUAL NARRATIVE

> There is no worse lie than a truth misunderstood by those who hear it.
> —William James

Some people use the word "plot" as a synonym for "story," but others will distinguish between the two. A *story* is more precisely the narration of events: the answers to "who, what, when, where, how, and how much." The *plot* explains the reasons behind those events. Plot answers the "why" question, providing the purpose (and perhaps the larger truth) for events that happen in a story. Plot gives a story intrigue and motivation. It's hard to imagine a story without a plot, but some stories, particularly those written for very young children, do not have problems, conflicts, or plots. Such stories typically describe places, characters, and actions such as a visit to a park, what a brown bear sees, what a very hungry caterpillar eats, or the ritual of saying goodnight to the moon. However, most stories and even most children's stories will involve plots and characters with conflicts and problems to solve.

Structure is neither plot nor story but can influence how both are understood. The *structure* of a story is the container that gives the story and plot their form. Structure is the framing and order in which those story events unfold and the plot surfaces. In Chapter 1, our search was for story ideas, the events and the settings in which actions might occur, allowing for the potential tones or qualities that a genre can provide. In Chapter 2 we considered the drives, traits, and perspectives of those characters who stimulate the plot and provide the reason (or why) things happen in the way they do. In the next two chapters we will review choices a writer makes about structure, deciding when a story begins, how the plot will unfold, and when as well as the manner in which it might end.

Linear Three-Act Structures

One of the clichés of the student film is the opening with a ringing alarm clock rudely awakening the protagonist, who slaps at the clock in a futile attempt to delay time and sleep away a little more of it. The student writer has recognized the familiar reoccurring patterns in the days that structure our lives. We wake, we follow the usual morning routines until something happens to disrupt them, we confront the challenges, until at the end of the day the routines are restored, changed, or completely upended, but the day is over.

Our days essentially follow a classic structure.

Three-act structure is one of the more enduring story containers, dating back to the ancient Greeks and Aristotle's observation that a story should have a beginning, middle, and an end. Three acts as a story structure have biological impetus. They follow a familiar pattern. Beginnings, middles, and endings seem natural. A child is born, struggles to grow and develops into an adult. The adult then confronts the many challenges of mature life, until finally, old age arrives, then death, and the story of that person's life is over. A business meeting has its kickoff with introductions of those at the table and the topic of concern. The meeting continues while participants discuss or debate the issues, until finally, maybe glancing at a watch, the person presiding over the meeting brings it to a close with a summary of concerns and perhaps a decision or a vote. The linear, three-part structure survives because it is familiar and instinctive.

Just because waking up is a natural beginning for the day doesn't necessarily make the annoyed alarm clock routine a compelling start to a story. The three-act structure doesn't need to start when the protagonist wakes up and rolls out of bed, unless there is something unusual in that familiar routine that reveals essential information about protagonists and their circumstances. A writer might instead choose to begin with a confrontation that better defines the protagonist's situation. In the classic musical based on the L. Frank Baum children's book, *The Wizard of Oz* (1939), Dorothy's story doesn't begin as the dog Toto licks her sleeping face to wake her when Aunty Em calls Dorothy down to breakfast. The story begins with Dorothy and Toto on the way home after a confrontation with their neighbor, Miss Gulch. Audiences don't see Toto bite Miss Gulch on the leg (though that might have been a dynamic scene). Instead, Dorothy returns to her aunt and uncle's farm and frantically tries to tell them about the fracas with Miss Gulch, who will soon arrive with an order from the sheriff to have Toto euthanized. Dorothy's story is strictly linear, flowing chronologically from beginning to conclusion without any flashbacks or side trips, unless audiences consider act 2 to be one long side trip deep into a technicolor concussion.

The classic three-act structure for a film tends to be linear or chronological. We experience the story the way we experience time. There may be the occasional flashback to explain an element of the plot or a character memory that can't be revealed with the forward flow of events, but the story generally flows temporally from beginning to end. For a film, the classic three-act structure devotes about a quarter of the film's total length to the first act, about half of the film's total length to the second act, and the final quarter of the film to the third act. In a two-hour feature film, act 1 will be about thirty minutes; act 2 about an hour, and act 3 about thirty minutes. In a twenty-minute short film, the first act will be about five minutes, the second act will be about ten minutes, and the third act about five minutes. Some critics suggest that three-act structure is more accurately a four-act structure and proceed to divide act 2 so that each of the four acts in a screenplay is a similar length (Tobin, 2007). The overall structure remains the same, but those who advocate a four-act structure argue that the beginning of act 2 (or act 2a) is more about how a protagonist reacts and survives to the new circumstances, challenges, and dilemmas of the story, whereas in the new act 3 (or act 2b) the protagonist is more knowledgeable and confident and has become more proactive than reactive as tensions and the difficulties of challenges continue to escalate.

In extremely short scripts, such as skits, and extremely long projects, such as episodic and interactive stories, scripts will generally use a structure other than three acts, adapting the work of three acts (or four acts) to better support unique features of their stories, just as a plate, a bowl, and a cup are each designed to support the particular kind of food they will deliver. Just as soup served on a plate would be a mess, some ensemble stories may not fit neatly into three acts.

Because the three-act structure is still prevalent in popular film and its elements are critical to understanding other storytelling structures in other media, I will review the work of three acts as this structure historically applies to film before discussing other structural dishes in which writers serve their stories in Chapter 4.

The Work of Act One

In the classic three-act structure, each act has specific jobs to do. Act 1 introduces the characters and their circumstances. It should show audiences what the protagonist's ordinary life is like before it is interrupted with the conflict or inciting incident that disrupts the protagonist's routine, forcing the protagonist to make decisions that will inspire the events in act 2. Sometimes the character's decisions may solve the original conflict, but also create new dramatic situations with additional problems for the protagonist to overcome. Act 1 also has the work of introducing the protagonist's goals, indicating the protagonist's needs, and revealing those qualities in the protagonist that will make an audience care about what happens to this character.

In *The Wizard of Oz*, the act 1 problem for Dorothy is Toto's imminent doom. Miss Gulch's order from the sheriff to have Toto euthanized is also an example of a *ticking clock*. A ticking clock is a threat, obstacle, or problem the protagonist must overcome by a specific date or moment, otherwise there will be a disaster. Toto's time on this earth is quickly vanishing unless Dorothy can do something to stop Miss Gulch. Dorothy gets audience sympathy in act 1 largely through her love for Toto and the threat to the little dog, but the other characters on the farm, Uncle Henry, Aunt Em, and the hired hands all care about Dorothy, so audiences can surmise that Dorothy is someone worthy of our concern, too. For Dorothy, the problem of Miss Gulch and her mandate to euthanize Toto will be temporarily resolved when Toto escapes from the basket on the back of Miss Gulch's bike and returns to Dorothy's arms. Dorothy wants a more permanent solution. She chooses to take her dog and run away from home. When Professor Marvel helps Dorothy realize how much she loves her home and how much running away would hurt her Aunty Em, Dorothy knows running away is not a viable solution. Dorothy can't follow through with a decision that would cause her family to grieve. She must go home and find another answer for Toto's dilemma.

Act 1 should also set the tone for the story that will unfold. The atmosphere of the first act of a murder mystery with the discovery of a dead body creates a very different mood than the first act of a comedy, when joking among characters helps an audience orient to comic tensions. Audiences watching *The Wizard of Oz* learn that life on the farm where Dorothy lives is hard work: wagons must be mended, chickens must be moved from a failing incubator, hogs must be penned and fed, and fences must be painted. When the protagonist expresses her yearnings through a song, audiences quickly realize that this is a musical and not a realistic drama. The song is also an example of *telegraphing*, where the script explicitly signals what will happen in the story. Dorothy will literally go "Somewhere Over the Rainbow" and have adventures washed in rainbow colors. Telegraphing is not a necessary device that must be used in act 1; telegraphing can happen in any act. However, like the three-part structure of a good speech (tell the audience what you're going to say, say it, and then tell them what you've said), telegraphing often happens in act 1.

It takes the external intrusion of a tornado to create Dorothy's new problem, which arrives before Dorothy has figured out the resolution for her old one. The arrival of the tornado is an example of *deus ex machina*, or "god from the machine." The phrase comes from the ancient Greek use of a mechanical device that brought the actor playing a god onto the stage to miraculously settle conflicts, usually at the end of the drama. In modern use, *deus ex machina* is frequently a derogatory term, referring to contrived maneuverings of the plot that resolve a story situation unnaturally. Critics often see it as the too convenient and clumsy gimmick of writers who don't have the imagination capable of logically resolving the story's issues. Though a tornado arrives in the *Wizard of Oz* like a god out of the sky to suddenly change events for Dorothy and Toto, it doesn't appear to be the clumsy device of the typical *deus ex machina*. Kansas is a tornado-prone state, so the abrupt appearance of the storm in act 1 of *The Wizard of Oz* seems less like a plot stunt. The tornado also doesn't end the story or solve the conflict but is the device that moves the story from act 1 to act 2 and creates a major new problem with a new conflict for Dorothy to solve without really solving the old problem.

When contemplating the sudden appearance of an external force, consider if this abrupt new event is reasonable or likely, if it could be an important metaphor or symbol, or if it is simply a convenient trick to solve a tough story problem. The abrupt appearance of an external force unrelated to previous events should at least seem logical to the world that act 1 has created. The shock of a forceful surprise like a tornado, a significant revelation, or a disruption of the protagonist's plans at the end of act 1 will set up the action for act 2.

The Work of Act Two

If we use dinner as the metaphor for three acts, act 2 is the main course of the script, half of the total length of the screenplay with the biggest caloric impact. The second act involves the protagonist's search for solutions to the new problems or the new conflicts introduced toward the end of act 1. The protagonist may have some successes in the beginning of the act, but fresh obstacles and challenges will appear, bringing with them new encounters, obligations, struggles, and dilemmas. The events and hardships of the second act might increase in urgency or danger for the protagonist until the point where all appears lost and the protagonist must make a desperate decision.

For Dorothy, act 2 begins when the tornado drops her house in Munchkin Land. Just as Dorothy had resolved to go back to Aunt Em and the home she loves, Dorothy is forcibly taken away. Her new goal is to figure out where she is and find her way back to her Kansas family. The breathtaking strangeness of this new world is visually enticing but a new conflict adds to Dorothy's problem of finding out where she is, creating even more interest. Dorothy's falling house has killed the Wicked Witch of the East, causing Dorothy to be the accidental hero of the Munchkins but also making her the sworn enemy of the Wicked Witch of the West. Before the Wicked Witch can claim her dead sister's ruby slippers, Glinda the Good Witch transfers them to Dorothy's feet. Glinda advises Dorothy to keep the shoes on her feet as she travels down the Yellow Brick Road to the Emerald City, where Dorothy should be able to find the powerful Wizard of Oz who will help her get back home. Glinda provides Dorothy with her primary goal for act 2 and simultaneously provides the Wicked Witch of the West with her objective. Vengeance motivates her animus for Dorothy and Toto, but the Witch also has the physical goal of claiming her dead sister's slippers, which she considers to be her rightful inheritance. The Witch and Dorothy have goals that are in direct conflict.

The bulk of act 2 deals with Dorothy's adventures on her trek to the Emerald City as she makes new friends of the Scarecrow, the Tin Man, and the Cowardly Lion. *Recapitulation*, or those scenes in which characters reiterate important story information, can occur in any act, recapitulation is particularly useful when characters need to reassess what has happened and try to figure out what they should do next. Recapitulation reminds audiences of important events and can create tension or anticipation for the next scenes. In *The Wizard of Oz*, some recapitulation occurs when Dorothy encounters each new character and explains that a meeting with the Wizard is the goal of her journey and the resolution to her problems, and possibly the solution to their issues as well. Act 2 is where the protagonist is continually tested. Dorothy demonstrates wisdom, consideration, and great courage in her interactions with her new friends. As they join her journey, her new companions depend on Dorothy to succeed.

Dramatic irony happens when an audience understands the situation, but characters don't. It is dramatic irony when audiences know the Wicked Witch uses her crystal ball to monitor everything Dorothy and her friends do. Dorothy and her companions don't realize they are so closely watched, yet they still manage to overcome obstacles the Witch creates for them. They arrive triumphantly in Emerald City, only to have the Wizard set them a new task of getting the Witch's broomstick before he will agree to grant any wishes. A four-act structure would divide act 2 here, where the protagonist has responded to her puzzling new world and appears to have triumphed. In the second half of act 2 (or act 2b), Dorothy and her friends are presented with another obstacle that will put them in direct confrontation with the story's villain. Dorothy is no longer simply reacting to events, now she intentionally ventures forward to meet them with a better understanding of the danger she faces.

As Dorothy and her friends travel to the Witch's castle to fulfill this new task, the Witch captures Dorothy. The Witch shows Dorothy an hourglass, introducing another ticking clock that will announce when Dorothy shall die, and the Witch can get her ruby slippers. Ticking clock devices increase the tension in a story, driving characters toward the inevitable deadline when something catastrophic is supposed to happen. Dorothy's friends come to her rescue, but the Witch sets Scarecrow on fire. When Dorothy tosses a bucket of water to douse the fire and save Scarecrow, she inadvertently splashes the Witch, who melts away. Freed from the Witch's enslavement, the guards of the castle celebrate Dorothy much like the Munchkins did in the beginning of act 2, rewarding Dorothy with the Witch's broom.

The job of act 2 is to confront the protagonist with obstacles and conflicts until that moment when it seems as if all has failed, and the protagonist may be doomed. With the exception of a few successes and revelations and perhaps meeting new friends and developing new relationships, protagonists generally have a bad time in act 2. The pace of action and risks intensify. There are many more problems and conflicts to resolve. What Dorothy learns in act 2 is that "Somewhere over the Rainbow" is a place beset with troubles and these troubles won't simply "melt like lemon drops."

The Work of Act Three

The work of act 3 is the resolution of the remaining problems, the *denouement* that explains or reconciles various elements of the plot. But act 3 will also introduce new setbacks and difficulties and a final dilemma before the primary problem is finally resolved. Protagonists will face yet another problem that becomes the initial work of act 3. Dorothy, who learned at the end of act 1 that she didn't really want to leave her home and her Aunt Em but is forcefully set down in a strange place, navigated that new world and defeated the Witch in act 2, now learns in act 3 that the Wizard has no magic, and she is faced with the possibility of permanent residency in Oz.

Dorothy and her friends arrive triumphantly in Emerald City, only to learn that the Wizard does not have the power to help them. This discovery that the Wizard is an ordinary man without any potent magic is an example of *false telegraphing*. When Glinda told Dorothy in the beginning of act 2 that the wonderful and mysterious Wizard of Oz would help, she created an expectation that audiences would see some wondrous magic from the Wizard. *Situational irony* and false telegraphing are similar. They are the disparity between what an audience expects to happen and what actually does happen. For example, earlier in act 2 when Dorothy and her friends are walking through a dark and creepy forest and the Cowardly Lion ambushes them and tries to bite Toto, Dorothy slaps the Lion. The Lion cries. Audiences don't expect this behavior from a lion. However, when the going gets tough, the Lion will act courageously to help his friends. The dramatic irony in act 1, where audiences know that Professor Marvel is a charlatan even if Dorothy thinks he has miraculous powers, is repeated when the Wizard of Oz is also revealed to be a con man. With both characters played by Frank Morgan, audiences know the Wizard is offering Dorothy's friends placebos rather than actual cures for their problems, but at this point the characters don't need the Wizard's magic to be smart, loving, and brave. Dramatic irony suggested in act 1 can be repeated or sustained in act 2 to excite audience interest as they anxiously wait to see what happens when the characters discover the truth of their situation.

Act 3 is where a new conflict is overcome, where most plot questions are answered, and most remaining conflicts are resolved. For Dorothy this is discovering that she might get back to Kansas with the Wizard in a hot-air balloon, but once again Toto jumps out of her arms and the balloon's basket so that Dorothy must go after him. The Wizard cannot control or stop the ascent of the balloon. Just as it seems Dorothy will surely be forever stranded in Oz, Glinda reveals the secret of the ruby slippers (another *deus ex machina*) and Dorothy is able to safely return to the bleak but comfortably predictable black and white of a humble Kansas farm and the knowledge that "there is no place like home."

The *Wizard of Oz* underscores the divisions between acts with stylistic choices. Act 1 appears in black and white, act 2 appears as a colorful and fantastical adventure, and act 3 is a combination of color that returns to black and white once Dorothy is safely back in Kansas. It's interesting that act 3 in *The Wizard of Oz* never makes it clear that the original problem of Miss Gulch and the sheriff's order to euthanize Toto has been definitely resolved. Because Miss Gulch's equivalent in Oz is the Wicked Witch of the West, and because the witch melts away, audiences might assume that Miss Gulch is also gone, lifted up and spun away on her bicycle by the fierce winds of a tornado and no longer a threat to Dorothy or Toto.

Sequence Structure

In a two-hour feature film, sequence structure further divides the acts into eight sequences of about ten to fifteen minutes each, so that act 1 has two sequences, act 2 has four sequences, and act 3 has two sequences. Using sequences as a scripting technique for writers has been credited to Czech film producer Frank (František) Daniel, who taught screenwriting in the University of Southern California's graduate screenwriting program (Gulino, 2004). The recognition of sequence structure dates to the origins of early silent movies and reels that could only hold about ten to fifteen minutes of film stock. To make the transitions between switching reels on the projector seem more fluid and intentional, early silent films would fade out at the end of one reel and fade in at the beginning of the next reel. Each sequence was like a mini-movie, with its own beginning, middle, and an end that would tease or connect to the following sequence. Instead of watching the entire feature at one sitting, sequences could also be watched as episodes, the same way audiences would watch episodic television in later decades. In early cinema history, such serial films resolved one story problem and then created a new problem with ample suspense to lure audiences back to the theater the following week.

The practice of dividing a two-hour movie into eight sequences continues into the twenty-first century even though its technological necessity in cinema projection is long gone. Sequences build larger stories from smaller episodes. Adapted forms of sequence structure have been useful for commercial television, when anticipation for the wrap-up of a suspenseful sequence must hold audiences through the interruptions of commercial breaks. The practice of binge watching episodic television on streaming devices makes the episodes themselves seem like extended sequences nested within the larger structure of a season, with the episodes composed of even smaller sequential story moments.

As it conforms to the three-act structure, *The Wizard of Oz* also conforms to sequence structure. The first sequence begins with the trouble of Miss Gulch and her order from the sheriff allowing her to take Toto and ends with the dog's escape. The second sequence begins with Dorothy's decision to run away and ends when the tornado sets her house down in Munchkin Land. The third sequence, which begins act 2 in color, features the triumphant success of killing a witch and ends as Dorothy starts her journey down the yellow brick road. Each sequence introduces new problems, solves others, and creates fresh tensions as one sequence ends and a new one begins. Some writers find it useful to think of the three acts of a feature film in the shorter, connected stories of sequences. Bigger stories created from the concise moments of smaller ones can help keep audiences engaged and help writers feel less overwhelmed by larger projects.

The Three Acts of the Hero's Journey

As we mentioned in Chapter 2, American mythologist Joseph Campbell believed that much of human storytelling can be distilled into one single mythic journey that is told and retold with varying details, a similar hero on a similar journey but with a thousand different expressions (1949). The important moments of this journey involve the protagonist's travels from the exposition of the protagonist's ordinary world (the background information audiences need to properly understand the protagonist's character and situation), to the point of attack (or inciting incident where a major conflict rears its head), to rising action (where more tension arises and conflicts occur), to climax (the turning point in the protagonist's principal dilemma), to the falling action leading to the resolution of the conflict (dénouement, "happily ever after," death, disaster, or return home). In the *Writer's Journey*, Christ Vogler describes how the elements of the hero's journey are directly related to the three-act structure (1998, p. 14). Vogler also makes extensive references to *The Wizard of Oz* because it is a classical film many audiences have seen, but also because it follows this typical hero's journey (1998). Applying the structure of myth to the structure of a script, the story's journey does not need to involve literal physical travel to some other place, though for many stories like *The Wizard of Oz* it does. The journey may instead refer to the protagonist's pursuit of answers to a problem, such as a kidnap victim's search for escape or a secret agent's hunt for the clues necessary to unlock the riddle of an enemy's hidden code. The journey might concern a character's response to serious trouble that has invaded the character's home and community, a competition the character has willingly entered, or a protagonist's development through the special choices and challenges of unusual life circumstances.

As Campbell describes it, the first part of the mythological journey takes place in the *world of the common day*, showing audiences those usual routines in the protagonist's life. If this world is significantly different from what audiences would expect, the routines familiar to the protagonist and unfamiliar to the audience need to be established. These routines represent the protagonist's common life in contrast with the world of adventure the protagonist will face in act 2. The *call to adventure*, where protagonists face a challenge that disrupts their ordinary world, is one of the early steps of the journey that would ordinarily fall in act 1. The protagonist may *refuse the call* because of fears or doubts about undertaking this adventure. Something will then happen to convince the protagonist that this journey is necessary or unavoidable, *upping the ante*. It is also likely the protagonist will meet a *mentor* or guide, a character who will help with the decisions the protagonist faces. The mentor may give the protagonist a supernatural aid, talisman, or special insight to help with the mission. For Dorothy, the mentor in act 1 is Professor Marvel, who gives her the "supernatural vision" of her grieving aunt, helping Dorothy understand that she really wants to go back home rather than run away. By the end of act 1, the protagonist will be forced to commit to adventure, *crossing the threshold* that makes the beginning of the journey, just as Dorothy had to literally step across the threshold of her black-and-white, wind-blown house into the colorful land of Oz.

Once across the threshold and in the uncommon world, the protagonist faces the complications and conflicts that are typical tensions of act 2. Campbell refers to these as *trials* in an environment that is strange and disorienting, a place in sharp contrast to the ordinary world. It is a situation filled with danger and obstacles, but the protagonist might also encounter new friends and supporters who will help with the mission. Protagonists might have buddies or sidekicks who accompany them on the journey as Dorothy has Toto, and later encounters Scarecrow, Tinman, and Lion, who also become her companions and saviors. If the mentor from act 1 dies or disappears, protagonists may encounter other helpful guides who will reveal the tricks of survival in this strange new world. Dorothy will meet Glinda the Good Witch, another mentor who gives her the supernatural gift of the ruby slippers and the false knowledge that the Wizard in Emerald City will help her to get back home to Kansas. Other characters a protagonist might encounter include *threshold guardians*, who may attempt to thwart the hero's progress, *heralds*, who provide warnings, and *seducers*, who provide distractions or romantic interest. A protagonist might come upon *tricksters*, who could be either friends or enemies but are rarely who they seem to be. Dorothy's Wizard is a trickster as is Professor Marvel. The *Belly of the Whale*, the *Inmost Cave*, *Apotheosis*, and the *Supreme Ordeal* are descriptors for the major tests a hero will face toward the end of an odyssey of challenges, incidents, and adversities that the protagonist has encountered and largely overcome. For Dorothy, the supreme ordeal comes when she is imprisoned in the Witch's castle and watches the seconds of her life slip through the *ticking clock* of an hourglass.

Act 3 will involve the hero's return to the world of the common day, or *the road back*. After surviving the last ordeal, the hero is resurrected or reborn, cleansed of any ugliness from the agonies of the journey and all the many troubles that were endured. The *elixir* the protagonist brings home is that prize or reward, which might be a tangible object but might also be a valuable insight.

Joseph Campbell did not intend to provide writers with the unfailing recipe for successful storytelling to corner the Hollywood market. Campbell was a mythologist. He was describing some of the typical or more universal and reoccurring elements that he discovered in the myths he analyzed. Not every element Campbell describes appears in every mythological journey of every culture. However, the ability to identify these old patterns resurfacing in contemporary storytelling suggests that human beings enjoy the repetition of certain patterns as much as we enjoy disruption and surprise, as long as the challenges of disruption, surprise, and conflict happen to a protagonist and not to us. The realization that the structures of ancient myths seem to correspond to three-act structure reinforces the idea that this particular story vessel has been around for a very long time.

The Heroine's Journey

Critics of the hero's journey as a guide to contemporary storytelling have noticed that in a patriarchal world, a differently gendered hero has extra complications that can hinder the journey and may deny protagonists the higher heroic purpose that heterosexual male protagonists have typically achieved (Murdock, 1990). In order for a female protagonist to have an external hero's journey, some heroines must first travel inward to confront the illusions a patriarchal culture creates to limit them. The heroine must make a deliberate choice to change, to rediscover the animus she has denied and locked away. This inward journey is important because the heroine will need all her abilities to face her ordeal.

As we mentioned in Chapter 2, the *animus* combines those human traits that some patriarchal cultures mark as exclusively male and deny to females. These traits include such human abilities as logical reasoning, courage, independence, confidence, determination, intelligence, strength, power, and aggression. In preparation for her journey, the protagonist must recognize that her culture has methodically denied her those human qualities labeled "male," which might come in handy on her journey. Whether she wants to or not, a heroine must acknowledge her animus. She must also be willing to put aside a life that nourishes other people's ambitions and pick up the destiny of her own. Though in some stories this voyage inward can seem like the initial refusal of the call of the hero, it is a necessary preparation for the heroine's journey not necessarily the refusal of it.

When she has initially freed herself from patriarchal restrictions, the heroine can begin her adventure, though gender limitations are likely to shadow her throughout her journey. The heroine will encounter trials similar to those of the hero, but she must additionally slay the false myths of female dependency and inferiority, which can become the fierce threshold dragons of each new trial or test. The heroine may also need to find a male mentor to provide guidance in this male-dominated world she has entered. However, she must not confuse this mentor with the seductive "Knight in Shining Armor," which is the false myth that a man will solve all the heroine's problems. If she waits for a man to come rescue her, the protagonist becomes a damsel in distress and is no longer the heroine of her story. To remain a heroine and complete her journey, the female protagonist must be determined and resist stumbling into the constant cultural debris and the stereotyping that will litter her road of trials.

Before her journey is over, the heroine must reacknowledge and celebrate those human qualities her culture marks as feminine and disparages. These traits such as compassion, intuition, generosity, ability to nurture, self-sacrifice, empathy, organization, feminine creativity, and aesthetic judgment are also important to her success. Once she has reconnected to the feminine, the heroine can complete her journey with balance, her new-found elixir healing both her community and her psyche.

One often heralded example of the heroine's journey is the film *Erin Brockovich* (2000), based on the accomplishments of an actual American legal clerk, environmental activist, and divorced mother, who became the key to winning a lawsuit against a large energy company. In the movie, Erin must leave the life of a dependent housewife and succeed in the traditionally male realm of legal battle, corporate detective work, and the tricky maneuverings of litigation. The biographical film *Hidden Figures* (2016) is another heroine's journey. Katherine Johnson and her colleagues Mary Jackson and Dorothy Vaughn have already embraced the mathematical skills patriarchy assigns as a male trait but to discover the mathematical answers that will rescue NASA missions, they must continually battle the demons of misogyny and racism.

The comedy film *Legally Blonde* (2001) is the story of a fictional Elle Woods, a "girly-girl" who surrounds herself in Barbie doll pink. She is graduating from college with the expectation of a marriage proposal, or M-R-S degree. When her boyfriend breaks up with her instead, Elle needs to examine her life for what is important. She thinks she wants to win her boyfriend back and stay on the accepted path to the traditional role of wife and mother, so she decides to follow the ex-boyfriend to law school with this plan to "win him back." Elle takes the Law School Admission Test (LSAT), passes with a high score, and is admitted to Harvard Law School, where she will encounter her road of trials. Here Elle learns that she has been living the big lie in a world where the illusion of security is a form of imprisonment. Elle's journey is played for laughs, so it isn't too threatening. Elle has an obsession with pink. She is eager to display her body for the heterosexual male gaze. Elle's concerns seem focused on her tiny comfort dog, her exercise classes, and her trips to the hairdresser. Finally, Elle's triumph is largely due to her understanding of fashion and hair treatments rather than a clever application of law. But underneath these chuckles are brief glimpses of what is a smart, capable, and impressive heroine.

The heroine's journey is subversive. It threatens the patriarchal status quo, so characters representing that masculine authority will fight against a heroine to regain power and squash the rebel feminine. However, just because a character is female doesn't mean she won't be a warrior for the patriarchal status quo instead of supporting the rebel heroine. Sometimes the most formidable villains and antagonists that heroines encounter on their journeys are other female characters. Based on Margaret Atwood's dystopian tragedy *The Handmaid's Tale* (1985), the Hulu television series features the characters of Serena Joy Waterford and Aunt Lydia who seem eager to participate in the oppression of other women and uphold the goals of a cruel patriarchy that is the foundation for the totalitarian government of Gilead (2017–). The wives and "aunts" of Gilead protect what tiny scraps of agency they have by tormenting and persecuting other women, the "handmaidens" and "Marthas" who are their servants. Through bullying and torture, Aunt Lydia trains the girls selected to become handmaidens in the arts of obedience and surrender. Guided by her dogmatic belief that submission is God's purpose for women, Serena Joy is one of the primary architects of Gilead's misogynistic policies. She is also the barren wife of Fred Waterford, a powerful leader in Gilead's harsh, authoritarian government. The protagonist of the series is a handmaiden sent to the Waterford household to become their sexual slave in a perverse religious ceremony intended to conceive their child. The protagonist, Offred, is not even allowed to keep her own name but like all handmaidens takes her master's name preceded by the preposition "of." For Offred to take the journey into rebellion, she must embrace her animus and continually resist the patriarchal regime that turns women into household slaves, ornaments, sex toys, and baby machines.

Though Dorothy is a female protagonist, her journey through Oz is not a heroine's journey. Dorothy doesn't threaten the patriarchal status quo. Dorothy's ordeal is the revolt of a young girl against strict adult rules and a sheriff's death order rather than an expression of the rebel feminine. Professor Marvel makes Dorothy realize she must honor her aunt's care and devotion; little girls shouldn't run away from home. Little girls should honor their home and not make their mothers or aunts cry. The tornado whisks Dorothy away before she can even consider whether or not she is equipped for heroic encounters. Dorothy skips the inward journey necessary for the rebel heroine, finding her success through intuition, good luck, and the help of devoted friends.

Many heroic journeys with female protagonists are simply hero's journeys. The female protagonists in *Alien* (1979), *Lara Croft: Tomb Raider* (2001), and *Wonder Woman* (2017) are not female characters who need to take that inward gender journey or put up a substantial fight against misogyny before becoming successful heroes. These characters have already embraced their animus and are fully equipped for the challenges of their adventures.

A Heterosexual Man on a Heroine's Journey

A protagonist does not necessarily have to be female in order to need that inward trip to face inhibiting cultural demons before crossing the threshold into heroism. A gay man, transgender man, even a heterosexual man who has harmfully denied and imprisoned the qualities of his anima, may need this extra inward journey before beginning the heroic one. For example, in the 1979 film *Kramer vs. Kramer*, Ted Kramer's workaholic aggressiveness has landed the successful advertising executive an important account and the admiration of his boss. When Ted comes home to share the good news, he learns that his wife Joanna is leaving him. He will have to raise their 6-year-old son, Billy, on his own. This is not a journey Kramer would have chosen and he resents the necessity for it. He will need to sacrifice some professional accomplishments to do the demanding work of childrearing that a patriarchal culture considers to be among the many demeaning domestic chores that belong to women. To be successful as Billy's parent, Ted must free his anima and connect to the traits of empathy, creativity, intuition, nurture, concern, and self-sacrifice that will be necessary for him to meet the challenges of parenting.

Kramer vs. Kramer received a great deal of critical success when it was released in 1979, winning Academy Awards for Best Picture, Best Director, Best Adapted Screenplay, Best Actor, and Best Supporting Actress. Yet, I can remember the uncomfortable responses of some ordinary audiences watching a heterosexual male protagonist undergo a heroine's journey. In 1979, some men found the character of Ted Kramer to be "pathetic." The thinking was that Ted should have just hired himself a sexy *au pair*; problem solved. Both women and men were outraged that a mother would abandon her family in the selfish pursuit of her own ambitions and then have the gall to return and demand custody of her son. For many in the audiences of that time period, Joanna Kramer was the movie's obvious villain.

The way to consider the function of gender in a fictional journey is to consider the culture in which the story unfolds. If a protagonist needs to rediscover traits and abilities that have been suppressed or otherwise slay the dragons of gender tyranny to be successful, your protagonist is on a heroine's journey. The structure of the journey is similar, but self-doubt and cultural gender restrictions will be the protagonist's constant companions. Before her journey's end, the protagonist will reconnect to all those human traits that make the protagonist a complete and balanced individual.

Children's Journeys

The Wizard of Oz is a musical fantasy that makes few attempts at realism. It takes considerable suspension of disbelief to accept that a man in a lion's costume is an animal searching for his courageous self or that a scarecrow can talk and dance. There is also very little subtlety in the actors' emotional responses to events. However, those acting choices are faithful to the musical genre. Vogler admires the film because, in addition to being such a clear expression of the hero's journey, *The Wizard of Oz* has many possible interpretations beyond explicit or referential meanings. The movie may resonate so deeply with children because of fears about the loss of home, the failings of adults, and the necessity for children to learn to face life's challenges on their own. The film's explicit meaning ("there's no place like home") is the manifestation of the larger values of individuals struggling to survive in a capitalistic society during the economic crisis of the 1930s. The movie is a reminder of the importance of those things whose value cannot be measured with money. The movie has also had an incredible shelf life, still captivating audiences more than eighty years after its 1939 premiere.

My fondness for *The Wizard of Oz* was cemented when I watched my 3-year-old daughter become obsessed with it. We repeatedly watched Dorothy's adventures. My daughter acted out the scenes, sang the songs by heart, and danced barefoot across the living room carpet imagining her own yellow brick road—until kindergarten. Then, without any warning, she replaced *The Wizard of Oz* with the *Mighty Morphin Power Rangers* (1993–2002). I was heartbroken and suspected the wayward influence of her peer group. I couldn't understand what she saw in the campy imitation of a Japanese television series, where teens in colorful Spandex outfits repeatedly fought against the aggression of the evil alien witch, Rita Repulsa. What seemed like tasteless kitsch to me captivated my daughter and her young classmates. Kimberly (the Pink Ranger) replaced Dorothy in my daughter's heart. She was impressed with the Pink Ranger's gymnastic talents, and Kimberly's teenage sarcasm triumphed over Dorothy's naïve earnestness. My daughter wasn't alone in her admiration.

In 1994, the Power Rangers action figures were the most popular toy, approaching one billion dollars in sales and causing Morphin Mania as the Christmas holidays approached (Collins, 1994). Though the series is based on an ensemble rather than a single heroic protagonist, it did have elements of the hero's journey that resonated with young audiences. Zordon was the wise mentor, giving the Rangers the supernatural aid to transform into a fighting force. Each episode was another trial in the Rangers' ability to keep evil at bay and away from their sacred home in the fictional town of Angel Grove, California. Throughout their adventures, the Rangers occasionally touched base with the common world of high school, the difficulties of clique culture, teen angst, and painful romantic encounters. Many elements of the hero's journey were evident even if the series didn't have a closed three-act structure or a single protagonist. The episodes repeated or rearranged the traditional order of the journey's events. The series also had a surprising shelf life with an expanding franchise. It inspired two feature films (1995, 2017), a fair number of toys and other merchandising, and spun off new series (*Power Rangers Samurai*, 2011).

Just as I had become resigned to the *Power Rangers*, my daughter replaced her fanaticism for fighting teens with an addiction to *Alias* (2001–6), another television series in which a young protagonist, a college student named Sydney Bristow, is recruited to work for the CIA in a secret "Black Ops" division called SD-6. When Sydney tells her fiancé about her new job, he is murdered. His death pushes Sydney across the threshold into a journey that will last for five tangled seasons. Sydney learns that SD-6 is actually a global criminal organization and becomes a double agent to prevent SD-6 from acquiring powerful artifacts or the wondrously advanced technologies created and left behind by a Renaissance-era genius. Sydney Bristow is a heroine as well as a trickster, putting on multiple disguises to carry out her missions, but she is also surrounded by tricksters. Even Sydney's mother is an undercover agent with the Russian KGB and her father is a double agent. Her parent's marriage was not inspired by love but by an international intrigue that uses marital intimacy as the weapon to get state secrets. Sydney Bristow inspired my daughter to set aside gymnastics and pick up the study of martial arts.

Today my daughter's abandoned bedroom is a museum of her childhood media obsessions, which also included the franchises of *Harry Potter*, *Twilight*, and *The Hunger Games*. Her room stores a bewildering collection of posters, books, action figures, gymnastic trophies, and the many colored levels of Tae Kwon Do belts from white to black. All are testaments to fantastical media excursions with traces of the hero's journey. Most of these media infatuations enjoyed a period of strong popular culture success and all share a common certainty: adults are a disappointment and so are the worlds they create. It will be up to young protagonists to acquire the skills, knowledge, and friends to help them deal with hypocritical, duplicitous grown-ups and navigate their dangerous, inadequate worlds.

The typical dragons and threshold guardians for the journey of child protagonists are tied to their age. Young protagonists must decide if youth and inexperience prevent them from having the necessary skills, courage, intellect, and other traits they need to be successful. These young heroes must be willing to venture down a road of trials and return with the elixir that can protect the fragile purity of childhood worlds or help change the corrupted adult ones. These stories are also evidence that the mythical elements of a hero's journey are not necessarily confined to the three-act structure of a feature film or even to fantasy stories. Television series, comic books, video games, as well as traditional and nontraditionally structured feature films can all reflect important elements of a hero or a heroine's journey.

These elements in a hero's journey are not a secret recipe to be rigidly followed or the magic elixir for a writer's success. They are tools to inspire the imagination. Many writers have embraced these devices of the hero's journey for the ways they lend support to a story's structure, especially if the story fits naturally in a three-act bowl.

Not every story does.

References

Atwood, M. (1985). *The Handmaid's Tale*. McClelland and Stewart.

Campbell, J. (1949). *The Hero with a Thousand Faces*. New York: Meridian Books.

Collins, G. (1994) "With Power Rangers Scarce, a Frenzied Search by Parents." *New York Times*. Section A, p. 1, December 5, 1994.

Gulino, P. J. (2004). *Screenwriting: The Sequence Approach*. New York: Continuum.

Indick, W. (2004). *Psychology for Screenwriters: Building Conflict in Your Script*. Studio City, CA: Michael Wiese.

Murdock, M. (1990). *The Heroine's Journey: Woman's Quest for Wholeness*. Boston, MA: Shambhala.

Tobin, R. (2007). "The Screenwriting Formula: Why It Works and How to Use It." *Reader's Digest Books*.

Vogler, C. (1998). *The Writer's Journey: Mythic Structure for Writers*. Studio City, CA: Michael Wiese Productions.

Chapter 4

THE STRUCTURES OF TIME AND PERSPECTIVE

If all time is eternally present, all time is unredeemable.

—T. S. Eliot

One of the lessons I learned listening to my southern friends and family tell stories is that spontaneous, oral narratives rarely come neatly packaged or planned out in three chronological acts, yet these other story forms can feel just as natural and organic as day leading to night, the start of a journey preceding to its end, or infancy progressing to old age. My mother's storytelling sometimes began with the main climax and its outcome, then backtracked to reveal some of the oddball family histories of the important characters in her story. Then her narrative might detour to tell a related side story with different characters and erstwhile shenanigans that would slowly progress forward, until the side story finally connected to the central climax where she began ... or maybe not. If you were to draw a map of my mother's story chronologies, they never proceeded from beginning to end with a couple of informative flashbacks. Her stories were a winding road going backward and sideways in time with many odd but related bypasses that might circle around to the beginning or simply dead end at a poignant moment. Yet, her stories somehow managed to be entertaining even when she was abruptly called away because something on the stove was burning, the phone was ringing, or there was someone at the door.

Southern storytelling didn't discover a new story structure. Novelists and playwrights have historically tampered with time, flashing backward, forward, and sideways in the chronology of events. As a professional journalist, the structures of my news stories routinely started with the most volatile moment or most critical facts. Those vital facts contained in a news story's climax have been a recognized journalistic "lead" or "lede" since the days of reporting on the American Civil War, when journalists learned to announce the essential facts of an explosive conflict followed by significant details in descending order of importance. This was a practical structure in case war violence destroyed telegraph lines. If an informed citizenry was fundamental to democracy, the vital information must come first. This organization became known as the "inverted pyramid," a form for news coverage that continues in contemporary newspaper reporting and digital news reporting that audiences must read as written text (Lieb, 2009). The assumption of the inverted pyramid structure is that as interest declines readers might scroll on or turn the page, but citizens will still know the most important information. This is a structure that can be death to broadcast news, where waning interest in one story might cause audiences to abandon the entire news program. So, radio and television journalists learned to adapt the inverted pyramid structure to better suit broadcast realities. Broadcast journalists continued to lead their stories with the lede or climax but endeavored to keep audiences engaged and interested until the end of the story, teasing and backtracking in a style similar to oral storytelling. Table 4.1 shows a typical structure for a breaking news story.

The broadcast news story might start with the climax, or the big "what," using this to hook audience interest or concern, and then follow with more details of the "when, where, who" to finish with the "how and why" or the causes of this disaster and what it might mean for watching audiences. Sometimes answers to questions are unavailable in a breaking news story. This is one fundamental way that a fictional story differs from news accounts. In fiction, the author knows all the answers, or should know the answers, even if those answers are intentionally withheld from the audience or from other characters to create dramatic irony. In news stories, answers may never be available regardless of how diligently a reporter continues to hunt for them. As of this writing, neither journalists nor law enforcement have conclusively resolved the 1971 D. B. Cooper hijacking or discovered who was responsible for the 1996 murder of Tupac Shakur. Fictional mysteries can also remain unresolved, though authors of these mysteries should know what happened even if they choose not to reveal it.

Similar to news, a nonlinear structure of climax to background to cause and conclusion is one that fictional storytelling employs very successfully, particularly as fiction backtracks to explore the human drives behind a story's climax. News stories will reveal causal facts such as the faulty wiring that sparked a fatal fire or deferred maintenance on a bridge that ultimately produced a structural collapse, but rarely does news reporting get very deeply inside the human decisions and complicated histories behind deferred maintenance or slipshod wiring. In nonfiction, this kind of examination is more often the work of longer-form documentaries. In fiction, this examination can

THE STRUCTURES OF TIME AND PERSPECTIVE 79

Table 4.1 News Story Structure

Climax	Background	Conclusion
What, When, Where	**Who, When, What**	**Why, How, How Much**
A deadly fire broke out in an apartment complex in Madison late last night, destroying multiple units and killing a small boy.	Firefighters arriving on the scene found the upper floors of the apartment engulfed in flames. It took firefighters about 30 minutes to bring the nighttime fire under control. The boy's grandmother, uncle, and sister were hospitalized and treated for smoke inhalation, but the 3-year-old boy was pronounced dead at the scene.	A Fire Department spokesman blames faulty wiring and old circuits for causing the fire. Many older structures don't have the breakers to prevent an electrical arc from starting a fire. This apartment complex was built in 1971. Every year in the United States, poor wiring is responsible for over forty thousand home fires. The fire department advises people living in older buildings to check smoke detector batteries and avoid overloading circuits with multiple extension cords. Smoke detectors more than 10 years old should be replaced.
VISUAL: FIRE VISIBLE THROUGH WINDOWS, DOORS OF APARTMENT COMPLEX	VISUAL: FIREFIGHTERS AT WORK; AMBULANCE; WORRIED NEIGHBORS HUDDLED TOGETHER	VISUAL: SCENES OF SMOLDERING REMAINS; COLLAPSED CEILING; SORROWFUL RESIDENTS AND NEIGHBORS

uncover interesting dramatic tensions that ultimately land characters in the wrong place at a catastrophic time.

Scholars like to graph the emotional intensity of traditional three-act structure, where the emotional intensity starts low, builds to the crest of its strength, and then drops again as resolutions calm the protagonist's situation. The graph looks like the line drawing of a steep and bumpy hill with a steeper decline or even a sharp drop after the emotional apex. Starting with the climax at the top of the hill means emotional intensity is high from the beginning of the story. Very often this comes in the form of intense visual action. For *dramatic contrast*, the intensity will need to change as the story moves forward, moderating the pace and emotion of scenes as writers fascinate audiences in more subtle ways.

Broadcast journalists always had to keep in mind the important questions behind audience interest. "So what? Why should I care?" Audiences might remain tuned in to a news story when they feel an intimacy with the storyteller, curiosity about the subject matter, have some connection to or concern for the personalities in the story, are curious to see if a withheld answer is revealed, or understand how this story is relevant to their own lives. Fiction writers can ask the same questions. Why should audiences care about this story and these characters once the explosive on-screen, attention-grabbing action is gone? What calmer scene needs to come next that eases the intensity but deepens the intrigue?

The authors of *Alternative Scriptwriting: Rewriting the Hollywood Formula* offer several structural alternatives to the classic three acts (Dancyger and Rush, 2013). Some of these structural choices have those organic, nonlinear compositions that mimic oral kitchen-table anecdotes, campfire tales, and broadcast news. When three-act structure dominates in storytelling, a different structure can seem novel, but none of these are uniquely contemporary. As nonlinear popularity continues to grow, some of these alternative structures have become fairly routine.

Nonlinear Structures

We cannot escape linear time. It ticks relentlessly onward, moving with grim, tenacious precision. Yet, the emotional perception of time can appear to alter that steady, forward flow. Boredom, pain, anticipation, and dread can seem to slow time to an agonizing pace, but when we are giddily hooked inside a joyful experience, moments can seem to speed away. Vivid memories transport us from the present to the past. Vivid imaginations bring us from the present to the future. These emotional qualities impact how we prioritize events and shape the way we tell stories. Furthermore, in contrast with the way we actually live time, media technologies can be paused, reset, and skipped forward. On a media screen, lovely moments can be replayed over and over, while moments that bore, upset, or disgust can be avoided altogether. Stories intended for screen media naturally lend themselves to this emotional exploration of nonlinear time.

Nonlinear structures grew in popularity in the new millennium, becoming more the rule than an exception. Nonlinear approaches to structure told stories in reverse; connected and disconnected story events in playful, random disorder; or presented a chaotic fracturing of timelines. It became popular to

Figure 4.1 A nonlinear hero's journey

engage audiences by introducing characters in the midst of a volatile crisis, then backtrack to reveal how the characters got into this predicament. In the language of the hero's journey, instead of the world of the common day, the script begins with characters in the unknown world, deep in the belly of the whale and at the point of succumbing to a crisis, then time abruptly resets to show how and why the protagonists answered the call to adventure. Once the road of trials reconnects to the crisis again, the story's structure progresses onward to show how characters survive and triumph or perhaps fail and what elixir they bring home if any. It has become familiar to see a film begin with pure chaos and characters in a dire situation only to have the action interrupted at its peak with an on-screen graphic announcing "one year earlier," or "one month earlier," or some other, calmer time before an inciting incident began to move characters toward this ultimate crisis. In this particular nonlinear diagram, the protagonist's path begins at 12 o'clock but isn't neatly circular as in the typical hero's journey model. However, the path still has many of the familiar elements of the hero's journey.

Other nonlinear stories are more disruptive of the elements of a hero's journey, allowing the writer to emphasize particular moments, raise audience curiosity, and tease the audience with the surprise answers to the why question. The 2016 science fiction film *Arrival* based on the novella, "Story of Your Life" (Chiang, 2002) is an example of a nonlinear film that questions the notion of linear time. The protagonist is a linguist, Louise Banks, who loses her daughter to an incurable illness. When extraterrestrial aliens arrive on Earth, the government recruits Louise in an attempt to communicate with the aliens. Louise is successful but her discoveries question the very validity of linear chronology. The dramatic question is whether people would choose a particular journey or path for their lives if they understood that they could not prevent the painful tragedies of that choice. Are the fleeting joys of that journey worth the eventual pain? Another science fiction film, *Edge of Tomorrow* (2014) also has alien characters that manipulate time only these aliens intend to conquer humanity but inadvertently bestow the ability to reset time on a human soldier instead, causing him to live in a continuous loop he learns to manipulate.

One reason for choosing a nonlinear structure is to emphasize the specific stages in a character's life story in contrast with expectations. In the movie *Slum Dog Millionaire* (2008), the questions of a television game show both frame and trigger the exposition of important moments in the many different episodes of the protagonist's life. The game show competition is its own story. It is inconceivable to the show's producers that a poor man could know the answers to all their sophisticated game show questions. Police accuse the protagonist, Jamal Malik, of cheating, then detain and torture him. Questions in the game show structure and trigger the separate stories of Jamal's memories as a child during the Bombay riots, as a street beggar working for a gangster, surviving as a pickpocket, and years later working at a call center, before the story of the game show is finally resolved.

Multiple Stories and Ensembles

A story's lack of a single protagonist and single perspective signals the alternate *multiple story structure*, which better serves the complexity of dealing with multiple protagonists and their various interrelated drives. Multiple story structure is similar to the journalist's instinct to present several points of view on a controversial topic. News stories might also be organized by opposing points of view or the different perspectives of eyewitness accounts. In a narrative film, if the stories are different perspectives on one event told chronologically, or different events that occur during a single period of time, they might be intercut in a "meanwhile" approach. The structure of half-hour episodes for television comedy series frequently take on a multiple story "meanwhile" structure with interwoven A, B, and C stories told chronologically. Each of these stories may have a different protagonist chosen from the ongoing ensemble cast or maintain that ensemble quality with several characters sharing the same ambition and working together to achieve a goal.

Season three of the successful 12-season run of *The Big Bang Theory* (2007–19) provides a two-story example in the episode called "The Adhesive Duck Deficiency," which intercuts two completely separate stories that happen concurrently. In the "B" story, Leonard is going on a camping trip in the desert with Raj and Howard to watch the Leonid Meteor shower. After scouting the area to check out other campers, Howard returns with cookies that are a gift from some older women wearing Grateful Dead T-shirts, who happen to be camping nearby in a VW Microbus. The three scientists accidentally get stoned on these cookies, have comically "profound" observations, get the munchies, search for food, and forget to watch the meteor shower. This story doesn't have a clear protagonist, but the three characters each share the ambition to see the Leonid Meteor shower and the experience the same conditions in their unique ways. In the "A" story of this episode, Sheldon is the comic protagonist. Sheldon even refers to himself as the "hero." Sheldon is alone in his apartment when he hears Penny calling from her apartment across the hall. She has slipped and fallen in her bathtub, dislocating her shoulder. Sheldon comes to Penny's rescue, observing that a bathmat or adhesive ducks on her tub's surface would have prevented the fall. He then helps her through a series of comic situations: getting Penny dressed, driving her to the emergency room, and filling out the hospital forms. When she is home again and loopy on pain killers, Sheldon assists her into bed and sings her the healing "Soft Kitty" song, which they end up singing together in a round. Comic scenes in both stories move chronologically, cutting between the two stories that are happening simultaneously. The two stories are related only because the

Table 4.2 Structure of a Television Episode: *The Big Bang Theory*

"A" Story	"B" Story
	Campsite: Howard, Leonard, and Raj anticipate the meteor shower.
Sheldon and Leonard's apartment: Sheldon enjoys his alone time but then hears Penny's call for help from her apartment.	
Penny's Apartment: Sheldon discovers Penny's dilemma. She's fallen in the shower and dislocated her shoulder.	
	Campsite: Howard shares homemade cookies, a gift from Dead Head "Grannies" camping nearby.
Penny's Bedroom: Sheldon helps Penny dress for a trip to the emergency room.	
	Campsite: Howard, Leonard, and Raj are now stoned from eating pot-infused cookies.
Penny's Car- Sheldon, who does not drive, must drive Penny to the hospital.	
	Campsite- Howard, Leonard, and Raj have desperate munchies.
Hospital Waiting Room: Sheldon fills out hospital information forms for Penny.	
	Campsite: Howard discovers a brisket in his backpack, a surprise gift from his overprotective mother. Munchie adversity averted.
Penny's Apartment: Sheldon and Penny return from the ER and Penny is on powerful pain medicine. He helps her into bed. They sing "Soft Kitty."	
	Campsite: The final campsite joke. The many distractions have caused the three friends to miss the main reason for their camping trip.

characters are all close friends and either live with each other, near each other, work together, or visit frequently. The characters are all members of the series' ongoing ensemble family.

Table 4.2 shows the chronology of the "A" and "B" stories from this episode. Many episodes in television series might also have an interconnecting "C" story. Each interconnecting story has its own beginning, middle, and end.

One segment intersects with another at a moment where a pause is logical, or where the action is less ripe with comic possibility. For example, audiences won't see a scene where a doctor sets Penny's shoulder or where Sheldon is alone in the waiting room passing time until Penny's medical treatments are finished. Those moments or other moments that might be painful, boring, or have less comic potential are "covered" with the exploits of the "B" story.

Characters in the "A" and "B" stories of "The Adhesive Duck Deficiency" don't interact in this episode, though it is possible for the protagonist of the "A" story to be a supporting character or even the antagonist of another story in multiple story structures.

Television series have the luxury of many episodes and sometimes even multiple seasons through which to develop characters and explore their perspectives. Entire seasons can be one long, overarching and continuous story, and the episodes of the season must be watched in succession so that the understanding of the bigger story won't be lost. Even though the entire series is one long, fundamentally linear tale, it might be composed of the interwoven stories of many characters to create a complex, ensemble narrative. In an extreme example, the eight seasons of the fantasy HBO series, *The Game of Thrones* (2011–19) featured an extremely large ensemble cast with numerous storylines in a complex, interconnecting narrative with the dark overtones of ancient Greek tragedy. Individual characters and labyrinthine plots involved personal intrigues and fights for survival or power in a medieval-styled Seven Kingdoms, where the forces of witches, dragons, and magic were limited but evident. The overarching story is about which personality from which dynasty will ultimately control the power of the Iron Throne in a world where icy zombies from a frozen northland threaten everyone. As complicated as the series was and as often as viewers complained about needing a score card to keep up with all the characters and plots, the series was extremely successful for HBO (Renfro, 2019).

Episodes in some television series can stand alone. The episodes of the successful television show *Law and Order* (1990–2010) are examples of independent stories that can be watched out of order without audience confusion. Every episode in the series has two distinct but related stories told chronologically. The first is the discovery and police investigation of a crime, which ends with the arrest of a suspect. The second story is the court room prosecution of the suspect, which ends with a verdict. The series inspired many spin-offs, binge-watch reruns, and was adapted for British television, *Law and Order: UK* (2009–14).

A major determinant for structure is the medium and screen that will deliver the story. A multiple story structure for an ensemble television series is a natural choice.

Multiple stories in a feature film can be interrelated narratives that intersect through characters, viewpoint, or theme. The award-winning screenplay for the movie *Crash* (2004) crosscuts between stories that connect only coincidentally, but each story has racism, misogyny, or bigotry as the core theme. All the characters have assumptions that prevent them from seeing beyond their categorical thinking to understand the actual people and situations they have encountered. The characters share the situation of being both the victims and the practitioners of prejudice. All the stories also share the motif of an accident, as the choices characters make cause their lives to crash into each other.

An auction in contemporary Montreal and the attempts of a collector to establish the authenticity of a rare, red-colored violin frame another example of a multiple story in the film *The Red Violin* (1998). The collector's story bookends a series of stories that unfold chronologically over centuries in different countries with unrelated characters, but the rare violin and the human idea of perfection connect all the stories. The first story takes place in seventeenth-century Italy, when the violin is initially crafted and stained a tragic red. The stories and the violin then move through the centuries and musicians from an eighteenth-century Austrian monastery, to nineteenth-century Oxford, and even to China during the Cultural Revolution.

The multiple stories of the film *Being Human* (1994) depict the experience of a single human soul through several centuries and various incarnations. The actor Robin Williams portrays each of the protagonist's incarnations: as an ancient Celt, a slave in Ancient Rome, a crusader, a Portuguese man during the renaissance, and as a modern man in New York.

Another application of multiple story structure is a single event told from multiple perspectives. The multiple perspective stories can be arranged back to back, so the story resets to the beginning and the overall structure is not strictly chronological. The classic Japanese film *Rashomon* (1950) tells one story, but from the perceptions of four different characters, providing contradictory versions of a single tale about rape and murder. In a film structured like *Rashomon*, there might be a prologue, where minor characters or witnesses to part of the story's main conflict explain what happened. The film will then show the A character's perspective of events followed in turn by the B and C character perspectives, ending with an epilogue that either reveals the truth or perhaps buries it deeper. To avoid a boring repetition, each character's perspective should reveal challenging new details or dramatically alter the way the familiar scenes will unfold when they are repeated. And, as in *Rashomon*, it is possible that one or more of the characters is lying or a character's understanding is too limited to know the truth. Characters might share scenes in these multiple accounts, so that the protagonist in one version is a secondary character in another account, where the perspective has clearly shifted.

A multiple perspective story might use a "meanwhile" approach, intercutting and overlapping the different character perspectives at significant moments in the story to maintain one chronology and minimize excessive repetition. This multiple protagonist structure might use the same organizing devices as three-act structure with some adaptations. Different characters share the role of protagonist as the story's perspective shifts, but the chronology stays intact with the possible exception of some overlapping in scenes where the perspective shift occurs.

Multi-Story and Nonlinear Combinations

Many scholars have written about the film *Pulp Fiction* (1998), which is both nonlinear and multi-story in structure and was an Academy Award–winning screenplay. The film features four interconnecting narratives that are not concurrent, but counterparts. This is not a "meanwhile" approach, since the stories occur at different moments in time. The element connecting all the stories is a character, the gangster boss, Marsellus Wallace. Wallace is a force in each story even when he isn't present, yet Wallace is not the protagonist in any story. Other characters may be the protagonist of one story but a supporting character in another.

The "A" story of *Pulp Fiction* is about two gangsters who work for Wallace—Jules and Vincent—assigned to retrieve a briefcase and execute the men who attempted to swindle their boss. Jules is the protagonist of the "A" story. Jules believes that because he and Vincent were spared in the gunfire of a deadly shootout, this was God's message for Jules to retire as a hitman. Vincent is the protagonist of the "B" story. Wallace has assigned Vincent the mission to show his wife Mia a good time while Wallace is out of town, but Vincent must be careful to treat Mia with platonic, gentlemanly respect. Wallace has a reputation for ruthlessness and Vincent doesn't want to get on the bad side of his gangster boss. The "B" story is the only one that plays without interruption from the beginning of Vincent's date with Mia to its end. In the "C" story, Marcellus Wallace asks an aging boxer, Butch, to throw a fight. The "C" story includes a lengthy flashback to the childhood of its protagonist, when Butch receives a gold watch that belonged to his father. This talisman representing his father's honor inspires Butch to double-cross Wallace and win his fight rather than intentionally lose. Butch must return to his apartment and get his father's gold watch before he can leave town and escape the wrath of his ruthless boss. Vincent has been waiting in the apartment to exact Wallace's vengeance, but Butch kills him. As Butch is making his getaway, he accidentally

Table 4.3 A Nonlinear Multi-Story Structure: Pulp Fiction

Film Structure Chronology	Events in Linear Time
"D" Story: Diner—Pumpkin and Honey Bunny stage the hold-up of a diner.	**"C" Story:** Butch as a child hears the tragic tale of his father's watch.
"A" Story: Philosophical hitmen, Jules and Vincent go to retrieve a briefcase belonging to their boss, Marcellus Wallace, and kill the men who tried to double-cross Wallace in a big gunfight.	**"A" Story:** Jules and Vincent go to retrieve briefcase—a big gunfight ensues.
"C" Story: Topless Bar—Marcellus wants Butch to take a dive in an upcoming fight. Vincent enters with the briefcase.	**"A" Story:** Jules and Vincent survive the gunfight but make a bloody mess of their car when Vincent accidentally shoots and kills their informant.
"B" Story: Vincent and Mia go on a platonic date. They eat, dance, and Mia overdoses but survives and Vincent takes her home.	**"A" Story:** Jules and Vincent deal with the cleaner situation and after all is hygienic and clean again, they decide to get breakfast.
"C" Story: As a child, Butch receives his father's gold watch as an heirloom and hears the tragic tale of his father's heroism.	**"D" Story:** Diner—Pumpkin and Honey Bunny begin the hold-up of a diner where Jules and Vincent are eating.
"C" Story: As an adult, Butch refuses to throw the fight as Marcellus asked. He is going to skip town with his girlfriend, but she left the gold watch at their apartment and he must go back after it.	**"D" Story:** Jules and Vincent have a Mexican standoff with Pumpkin and Honey Bunny but Jules talks them into letting them leave the diner with the briefcase.
"C" Story: Butch goes to the apartment for the watch and kills Vincent, who was in the bathroom.	**"C" Story:** Topless Bar—Marcellus wants Butch to take a dive in an upcoming fight. Vincent enters with the briefcase.
"C" Story: Butch and Marcellus have a confrontation, but when Butch saves Marcellus, the crime boss grants Butch his freedom. Butch and his girlfriend make their getaway.	**"B" Story:** Vincent and Mia go on a platonic date. They eat, dance, and Mia overdoses but survives and Vincent takes her home.
"A" Story: Jules and Vincent escape the gunfight and retrieve the briefcase, leaving with their informant, Marvin. Jules decides to give up crime. Vincent accidentally shoots Marvin, leaving the car a bloody mess.	**"C" Story:** Butch refuses to throw the fight as Marcellus asked. He is going to skip town with his girlfriend, but she left the gold watch at their apartment and he must go back after it.
"A" Story: Jules and Vincent deal with the cleaner situation and after all is once again hygienic, they decide to get breakfast.	**"C" Story:** Butch goes to the apartment for the watch and kills Vincent, who was in the bathroom.
"D" Story: Jules and Vincent are in the diner that Pumpkin and Honey Bunny decide to rob. After a Mexican standoff, Pumpkin and Honey Bunny allow Jules and Vincent to leave the diner with the briefcase.	**"C" Story:** Butch and Marcellus have confrontation, but when Butch saves Marcellus, the crime boss grants Butch his freedom. Butch and his girlfriend make their getaway.

runs into Wallace, who gives chase. Butch has an opportunity to save Wallace's life, which he does, and the gangster boss forgives him. The film's return to the "A" story is initially disconcerting, because Vincent is alive throughout the "A" story and audiences had watched him die in the "C" story. It takes a moment to understand that the chronology has been disrupted. Table 4.3 shows the outline of the film's narrative structure compared to the story's chronology told in linear time.

Brusque Endings, Curt Beginnings, and Slices of Life

It may seem pretentious to impose a solution on a story idea involving an ongoing, complicated issue. A structure with an abrupt, unresolved ending emphasizes the unsettled aspects of this type of story. This is a hero's journey without a road back, resurrection, or healing elixir. The story ends with a protagonist still facing an ordeal. One caution is that audiences accustomed to resolutions may be frustrated with a structure that doesn't offer one. When choosing this structure for a story, consider your motivations carefully. Does this structure underscore the authentic persistence of a stubborn conflict or is it an inability to imagine a satisfying solution? *Three Billboards Outside Ebbing, Missouri* (2017) is one example of a film with an unresolved ending. The protagonist is a mother, Mildred Hayes, who is still grieving over the rape and murder of her daughter seven months earlier. She rents three billboards to advertise the fact that there are no arrests in the case and calls out the town's police chief Bill Willoughby for this failure. Willoughby suffers with terminal cancer and decides not to wait for the progress of his disease but commits suicide. He leaves a note for Hayes, explaining that her billboards had nothing to do with his decision. Willoughby even pays the rent to extend the life of the message on the billboards, hoping to keep public attention on the murder and authorities motivated to solve it. At one point characters think they may have solved the crime and plan their vengeance, but new facts show that while Mildred Hayes may have discovered a rapist and murderer, this is not the same man who killed her daughter. The movie ends with no resolution to the crimes and no clear understanding about what Hayes will do next. In a comparable lack of resolution, the film *Broken Flowers* (2005), ends without audiences or the protagonist understanding what has happened. When a retired philanderer, Don Jon gets an anonymous letter telling him that he has a 19-year-old son, he begins a cross-country journey with the goal to find his old girlfriends and the mother of his son. The movie ends without the satisfaction of that discovery.

Similar to the unresolved ending are stories that have no discernable exposition. Audiences are plopped into the middle of action without knowing who the protagonist is, which of the characters are important, the nature of the dilemma, or understanding any of the decisions that have brought about the explosive actions they witness. The world of the common day and its establishing features are missing and there will be no backtracking with an informative graphic bringing audiences to an earlier time period to explain what is going on or why and how this crisis happened. Audiences may be more forgiving of an abrupt beginning if crucial elements of exposition can be naturally revealed as characters learn to deal with the tense situation already in progress. In one example, the first act of *Swiss Army Man* (2016) pairs a man stranded on an island with a flatulent corpse without explaining the reasons for either character's predicament.

Stories that have both an abrupt beginning as well as a vague ending are sometimes called a *slice of life*. This is a type of story that is generally naturalistic and confined to a period of time and may also be constrained to a limited space or event. A slice-of-life story appears to consist of routine life activities interrupted by curious events. A slice-of-life structure may not have an obvious character arc.

The Florida Project is a 2017 film in which the protagonist, a 6-year-old girl named Moonee, lives with her extremely young, unemployed, single mom in a low-rent motel near Walt Disney World called Magic Castle. Mother and daughter are one missed rent payment away from homelessness. The movie is a chronological account of random moments in Moonee's life in a community that survives in the thin, disposable margins of the Magic Kingdom. This is a community of waitresses, janitors, cooks, vendors, prostitutes, and drug dealers who live off the scraps of the Disney Empire's more privileged entertainment buffet. The movie is confined to the early days of summer, where 6-year-old Moonee wanders unsupervised around cheap motels and strip malls with other children who live in the Magic Castle or the nearby Futureland motel. The movie is confined to walkable spaces. The children pull pranks, have a spitting contest, beg for change from tourists, spy on a nude sunbather, go on imaginary safaris, and get into some serious mischief, including setting a fire in an abandoned condominium complex, which swells into a dangerous blaze. This "slice-of-life" also observes the routine jobs of the motel manager, Bobby, as he disposes of a bug-infested mattress, shoos cranes off the driveway, deals with a broken ice machine, touches up the purple paint job on the motel's imitation Disney exterior, and chastises children and residents who violate motel rules. Moonee and her mother live in the moment, scamming, stealing, and conning their daily existence without the driving ambitions of typical protagonists. While her mother turns the tricks she solicits online, Moonee plays in the bathtub, washing the hair of her dolls and listening to loud music.

The Department of Children and Families eventually comes to investigate Moonee's situation, but the movie offers no distinct resolution to her condition just as it offers no background on the why of her circumstances. The movie concludes with the characters holding steadfast to the same attitudes they had at the beginning of the film, no character arcs or dramatic revelations. The meaning behind the film's sometimes haphazard incidents are left for viewers to interpret without any overt clues.

Writers choose a slice-of-life structure because it seems less editorial, less contrived than a three-act structure. It appears to reveal the random trivialities of real life. However, the writer's perspective is always there and events still happen because of choices writers have their characters make, but the moral of the story is not obvious or didactic.

Another film with slice-of-life elements is *Nomadland* (2020), a year in the life of a middle-aged widow living in a dying town where the local industry has closed. She makes the decision to buy a van and travel the country looking for work. The film shows the routines as Fern migrates from job to job, one camp after another, learning survival skills of itinerant life. The film also reveals the warmth and comradery of friends encountered on the road, where goodbyes are never absolute. Fern's home might be confined to the cramped space inside her tiny van but it's also wherever she parks it. After a solemn visit to the derelict neighborhood where Fern once lived with her husband, she makes a definitive commitment to nomad life. The movie ends with Fern on the road. Though Fern's commitment to the itinerant life gives this film more arc and resolution than normally expected from a slice-of-life structure, *Nomadland* does show the everyday, chronological, and sometimes banal events of an unusual life choice.

The Terminal (2004) has slice-of-life qualities, showing what happens when a tourist is stranded at an airport for an extended period, unable to leave. Viktor an Eastern European visitor to the United States is stuck in New York's John F. Kennedy International Airport, when his invalid passport is seized. Viktor cannot enter the United States or return to his home country. Inspired by the story of an Iranian refugee who lived in the Charles de Galle Airport for 18 years, the movie is generally confined to the airport and Viktor's time there, showing how he lives his life, finds work, creates a makeshift shelter, and interacts with travelers as the airport becomes his home and country. Tension comes from wondering how Viktor will survive these conditions with the direct, formidable threats coming from a customs director at the airport, who wants to deport Viktor to his fictional home country, which is entangled in a civil war. The film departs from the slice-of-life structure when Victor's off-terminal excursion reveals the "why" behind his initial trek to New York. The movie ends when Viktor tells a taxi driver that he is going home but doesn't clarify what "home" means.

The Unmotivated and Disenfranchised Protagonist

A prevailing wisdom about story structure is that the protagonist's goals and needs will motivate the narrative's forward movement, whether the story's structure is linear and closed or has a less conventional structure. The thinking is that the story has no momentum without the protagonist's goals and the inciting incident that provokes that protagonist into action. However, there are *unmotivated protagonists* in compelling stories who make no plans, live in the moment, and wait for events or the ambitions of other characters to inspire decisions. This observation may seem to be more about the protagonist than the form a story will take. The relevance to structure is that other characters or chance events will determine the organization of the story when the protagonist is unmotivated.

The protagonist of the 2004 comedy film *Napoleon Dynamite* is a socially awkward teen who doodles and daydreams, impulsively answering to the ambitions of others rather than his own dramatic need. Napoleon's actions are more sporadic than planned. He tosses an action figure tied to string out the school bus window just to watch it bounce down the road behind the bus. Napoleon responds to life with whatever the moment inspires him to do. However, Napoleon's friends and relatives have ambitions, and it is the aspirations of these other characters that move the story forward.

The frequently stoned character of "The Dude" in the Coen brothers' 1998 crime comedy, *The Big Lebowski*, is another example of a protagonist who fulfills errands for other characters, and it will be these actions that push the plot onward. Dude is a *slacker hero*, an unemployed, easygoing, underachieving protagonist. He enjoys smoking dope and bowling. Dude accidentally becomes involved in the story's plot through mistaken identity and afterward the things that happen to Dude seem random or the result of decisions that other characters' make. Both Napoleon and Dude may seem like *id-dominated* characters and they are, but the id doesn't drive either character with absorbed ambition but only incidentally advances the plot. Both characters act in the moment to do the bidding of others or simply react to a capricious world. The slacker perspective of unmotivated protagonists will alter the way their stories unfold.

The *disenfranchised or oppressed protagonists* also challenge the wisdom that a protagonist's goals will motivate the story forward. However, the needs and goals of the oppressed protagonist are silenced and concealed rather than careless, indifferent, or lazy. The protagonist may have dreams, but these are ambitions that an oppressive culture, other characters, or the crushing events in the story will overwhelm. Disenfranchised protagonists are more often the victim of their stories than the heroes.

In her analysis of the character of Edith from the television movie, *If These Walls Could Talk 2* (2000), Rani Crowe examines Edith as an oppressed and disenfranchised protagonist. Crowe argues that the movie is already an alternative, multi-story structure intended to contrast the experiences of lesbian couples in three different American time periods (2020). In 1961, Edith and her partner Abby have been in their hidden, "illegitimate" relationship for 30 years. When Abby suffers a stroke and dies, Edith will not be allowed to be with her beloved and comfort Abby in those last moments because the dominate culture in 1961 did not recognize Edith as Abby's family. Instead, the couple is separated. Abby dies alone in her hospital bed and Edith spends the night in a waiting room, comforting a woman who tells Edith that she is "lucky" not to have a husband. She tells Edith that without a husband, Edith can't experience the heartbreak of losing a life partner. Even Edith's grief is illegitimate. Crowe suggests that Edith is not a protagonist motivated to cross the threshold into an unknown world filled with adventure because Edith's known world is and has always been a hostile road of trials. Edith will end her film journey without her home, her partner, or any "elixir" of enlightenment.

Similar to the unmotivated protagonist, the oppressed character is like a broken branch floating in a quickly moving stream. The currents and waves that other characters make and the random obstacles that disturb the smooth forward flow of the narrative will determine a journey the protagonist cannot control. As Crowe suggests, many of a culture's important stories are about protagonists with limited ability to act. Being able to take clear and visible action requires a certain amount of privilege. Edith has the desire to act but not the privilege. It is also worth noting that Edith is an older character at the end of her life's journey at a time when she might feel less capable of putting on the hero's mantle and fighting for agency in a system determined to oppress her.

Not all tyrannized and disenfranchised protagonists are without motivation. In the 1997 Italian comedy-drama *La Vita è Bella (Life Is Good)*, the protagonist, Guido is forced into a harsh Nazi concentration camp, where he must conceal his young son Giosuè from German soldiers and the gas chamber destiny where the other children have been killed. Guido's goal is to keep his son safely hidden by telling his young son that they are all playing a marvelous game and that Giosuè will lose points if he breaks the rules. Guido is highly motivated to successfully protect his son and his son's childhood and so Guido travels the harsh road of trials that the terrible tragedy of history and the Nazi regime has forced on him, but Guido's own personal goals to protect his son drive him and his story forward even as he reacts to oppressive external pressures.

An Alternate Perspective on Genre

One strategy for defying traditional structure is to intentionally challenge the elements, the typical perspectives, and the structural expectations of a genre (Dancyger and Rush, 2013). For example, the typical predator-prey structure of a horror movie might be upended in unexpected ways. The caution is that if audiences' expectations are disappointed, they may tune out. The potential reward is finding new life and new gratifications in old-genre constructs.

In an article mourning that science fiction as a genre may have lost its cultural reason for being, Bruce Sterling (1989) describes the mash-up of science fiction and fantasy genres as "slipstream," a form that is more the parody of a genre than a coherent identity that embraces the genre's conceptual aesthetic or form. It is a style designed to make the audience feel strangely confused. Sterling noted that slipstream has no real genre identity and predicted that these mash-ups would have limited commercial success. His complaint is that slipstream doesn't create new worlds to explore but rips at the foundations of the ones we know. Examples of odd-genre mash-ups produced as moving image media tend to play as comic parody. These include films such as *Abraham Lincoln: Vampire Hunter* (2012), in which the confederate army deploys vampires in the Civil War and Lincoln wields a silver ax and silver bullets in the Union's defense, or *Cowboys and Aliens* (2011), in which a pose of cowboys stop an alien spaceship arriving in 1873 Arizona to take over the earth, or *Pride and Prejudice and Zombies* (2016), in which Jane Austen's popular historical romance (*Pride and Prejudice*, 1813) is reimagined as a horror-comedy.

Defying a genre's conventions need not be an incongruous mix of genres but a story with unexpected choices that resist a pure genre identity. For example, *The Ballad of Little Jo* (1993) is a Western inspired by the real life of Josephine Monaghan, a woman whose family disowned her for giving birth to an illegitimate son (Lebow, 1995). The movie has the recognizable properties of the Western: a setting on the American frontier with cowboys and gunslingers, a loner for a protagonist, conflicts over land and livestock, and disputes between those with different ideas about what civilization should be. At the end of the eighteenth century, options for women were limited. Josephine embraces her animus and becomes a man so she can survive the rigors of the old West. The story's premise upsets expectations by making a woman the gun-slinging protagonist, making her lover a Chinaman, and keeping her secret until she dies. While it challenges the expectations of the Western, the story's structure is also a heroine's journey, as Little Jo embraces her animus and crosses the threshold into the challenges of life as a man.

Another example that defies genre is the Academy Award–winning German film, *The Tin Drum* (1979) based on the novel *Die Blechtrommel* (1959) by Günter

Wilhelm Grass. The film's protagonist, Oskar Matzerath, decides to stop growing. Oskar refuses to mature and become an adult in a cruel adult world. Oskar falls down the basement stairs, which provides the explanation for how he remains a perpetual 3-year-old who pounds his toy drum and shatters glass with his screams. The film has elements of bawdy comedy, fairy tale, satire, surreal fantasy, and experimental film.

Pseudo-Documentary, Mockumentary, and Found Footage

The pseudo-documentary is considered a genre of narrative filmmaking but also has structural as well as style implications borrowed from news and documentary forms. Pseudo-documentaries or mockumentaries are fictional films that can mimic a wide range of documentary or reality media practices. The mockumentary caricatures the documentary form as well as its subjects in humorous or satirical ways, acknowledging that even from its earliest days, nonfiction films played loose with the truth, staged events, and might verge into fiction. For example, the silent documentary *Nanook of the North* (1922) was a collaboration with the Inuit people, staging events that filmmaker Robert J. Flaherty would advertise as "true."

The pseudo-documentary can take its style from direct cinema, *cinéma vérité*, more formal educational documentary styles, reality competition shows, or various combinations of these. In a *cinéma vérité*-style mockumentary, the character of the documentarian will both observe events and participate in them, becoming an on-screen character in the film. The film *This Is Spinal Tap* (1984) is a *cinéma vérité* style that includes the character of an on-screen documentary filmmaker, who interviews and records the antics of a fictional heavy metal band, Spinal Tap, as he follows them on tour.

In a *direct cinema* style, the fictional filmmaker is largely absent as a character, becoming the eye behind a camera, a passive, unobtrusive observer the audience will not see but whose gaze the audience will adopt. The mockumentary *The Baby Formula* (2008) reveals the story of a lesbian couple who use an experimental process to conceive each other's biological children. This fictional film mimics more of a direct cinema approach, even though characters openly address the fictional filmmakers, at one time insisting they stop the cameras.

A more formal pseudo-documentary approach pretends that the fictional story is an educational or a historical program and may involve such devices as voice-over narration, title cards, still images, and on-screen texts. *The Gods Must Be Crazy* (1980) is a South African comedy set in Botswana that uses a formal documentary style to emphasize the comic predicaments of humans and the absurd mistakes of civilization. Voice-over narration in the style of an anthropological documentary tells the story of a Bushman, who travels to the ends of the earth to return an empty coke bottle to the gods, who clearly made a terrible mistake by dropping this unwelcome gift on his native tribe. Traditional documentary forms allow the writer to frame the narrative with an *expert voice* or an authoritative V.O. to provide context and interpretation for the story.

A recent example of the mockumentary *Death to 2020* (2020) is a strictly chronological retelling of a globally awful year, beginning with the Australian brushfires in January of 2020 that were so terrible that they could be seen from outer space. The mockumentary continues with news footage concerning the development and spread of the coronavirus, the first impeachment of Donald Trump, the police murder of George Floyd in America followed by worldwide protests for social justice, the antics of the American presidential election, and Trump's many constant attempts to have the election overturned. The mockumentary uses actual news footage. However, the "experts, scientists, historians, and average people" who provide commentary on the footage of these real news events are actors playing fictional, scripted characters. These imagined characters end the satirical mockumentary with joke predictions about 2021. None of the fictional characters predict that a few days after the release of the mockumentary, Trump supporters would convene in Washington on January 6, 2021. Incited by the president's rally at the Ellipse park, these Trump devotees would storm the American Capitol to try and stop certification of the election, disrupting the government and shouting their desires to murder Vice President Mike Pence, the Democratic Speaker of the House, Nancy Pelosi, and her staff. The critical responses to this mockumentary provide a cautionary tale about choosing this format to mock the scary realities of a painful year in a post-truth era.

For writers thinking about using one of these "actuality" forms for storytelling, not only can the scripts mimic a variety of documentary styles, but they can also take on alternative structures. A pseudo-documentary can follow the structure of a multiple story or multiple perspective film as the fictional filmmaker interviews different characters about the same event or combines different but thematically related stories. The pseudo-documentary can use a nonlinear chronology if the "documentarian" begins with the story climax and then backtracks to uncover the causes of this incident, in a format similar to many news stories. Other pseudo-documentaries may incorporate abrupt beginnings or missing endings if significant footage is not "found," leaving major story questions unanswered. The pseudo-documentary might even be linear with interviews and footage loosely following a chronological, three-act structure. A challenge with this form is creating characters whose voices, traits, and perspectives are unique enough that they can come alive in a soundbite.

Considered a subgenre of the pseudo-documentary, the *found footage film* suggests that the fictional movie is the raw film footage, video recordings, or audio files that a character has discovered or unearthed. This footage has been left behind by another character who has disappeared or died. Characters will consider this footage to be the evidence that a strange event occurred or some previously unknown history has been discovered. Examples of this style of film include many in the horror genre such as *The Blair Witch Project* (1999) and its sequels, *Paranormal Activity* (2007) and its sequels, *Alien Abduction* (2014), *The Gallows* (2015), and *Phoenix Forgotten* (2017).

The often raw, amateur production style of mockumentaries, pseudo-documentaries, and found footage genres that mimic news or home videos make these forms attractive to productions with lower budgets. A writer dealing with supernatural or fantastical subjects might decide that a documentary style with emphasis on footage and interviews helps with suspension of disbelief in a clever way. One concern about choosing a pseudo-documentary or found footage style might be contributing to the erosion of the already perilously thin confidence audiences have for news and documentary. However, choosing a documentary style for fiction invites audiences to consider the relationship of a fictional narrative to the larger argument about what is real. These forms also allow characters to be interviewed, telling audiences their thoughts directly. However, characters might still lie to an interviewer, the audience, and each other.

Familiar Structures and Interactive Stories

Although alternative structures are not new, technological developments that encourage audiences to endlessly explore stories and characters may have nurtured the popularity of structural forms that resist three acts, creating a new instinct to examine a story vertically rather than horizontally, emphasizing depth and detail rather than pace and progression. The "if-then" writing style of computer games allows for very dense, sideways movements, and the exploration of environments through otherwise extremely simple stories. A player can even reboot, go back to the beginning, and choose an alternate path of action, experiencing a different version of the same story. Because games involve audiences actively making decisions that determine the story direction, the popular thinking is that games and interactive stories are vastly different forms, disconnected from the long heritage of human storytelling. Technology may have undermined Aristotle or at least challenged him (Allen, 2013).

In interactive stories, the storyteller or game creator seems to disappear beneath the power of the player. It is true that some games are largely sandboxes or digital environments where players take their avatars or playable characters (P-Cs or PCs) to explore, encounter other players, create something, or just meander, acting on impulse and ignoring the stated goals and rules of the game if there are any. Yet, the similarities between the story structures of many games and the story structures in other screen media are obvious. Interactive stories also provide a dramatic goal or an objective to motivate players. Like the hero in a hero's journey, the protagonist in a game makes decisions (if this) resulting in an action or outcome (then that), which the player hopes will get the P-C closer to the goal. Many interactive games will reflect the specific characteristics of genre, such as a murder mystery, where players search for clues to a killer, or the action-adventure, where the player encounters dangerous obstacles and foes in the completion of a task. Science fiction, fantasy, and war are all popular genres for games and have the traits predictable to those genres.

Like a movie, games are organized by scenes, or the time and location where actions occur. An interactive story may refer to these scenes as *branch targets*, which are the specific locations in the story where a player can make specific choices that trigger particular actions. Also, as in most stories, the choices a protagonist or player makes in this specific environment have consequences: direct, indirect, delayed, or random results. If a player makes a certain choice, there may be a specific result or perhaps new choices become available to the player. With a *direct link*, a player makes a choice, and that choice produces a precise response, usually one the player expected. A simple direct link might involve players choosing something from a visual menu, such as selecting which of several doors their P-C will open. There can be many options with direct links within one scene.

Indirect links involve the choices a protagonist or player makes that have unknown and often unintended consequences. A *delayed or intelligent link* in a game is a postponed response. The game remembers the action but does not respond until certain other conditions are met. A P-C might pick up and pocket a key in one scene without any direct consequences until that player encounters a locked box in another scene, at which point the player can open the box and retrieve something that aids or perhaps hinders the journey. *Random events* are those choices programmed to have a wider range of chance consequences.

Like narratives in older media, games can include devices such as telegraphing and recapitulation. Clues in the game or dialogue from non-playable characters (N-P-Cs or NPC) may have falsely telegraphed to the player that an object is important only for the player to learn otherwise. The N-P-Cs in a scene might be mentors helping with clues or advice, or antagonists, trying to prevent the player from achieving the goal. The N-P-C might simply add to the mood or color of the scene, be a distraction to the player, or provide insights for the journey. In multiplayer games, P-Cs encounter other P-Cs, who can also become antagonists, helpers, or simply characters in passing. Like other fictional screen media, interactive stories can also employ devices like ticking clocks and dramatic irony.

Movement in interactive media is not always forward. The player might be allowed to backtrack, returning to an old scene or location. Since choices have already been made in that location, returning to the old location in a different time period creates a new scene, just as it does in film and television. The player may simply be returning to make sure something important wasn't missed earlier. In some interactive media, returning to a previous location may have changed the player's options or trigger new choices of a delayed or intelligent link.

Instead of the acts of three-act structure, games tend to be organized in *levels*. Once a player has become familiar with the world of the game, its rules, goals, and the other characters (the work of act 1), mastered these and achieved certain tasks, the player can move forward to a higher, more challenging level. Levels are not defined by time the way film acts are but might be defined by complexity, the number of choices offered to the player, obstacles in navigation, and player skills. One of the biggest differences between the interactive stories in video games and the predetermined stories of movies and television is that players establish the amount of time spent in a scene or on a level. Interactive media are generally not time bound. Yet, writers do have control over interactive stories. Writers determine the player's purpose, provide the scenes, tasks, choices, N-P-Cs, and the levels a player encounters in the journey toward the game's completion. Unless the game is primarily a sandbox, it is the writer who decides how each of these elements are linked and how a player can be successful. While there are significant differences in the production and delivery systems of different screen media such as film, television, games, virtual reality, and augmented reality, they share many basics of fictional storytelling and innovations of these different media influence each other in structure and content.

Choosing Structure

As you consider the shape and structure of your original stories, their form, ultimate audience, and media screen, it's helpful to pay attention to your own natural inclinations toward story structure. Listen to your own voice as you tell friends about something that happened to you. Where do you naturally begin a story? Do you open with the background, the climax, the outcome? Do you often detour to tell a related side story? Consider what forms seem the most organic to the story you want to tell. Though some forms may seem popular, they could detract from the story if they appear forced, artificial, or confusing.

As a structural exercise, attempt to reorganize the sequences of existing films. Would it be satisfying to reconstruct the *Wizard of Oz* as multiple stories, interweaving the perspectives of the female characters of Miss Gulch, Aunt Em, Dorothy, Glinda, and the Witch? What would happen to the story if it was told from Toto's perspective?

Important considerations for structure are whether or not that structure supports or distorts the story and the screen on which the story will be delivered. Forcing a story to conform to a nonlinear or multi-story structure because that architecture seems to be trending or innovative puts the story in a back seat when the story should be driving this decision. Similarly, forcing a narrative into three acts just because it is a familiar structure may not be recognizing unique aspects of the story that would have more impact with an alternate form.

References

Allen, R. (2013). "Beginning, Middle, and End of an Era: Has Technology Trumped Aristotle?" *Journal of Film and Video* 65(1–2): 9–22.

Chiang, T. (2002). "Story of Your Life." In *Stories of Your Life and Others*. New York: Tor Books.

Crowe, R. D.. (2020). "Strategies of Activating the Oppressed Protagonist in Jane Anderson's '1961' of *If These Walls Could Talk 2*. 74th Annual University Film and Video Association. Virtual Conference. July 28, 5–6:45 EDT.

Dancyger, K., and J. Rush. (2013). *Alternative Scriptwriting: Rewriting the Hollywood Formula* (5th ed.). Boston, MA: Focal Press.

Edwards, E. D. (2013). "Introduction to the Special Issue on Media Writing." *Journal of Film and Video* 64(1): 5–8.

Lebow, B. (1995). *Little Joe Monaghan*. New York: Dramatists Play Service.

Renfro, K. (2019). "A Quick Guide to Every Game of Thrones Character You Should Know." *Insider*. April 20, 2019.

Sterling, B. (July 1984). "Slipstream." *SF Eye No. 5*. Reprinted by the Electronic Frontier Foundation. Retrieved June 7, 2019.

Chapter 5

OUTLINES AND THE SPINES OF STORIES

> In telling a story, it should be just true enough to be interesting, but not true enough to be tiresome.
>
> —Saki

As we've explored in Chapters 3 and 4, screen stories come in many structural shapes. Three-act structures, sequence structures, and journey structures have some historical dominance and familiar advantages. However, non-linear, multi-story, genre-defying, reality-mocking, unmotivated, episodic, disenfranchised, broken, and abrupt structural forms or some combination of these alternatives have all made provocative screen narratives. An author's natural inclinations, the screen that delivers the story, and the story's needs drive decisions about a story's structure, where the story starts, where it ends, and how all the pieces connect. If a story is complex, an established and recognizable structure might better support and clarify the developments in that story's truth. If a story's truth is simple, experimentation with an alternative form might give that more ordinary, uncomplicated account a new life, helping audiences to understand it differently. The decisions about what form a story takes belong to the author and to the needs of an author's characters and their struggles.

Step Outlines for Any Structure

Many writers like to construct step outlines as the skeletal form of their stories from beginning to end before they begin constructing scenes. Some professional groups expect this. Impatient to get submersed in their stories, other writers skip outlining altogether for a more impulsive approach to their stories. However, constructing some sort of story spine prior to scripting is standard advice. Outlining doesn't need to be viewed as a heinous chore. It's an interesting part of the creative process and an exciting early glimpse of the possibilities for that finished script.

Once writers have considered their story concept and developed the characters who determine how the story will move forward, the next logical step is to list the specific, important moments of the plot. The *step outline* is a catalogue of these significant moments and potential actions, a skeletal sequencing and summary of those important events that happen in a script in the order that they might appear on screen.

A *step* in a step outline is a critical moment or an important incident in the plot. Steps don't necessarily correspond to scenes at least not in the first drafts of an outline. A *scene* is confined to those things that happen in a particular location at a particular time. It may be that more than one important idea happens within one scene. It may also be true that a complex step or critical event requires more than one scene to set it up or flesh it out, so a single step in an outline might ultimately generate multiple scenes.

Writers who choose a traditional structure can go back to Chapter 3, examine what work should be done in each act and see if the specifics of their story can fit within this traditional outline. A writer might believe a narrative fits more comfortably in an alternative structure. For example, a writer dealing with multiple protagonists must decide the order in which each character's stories are revealed, the order of events in each character's story, and how those stories are interconnected. In this case, a writer might construct a condensed three-act structure for each character's story, then decide if these three stories are interconnected, interrupting each other in a meanwhile approach, or if they will be delivered sequentially, one after the other. Writers who want an abrupt opening with a catastrophic event might choose to create an outline based on the traditional three acts, then move to events that normally happen as the establishing work of act 1 to moments later in the script where that information can be revealed plausibly.

An outline is a way to look at the spine of a project to see if it supports the story an author wants to tell and works for the media that will deliver that story.

Usually no one but the author or perhaps the author's writing partners see this outline, so there are no formal or professional demands for how it must look. If writers are part of a professional group, there may be expectations for contributions to a mutual outline, but these tend to be specific to the unit, are willingly shared with new writers to the group, and are always subject to change. Some professional groups like to use *scene cards* and bulletin boards, with each separate event important to the story written on a single card. These are tacked to a board, where an event can be easily moved and studied in a new context. Other groups use combinations of cards, white boards, and digital pads. Even among professionals, rules at this stage are imposed only for the sake of group clarity. The outline creates a road map for the conceptual inspiration that will eventually guide the writing of the script.

One important value of the step outline is the protection it offers against the Athena fixation, or the delusion that great scripts emerge from a talented writer's mind in that first draft without any prior planning, just as Athena appeared from Zeus's forehead, fully developed, stunningly beautiful, and with her armor already polished to a magnificent sheen. When the writing of the first scenes in the first drafts of scripts is rough and wandering, the Athena fixation inspires dangerous self-doubt, conceptual disappointment, and even writer's blocks. First drafts of scenes are much less likely to wander with an outline to lead them and no one expects to see wondrous beauty in the skeletal form of a step outline. An outline is supposed to have bony bits and rough edges exposed and, depending on how new the draft of an outline is, a skeletal outline might even stink a little.

An Example Process for Developing a Step Outline

As a case study of how authors can approach an outline, I'm going to return to the character of Jaz from Chapter 2, and the *Little Lame Prince* that inspired his story to demonstrate how an outline could be structured and the ways that outline can be helpful for structuring a narrative. The concept for this example was motivated from the fairy tale, the setting of a competition, and the genre of family drama. The concept then veered away from a strict adaptation to use elements of the fairytale as inspiration. The new story will be a contemporary tale—a boy with a birth defect and an economically disadvantaged family dreams of leaving home to compete in a skateboarding tournament.

Because all scenes and events in an outline are connected in some way to the story's conceptual core, it's helpful to begin outlining a narrative project with the logline at the top of the page or at least on a card nearby. If answers to who, what, when, where, how and how much questions surface in that conceptual logline, having it handy for inspirational reference is useful.

Some writers also like to have a one- or two-word *title* that relates to the setting, a character, or one of the script's core questions. Titles at this stage are *working titles*, meaning they will most likely change, and even loglines might change if new ideas surface during the outlining or the writing process. For this example, I'm going to choose a one-word title that connects to the sport of skateboarding, "Kickturn." I initially considered "Kickflip," but the title *Kickflip* has already been used by a couple of screen projects, including several student shorts, instructional videos that teach the move, and a respected Malaysian film that began streaming in 2020. So, "Kickturn" will be the working title for this example. As a working title, "Kickturn" suits the concept because informants tell me that the kickturn is considered a more basic skateboard move and the main character is young, inexperienced, and disabled.

The phrase also suggests a change in direction, though maybe not as dramatic a change as a flip. Again, this is a temporary or working title. It'll do for now.

> Title: Kickturn
>
> Logline: When a disabled boy decides to leave home to compete in a skateboard competition, he must be able to excel against skillful athletes, but his own father is his toughest challenge.

I'm going to choose a three-act structure for "Kickturn" for this first draft of the step outline. If this structure doesn't set comfortably with the story, an outline can always be changed with less pain than rewriting 90–120 pages of a feature script. I've already determined that this story will be a television or streamed movie, not an episodic series or a game, which a three-act structure would not support particularly well. With this decision made, I can begin with a review of a general outline to see how and where my specifics would fit.

A very generalized outline might look something like this:

1. Act One. Introduce the characters and their circumstances, tone, setting. Reveal the protagonist's ordinary life, goals, challenges, needs, qualities, initial problems. Disrupt events or routine with an inciting incident, the big problem or opportunity.
2. Act Two. The protagonist solves the problem, or attempts to solve the issue, or a solution presents itself only to have that solution create more issues, which can overshadow the initial challenge. Each new problem tests the protagonist's resolve as the protagonist encounters new characters and difficulties. Some parts of the why questions are answered but these answers create a twist in the protagonist's expectations. Toward the end of act 2 the protagonist is more aggressive, has successes, and gains new confidence, but additional problems undermine any definite triumph. Then the situation goes dark. The protagonist must take action.
III. Act Three. There is a light at the end of the dark tunnel, but just as triumph seems within reach, other obstacles and the final dilemma emerge. Once again, the protagonist takes action and the goal is achieved (or lost), the biggest issue is either resolved (or not). The protagonist may have mended a sad psychological flaw.

Turning these general guides into specific steps means examining where a particular story about a boy with a birth defect fits into this general outline. It means deciding which elements in a story about a boy's goal to be a talented skateboarder and his need for his father's love and attention match with this general description. In the outline below, general explanations about the work of each act are replaced with the corresponding proposed events of a developing story.

I. Act One

A. Sequence One

1. A skateboard park. Jaz—(protagonist) - economically disadvantaged, clubfoot, admires the physical skills of the skateboarding community. Jaz wants to prove that he can accomplish skills that challenge sure-footed athletes, but an older athlete, Couper (villain, id-driven), subjects Jaz to ableist bullying. Couper calls him "Gimp," an insulting nickname.
2. Among the gifted athletes is a girl, Ciel (tritagonist). When Couper openly criticizes one of her moves, she makes the next attempt spectacular. Undaunted (ego-balanced). Not overly proud or haughty.
3. Jaz's attempts at a modest skateboard move are met with ridicule from Couper and his crew. Couper intimidates Jaz into leaving the park. Couper and his elite skateboard pals dominate the park, for now.
4. Jaz's home life.—Overbearing father (antagonist, super-ego). Many economic challenges.—Can't afford to replace the orthotics and leg braces Jaz is outgrowing. The concern:—skateboarding may damage the corrections Jaz's therapy achieved for his bad foot.
5. Father's perspective:—skateboarding is useless and harmful. Jaz needs to own the reality of his birth defect.
6. Hurt, Jaz returns to the park. It's closed. Gate on the fence is padlocked. Jaz meets his sidekick for the first time. Sauter (deuteragonist, id-driven) takes a bolt cutter to the lock on the chain link fence. They open the gates and have the park to themselves.
7. Sauter appreciates how Jaz accommodates his disability to achieve the basic moves. Both boys dream of leaving the oppression in their tiny town to compete in a big skateboard tournament.

B. Sequence Two

1. At a skateboard shop, Sauter and Jaz befriend Ciel and learn she has already entered an important skateboard competition. Surrounded by his crew, Couper shows off a new board he acquired for the same competition. Couper embarrasses Jaz, calling him "Gimp." Sauter steals the colorful competition poster from the wall.
2. Sauter now has a specific goal: to compete in the junior series in this respected skateboarding event in New Hampshire, many miles away from home. Jaz says he would be happy just to see such an event, performing in it would be icing on the cake. Problem: how to fund the trip, entry fees, and basic necessities during their stay. And neither boy has a worthy skateboard.
3. Jaz wants to excite his family with the idea of the skateboard competition, but—of course—Dad won't have it. A waste of time and money. Dad's own dreams of athletic glory were squashed, and Dad didn't have a disability to overcome. Jaz needs to face facts.
4. While performing a move with his new skateboard, Couper takes a spill. Not hurt but angry. The board must be defective.
5. Skateboard shop. Couper returns his "defective" board. While the shop owner is distracted with Couper's demands, Sauter steals money from the register, but it won't be enough to get them to New Hampshire. Dismayed at the theft, Jaz agrees to hide the money for safe keeping anyway.
6. Ciel, Sauter, and Jaz meet after hours at the skateboard park. Friendships deepen. Ciel teaches Jaz some new skills. (Montage?).
7. Dad discovers the stolen money in Jaz's bedroom. Dad forces Jaz to return the money to the skateboard shop, though Jaz was not the thief. "You are the company you keep. If your friends are gangsters—guess what, you're in a gang." The

other penalty for Jaz: no more skateboard. Dad's disappointment is profound.
8. Jaz doesn't think he can cope without his skateboard or his friendships. He defies Dad and sneaks away to the park.
9. Ciel is excited. Wanting her new friends with her at the competition and because she is financially able, Ciel finances round-trip bus tickets for Jaz and Sauter. She presents them with the tickets. They'll meet her in New Hampshire. Jaz is running away from home.

II. Act Two

C. Sequence Three

1. The Road Trip. —Jaz and Sauter at the bus station. The small hiccups and large excitements of traveling on their own, setting their own rules. Sauter attempts to jimmy a vending machine for a snack. No such luck.
2. Transit Station Security apprehend Jaz and Sauter for skateboarding inside the bus station, but the boys manage to escape. Sauter kicks the vending machine as they run past, and it delivers a snack food payload.
3. Outwitting security, the boys find their bus in time to board, arms full of snacks, but Sauter's skateboard is locked in the office of Transit Station Security. Both boys are going to a skateboard tournament without boards.
3. Dad discovers Jaz is missing. Files a missing-persons report. Big discussions with the local police. "My son has a disability."
4. Home again, Dad is upset, worried, angry. Takes his anger out on the skateboard he confiscated from his son. He notices photographs of Jaz as a toddler using the skateboard to get around because Jaz couldn't toddle properly on his defective foot.

5. On the road, Jaz looks at the sights from the bus window. He's never left his neighborhood or his hometown.

D. Sequence Four

1. Excitement. Jaz and Sauter arrive in New Hampshire and find the venue where the event is underway. Their old nemesis, Couper, is at the competition, performing in the same age group with Ciel. Couper and his crew manage to be verbally abusive. The boys are reunited with Ciel.
2. Meanwhile, from clues discovered in the history of his son's Internet searches on the family computer, Dad learns that Jaz is likely in New Hampshire.
3. Hometown police alert the managers of the skateboard tournament about the missing runaways. Authorities search the entry forms for Jaz or Sauter. The boys aren't listed as competitors, but the managers of the event will watch for them.
4. Couper discovers a flier with their fuzzy photos on it, "Have you seen these boys?" Couper make jokes and threatens to turn "Gimp" into event security.
5. At a nearby elementary school, Jaz and Sauter manage to break into an empty school bus, where they spend the night.

E. Sequence Five

1. Next day. Jaz, Sauter, and Ciel meet at a practice park. Spectacular skateboard tricks abound. Ciel has perfected something impressive for the competition.
2. Couper and his crew observe Ciel's spectacular stunts and Couper becomes worried for his own standing in the tournament.
3. Ciel's father doesn't realize that the boys who form Ciel's fan club are runaways, and he has no idea that his daughter financed their trip. He

just knows that Jaz and Sauter came all the way from Mississippi to watch Ciel perform. Ciel's father is glad to see his daughter have hometown support and treats all the kids to lunch.
4. Meanwhile, disappointed and upset that police haven't found Jaz, Dad takes off work to drive to New Hampshire and the skateboard competition to look for his son himself. Something he really can't afford to do.
5. Red herring as police mistake some skateboard contestants for Jaz and Sauter but the limping boy they apprehend doesn't have a club foot, he had just taken a nasty spill in the competition.
6. Wearing a silly hat as a disguise, Sauter approaches a competition official to ask about a late entry in one category and learns this is possible. In spite of—or because of—his crazy disguise, the official thinks he recognizes Sauter. On the run again. The boys still don't have boards or the money for competition fees even if they could get away with entering under a fake name.

F. Sequence Six

1. Day three of competition. Dad arrives in New Hampshire and discusses his son's problems with the security on the venue site. Security gives Dad a V-I-P pass to search the venue for Jaz, but don't have resources to escort him around. Dad is on his own.
2. More spectacular skateboard tricks. Dad pauses to watch, becoming mesmerized with the stunning skills and dexterity demonstrated here. Sauter and Jaz spy Dad and realize that Dad and the police are actively looking for them. Avoidance and Secrecy. They can't too openly act as the hometown cheerleading squad for Ciel.
3. Different heats are called to compete. It's Ciel's turn. With wicked stealth, Couper and some of his crew manage to blow little copper-plated B-Bs onto the track like spit-wads.

4. Sauter realizes what Couper has done but it's too late. Ciel has already started her run on the course. As Ciel is about to complete her breathtaking move, the wheels of her board land on some of the tiny, copper balls, which throw her off balance and send her into a nasty sprawl.
5. She doesn't get up. Medics are called. Ciel's father is frantic. Ciel knew this move in her sleep. What happened?
6. Sauter can't let Couper get away with this. Over the turmoil and the mad roar of an upset crowd, Jaz happens to lock eyes with his Dad. Jaz and Sauter need to ease on out of the arena before Dad gets them. No. They need to run. "Dad don't play."
7. How can they let the authorities know what Couper did when they must dodge those same authorities? As they leave the arena, Sauter nicks a couple of untended skateboards leaning against the bleachers.

III. Act Three

G. Sequence Seven

1. Jaz and Sauter watch as an ambulance screams away from the skateboard tournament. What to do now? It hits home. Jaz is in big trouble and Ciel could be seriously hurt. They decide they need to go to the hospital and check on their friend. Stolen skateboards for transportation.
2. At the hospital, Sauter pinches a keychain with a toy skateboard ornament on it from the hospital gift shop.
3. They find Ciel's hospital room, where her father is happy to see them. They learn the hard news that Ceil won't continue with the competition. She has a mild concussion, fractured ankle, and abrasions, enough injury to keep her sidelined for the duration of the event.
4. Back at the competition venue, order is somewhat restored, but it seems that Sauter wasn't the

only person who saw Couper and his crew spit B-Bs on the track. A woman videotaping the competition on her phone has video that shows Couper in the act. Competition judges sweep the track and discover the B-Bs.
5. Sauter gives Ciel the gift of the keychain he stole to cheer her up. She's charmed. Sauter tells them all that he saw Couper do and why Ciel had a misstep performing a move she knows so well.
6. Ciel's father decides he must talk to the judges about what happened to his daughter, but he will also see if Sauter can participate in Ciel's place, maybe not for the competition but for the experience. This is something Ceil wants. If she can't compete, she fancies watching Sauter perform.

H. Sequence Eight

1. Final day of competition. On crutches, Ciel and her father meet with the judges. Couper is disqualified for bad sportsmanship and endangering a contestant. He is angry and ready for vengeance.
2. Ciel and her father meet with Sauter and Jaz. The judges have agreed to let Sauter have the experience of skating, though he won't be allowed to take Ciel's place as a contestant. The judges have given Ciel's father a special waiver allowing Sauter to perform.
3. With some hesitancy, Sauter offers this opportunity to Jaz, which is okay with Ciel. Both Jaz and Sauter have seen Dad in the crowd looking for Jaz. Except for when Jaz was a toddler who couldn't toddle and Dad gave Jaz an old skateboard to scoot around the house, Dad has never seen his son on a skateboard. Sauter tells Jaz to "show him why it matters."
4. The announcer calls Ciel's heat. Jaz limps toward the arena with Ciel's skateboard and the judge's waiver. Dad makes his way through the crowd to

the area where Sauter, Ciel, and Ciel's father linger, watching as Jaz hobbles into the track. Dad and Ciel's father introduce themselves. Just as the two men begin to understand something about what their children might have done, the announcer explains over the speakers that Jaz is a new contestant in a special noncompetitive category.

5. Jaz takes his place at the top of a ramp as Couper sends a marble onto the track. All eyes are on Jaz. He takes a deep breath, looks out at the crowd, and sees Dad. Souter motions frantically. Jaz sees the marble but too late, he has already started his routine. He avoids the rolling marble with a dexterous move.

6. Jaz finishes a performance that is not astoundingly difficult, but flawless. He did not fall. Dad is impressed, even speechless. The crowd applauds; Couper sulks. Ciel's father remarks, "We fathers are the cracked and buckled sidewalks on which our children grind their moves, still it's our purpose. It's why we're here."

7. It's a rare moment, but Dad is so relieved when Jaz returns to the group safe and uninjured, he hugs his son. Jaz does not win the tournament, but judges present Jaz with a challenge spirit award. Couper pays a fine and is barred from future competitions at that venue.

9. At the bus station. With glib lies and a winning smile Sauter manages to get refunds on their bus tickets for the return home. They'll be riding back with Dad. It'll be an interesting trip.

What an Outline Can Reveal

One thing you may have noticed about the outline for *Kickturn*, not only does it indicate a three-act structure, but it's subdivided into eight sequences as well. The outline lists broad story events within a sequence rather than ideas for specific scenes. Some events described in the outline will need several scenes for setup with other scenes to reveal their full dramatic consequences. Other events could be brief moments combined together in one scene. The example is sparse; many details are left out. Sometimes sentences and even thoughts are incomplete. Character motives are sketchy. The story also needs more twists or *kickturns* in the action to earn its working title. The plot as it stands in this outline is too predictable.

You might have noticed some characters labeled as id-driven and others as super-ego-driven. The protagonist's sidekick (the deuteragonist Sauter) is also a compulsive thief, but a loyal and generous friend. However, the villain of the story, Couper, is more dangerously id-driven. He enjoys the pain and disappointments of other characters. The tritagonist, Ciel, who gives Jaz and Sauter the bus tickets is labeled as an ego character. She might make bad decisions, but she's generally balanced. Having her dreams frustrated at the skateboard competition is upsetting, but she has the strength to handle disappointment. Dad is a super-ego-driven character. Labeling characters in the outline is not necessary but some authors might find it helpful to keep in mind a character's dominant drive.

You may have noticed bits of dialogue here and there in the outline. Step outlines have no rules about what details to include. When they occur, ideas about dialogue might as well be included in an outline. This never means these ideas must be transferred to the script.

One of the significant things that will need some fleshing out in a second draft of this outline is the complex relationship between Jaz and his Dad. This bond is an important concept in the family drama and needs attention. The Dad is a major, super-ego-driven character, but in this draft of this outline he doesn't even have a name and there are no good clues about why his relationship with Jaz is so strained or why he is so authoritarian. We don't know from this draft if Jaz has a mother or siblings or what Dad does for a living. Some of this expositional information might be pulled from a character bio and slipped into a scene fully disguised so audiences will never suspect they are watching this obligatory stuff. The character of Ciel's father also needs considerable development in another draft outline if this character is to function as a counter to Dad.

The draft outline for *Kickturn* gears the narrative toward children or preteen audiences. The tensions between characters aren't too overwhelming and there isn't an on-screen body count. It seems to be family friendly and could easily develop with a G rating suitable for television. Changing the ages of these main characters into older teens or young adults would alter the story in new directions to reflect the concerns of individuals at this older stage in the human lifecycle. That change would move the story away from the genre of family drama. The narrative could still be situated within the world of skateboarding but would have adult themes. There might be love interests, more serious betrayals, dangerous hostilities, or riper tensions. Taking a cue from *Little Miss Sunshine*, the story could take a bizarre, comical turn if the main characters became the middle-aged adults and extended family members who accompanied the children to the competition.

Keeping the story firmly within the genre of family drama, a review of the outline might suggest that within the mix of the main characters as children, the id-driven Sauter might be more interesting as a flawed protagonist than the more balanced Jaz. Events of the story could have an obvious impact as Sauter matures from a petty thief or even a kleptomaniac into a generous friend struggling to control his impulses. Changing the story's protagonist means the mission changes. Unless the character of Sauter's father is developed in this new step outline, the main goal won't be to reveal the complicated love between father and son, but to show the influence of friends helping a young boy find balance. The outline stage would be the time to make those decisions and reflect the changes in a new draft of the step outline.

The example step outline looks like an outline. The sequences in each act are identified alphabetically. Steps are identified numerically. The next draft of the outline might divide the steps to show the proposed scenes numbered under each sequence and what will happen or be revealed in each of those scenes. Identifying items in an outline alphabetically and numerically is useful when the project involves writing partners, because the different elements will be easier to reference in a discussion.

If you're creating a story spine or map for your eyes only, use whatever works to fuel inspiration and drive your writing. Cards, photographs, drawings, post-it notes, markers, crayons, nothing is off limits as Figure 5.1 suggests. Do whatever you need to make this process exciting as well as useful. The job of the outline is to provide logical organization and guidance, but the outline is also an inspirational tool, a place to experiment and have fun with ideas. Sometimes what looks like a hot mess to others is just what an author needs. For some creatives, inspired mayhem is a first, playful step toward a more logical outline.

Challenging the Structure

The first draft of a step outline will also be the time to decide if the three-act structure is the best spine for this story. With a step outline transferred to analog or digital index cards, writers can experiment with the structure, rearranging from a chronological order to alternate compositions, experimenting to find a structure that seems the best fit for their story. In the above example, a multi-story structure might work better for the mission of a relationship drama, showing the two distinct and opposing perspectives of Jaz and Dad, going back and forth between their two separate stories to reveal their different

Figure 5.1 Hot mess

needs, observations, decisions, and transformations. If this is the decision, the next draft of the outline will need to develop Dad more fully, make him the obvious and sympathetic protagonist of his own story, and give him a name. In a multi-story concept, Dad is no longer simply the antagonist in Jaz's story. He becomes the hero of his own.

The story described in the outline might be interesting as a slice-of-life structure, confined to the three days of the skateboard tournament, showing the normal even banal routines of the competitors' lives and their reactions to disruptive events. However, choosing to make this story a slice of life with a less obvious purpose may not be the best decision if the target audience is young. The editorial hand tends to be evident in children's media. Producers of children's screen stories are careful to make responsible choices, so the consequences of a character's decisions are obvious and young audiences won't be confused.

A writer might also consider a mockumentary style, telling essentially the same story but with a fictional documentary filmmaker following young contestants to the competition, interviewing them, their friends, and families. Quirks and the oddball characteristics of the skateboard subculture can come to the forefront. Mimicking a documentary style will not only change the target audience but replace the story's genre with a comedy. Subversion of genre might also work for this story, as an unexpected or even unlikely event at the end of act 1 abruptly moves the characters from a naturalistic story into something odd and unanticipated, dropping the protagonist into a genre-defying predicament, where skateboards are not part of a competitive event but the devices on which characters travel through time, space, or pure craziness. Any of these changes will mean a drastic rewrite of the outline and a reconsideration of the story's mission, genre, and target audience.

Story Outlines and Awkward Truths

A thoughtfully developed step outline is useful for keeping a writer on track. When the story begins to wander, a step outline is a reminder of the original plan. Writers can have different approaches to finding a story structure. Some prefer to find their stories in more spontaneous ways during the writing of the script and then refine all the ragged edges, holes, and unfortunate choices through revisions. How authors choose to engage their creativity is a personal decision.

And one admitted potential problem with a step outline is being too rigid with it. If during the writing process exciting things happen with characters that make the story want to veer away from the predetermined structure, it could be limiting to deny those possibilities just because they weren't listed in the original outline. However, not having an outline can mean losing your way, the story, and its characters inside a cloud of ideas.

A clear outline is like a G-P-S for writing narrative fiction, you may need to recalculate, but it's comforting to have a guide.

Now for some truth.

I am not intimately familiar with the skateboard community, so if I was going to continue and develop the ideas in this outline into a feature script, I would need to do research, reconnaissance, and find a writing partner who could bring the physical expertise to the table that I don't have. My goal with this example case was to provide an illustration of a raw, unproduced idea fitted into the outline of a traditional structure. It might have been more interesting to share the step outline of a produced, award-winning commercial project, but I didn't have one available to me. Not too many writers in my acquaintance hang on to old note cards and outlines once their script is produced and boldly swimming through the cultural mix. Or perhaps they're not excited about sharing the humble, ragged beginnings of their award-winning script with their public. Without an existing preliminary outline from a produced script, I chose to use the preliminary development of an untested concept, which is where all outlines begin. Skateboarding developed as the "what" for this example by pure accident.

I was already noodling over *The Little Lame Prince* in Chapter 2, spinning a fable, setting, and genre to inspire a character in a logline, when I heard a terrible noise outside my office window. I looked out and saw three teenage boys using the sidewalk and stairs as an unauthorized skateboard park. I watched as one of the boys attempted the same trick over and over, a move his companions had already mastered. The performance involved starting on the landing area at the top of five stairs, jumping, flipping the skateboard mid-air, and arriving at the bottom with both feet solidly on the board. This boy fell on the concrete many times. He was bleeding but kept on trying to learn the move. He never quite mastered the trick while I was watching, but he was determined and I was impressed. However, I won't pursue the concept that this indomitable skateboarder inspired and write the script. Skateboarding is just not in my wheelhouse, I don't have the knowledge or bluster to pursue it, and my bones are too brittle to risk a tumble on the asphalt. The depth of my ignorance about the skateboard subculture became vividly apparent during the outlining process. I've never even been to a skateboarding tournament. Luckily, there are already a fair number of movies that feature skateboarding as a major "what"—*Skateboarding Revelations: The Skateboard Kid* (1993), *Journey to the Final Level* (2018), *Skateboard or Die* (2018), *Skate Kitchen* (2018), *Levelland* (2003), *The Smell of Us* (2014), *MVP: Most Vertical Primate* (2001), *Land of Skate* (2017), and *Skateboard Madness* (1980) among others. This potential story won't be missed. My final excuse to stop here is a nagging concern about possible social media shaming from angry parents who don't want more media stories glorifying a dangerous activity. The boy I watched outside my office window was bloody and helmetless.

But here is another sweet truth about outlines.

If the writing of an outline reveals huge holes in knowledge or a subject and a story that just won't work for you personally, and if it isn't commissioned work, there's not so much investment at this point that you can't just let it go.

Outlines, Flow Charts, Beat Sheets, and Treatments

Outlines are useful for the development of any screen story. Most game developers will begin the creation process with an outline of the major game story much like a step outline for film and television projects. The outlines start big and broad, describing the mission and cataloging major character choices and their outcomes. At each location of the story, the outline will list all the major events for every character and what sets up each possible decision and what that decision triggers. After the big overview of the story has been planned, the typical next phase is visual development of the game world and its characters. Flow charts follow later in the process. The first *flow charts* are not text outlines, but diagrams based on those text outlines. Flow charts use shapes, icons, images, and words to show how an interactive story moves from the start of the action to its conclusion. The biggest difference between final production documents for narrative interactive media and scripts for narrative film and television projects is that scripts for interactive media rely heavily on flow charts, detailed descriptions, and graphics as well as those scripted segments familiar to film and television production. Interactive scripts tend to be beefier and don't have the same literary attractions as a screenplay or television script. It's not quite the same thing to curl up in bed with a good flow chart. But similar to the scripts for film and television, the documents going forward for the production of an interactive story benefit from the guidance of an initial outline.

A *beat sheet* or a *scene breakdown* is similar to a step outline. They are another organizational tool for writers. A beat sheet is a list of ideas for a scene or sequence and is a term more often encountered in episodic television production. Some writers consider a beat sheet to be preliminary to an outline. A beat might not be expressed in complete sentences or phrases, but a single word. A beat might not fully answer the questions of a particular story event, but simply indicate the texture of a moment. Since early drafts of a step outline do comparable things, it's difficult to articulate major differences between a beat sheet and the first draft of a step outline. Beat sheets might be more detailed than step outlines, but they provide essentially the same guidance. The biggest difference is that the terms "beat sheet" and "scene breakdown" are more closely associated with scripts for sitcoms, soaps, and hour-long episodic dramas.

A *treatment* is a detailed summary of a script and reads more like a short story. Many producers will refer to a treatment as a *synopsis*. A synopsis is the script's narrative written in prose form, broadly describing the main characters in the story, the setting, the conflicts, important themes, how events unfold and the connections between them. A synopsis will help pilot the writing, but like a logline, a synopsis will also be needed for the purposes of promoting the finished script to potential producers. If authors haven't already written a synopsis as a conceptual guide, they will eventually need a well-written synopsis to entice potential producers to read a script.

The outline, beat sheet, and treatment can all provide writers the structural framing for how their particular stories unfold. Structure is not story, but one cannot happen without the other. Along with the familiar chronological sequencing of scenes and acts, disruptive sequences, multiple protagonists, violations of genre expectations, unmotivated protagonists, delayed or missing exposition, and unresolved conflicts are all possible choices for narrative structure. When it seems like story events and characters are making the decisions about the direction their stories take, a writer may have found the organization that works best.

Chapter 6

THE TRUTHS OF STYLE AND FORMAT

> In matters of grave importance, style, not sincerity, is the vital thing.
> —Oscar Wilde, *The Importance of Being Earnest*

Writing for fictional media is one activity where adults are permitted and encouraged to let their imaginations absorb them. Writers project their thoughts into alternate universes, different times, unusual worlds, unique circumstances, and become absorbed in the characters and conflicts they create. Writers are ready to connect their thoughts with their own creative landscapes or become deeply engaged with characters and situations adapted from researching news and historical events. Writers want to play. The "Rules of Writing," things such as grammar, style, and format conventions, are not the stuff of imagination. They are often painful reminders of elementary school English classes or embarrassing corrections on college themes. These rules are not the most lively and imaginative moments of scripting. However, many adult writers have ultimate professional goals for their stories. Writers want the people who read their work to become swept away by the events and characters described in their written texts. They hope to sell scripts to producers or produce their scripts themselves. They hope to involve media production professionals in the processes of shaping a universe on the screen, igniting the creativity of others to breathe life to the worlds where their characters live. For those reasons, grammar, format, and style are important. They are essential for revealing the places, actions, and characters writers have imagined to the cast and crew who will develop the story into the media that audiences can see and hear.

One important truth about grammar and format is that they are simply tools to help writers express creative ideas. These tools are not divine. People created them. As media develop and change, these tools—language, grammar, formatting, and style—are also likely to modify, adjusting to accommodate new practices in production, different ways of thinking, new media technologies, and different social realities. Language is itself an organic thing, evolving as life does. Creative people need the flexibility to pick up new tools when they become available and be able to adjust to the unavoidable facts of technological and social change. It is likely that traditional tools and formats will inform the way newer formats adjust to inevitable changes in media. Just as screenplay formats evolved from stage plays and as some forms of television scripting developed from screenplays and radio dramas, the formats writers currently use will adapt from older forms to serve new technologies and different production methods. Media production professionals will continue to have certain expectations for moving image scripts: they should be easily understood, they should follow the current conventions of professional scripting for the medium in which they will be produced, and they should take those abstract rules of grammar and language to create from them something that unites the imagination of the reader with that of the writer, igniting both with the story and its possibilities. Clearly Oscar Wilde was being facetious when he claimed that style was more important than sincerity. I am not being facetious when I add that clarity, not style, is the important thing.

Writers of all fictional media share the task of using words to create a story and its characters. Whether it's a short story, graphic novel, feature film, game, or television series, writers must make decisions about characters, plot, and structure. Because these media are distinctive in their final forms, the formatting of scripts, walkthroughs, and manuscripts will differ. These different writing formats reflect the needs and expectations of media production professionals and their methods, whether the final distribution of the finished work is a streaming platform, broadcast/cable channel, computer screen, VR headset, or theatrical cinema.

The Literary Screenplay

Among the oldest media script formats is the screenplay, which borrowed and adapted some conventions from stage plays to better serve the needs of film production. This formatting has been in place for many decades now and continues to function as the template for short films, feature films, television movies, and hour-long television episodic dramas. Certain conventions of screenplay formatting have even evolved to serve the development and production of cutscenes in video games and narratives produced for virtual reality (VR) technology. The emphasis in this chapter will be on screenplay formatting, with an examination of how this older format has adapted to serve other media. One truth is clear. The world is not a stagnant place. Writers need the flexibility to adapt, to take what they know about telling stories into different media forms. It is possible that a writer will work in one medium and one format for an entire career, but the ability to adjust to new situations and new technologies is a helpful survival skill.

Even if they are meant to be produced rather than read, reading a screenplay can be a wonderful literary experience. The more comfortable people become with the screenplay format, the more fun it can be to "read a movie," especially one written by a gifted writer. Because reading a script can be such a good experience, some literary magazines have even begun to publish short scripts or serialized versions of narrative feature films.

I have a colleague who worked for several years in Los Angeles, first as a script reader, then as a development executive for a studio, where she evaluated many scripts in a week. She generally enjoyed reading scripts, but most of what she read she rejected and many of these were rejected because the writer didn't meet her professional expectations. A script presented in the wrong format, with errors of grammar and spelling, was not likely to get sent forward because in the mind of this development executive, there weren't high expectations for the work of a writer who disrespected words, grammar, and industry expectations for how these are organized on the page. Such a script would most likely be "passed" (or rejected) even before she read all of it. Development executives are people, and people want a good read. They want that literary experience of escaping inside a mental movie without jarring reminders that they are reading a screenplay. Another studio reader said bluntly that he read, "to the first typo, then tossed." Too often that first typo was on page one. There might have been a good story somewhere in that script, but it was buried under sloppy or careless writing. There are many reasons why readers reject scripts, but errors of grammatical style and confusing formatting that cast a shadow over a story's creative potential should not be the primary cause for rejection, especially when these errors are so easily prevented.

Because a screenplay is essentially a guide for the production of a movie, such things as spelling, grammar, style, punctuation, and format may not seem important to writers who have no intentions of submitting their scripts to literary magazines and understand that audiences are not likely to see their words in written form. More than one novice has used this as an excuse for spelling and grammar errors, arguing that "the audience will never see this script, they'll just see my movie and I'm going to produce and direct this script myself. I know what the script means, so punctuation and format errors are unimportant." Even if a studio reader or an audience of readers will never see the screenplay in its written form, the actors, crew, and staff that are part of the production team will. Format errors, grammar issues, and misspelled words are distracting and confusing and damage the confidence a production team could have in a project.

Types of Film Scripts

Screenplays can be written on "spec" (a speculative script), as an "assignment" (a commissioned script), or for a writer's own reasons, which may include a production where the writer will also be the producer or director. A spec script is a script that will be shopped or sold on the open market, as opposed to one commissioned by a studio or production company. Spec scripts are "speculative" because they are written for the possibility of a future sale; they are not yet under contract. The master scene format is the conventional script presentation for both commissioned screenplays and spec scripts until the scripts are ready to be modified into the shooting script that guides specific production choices. In the master scene format, the writer concisely and imaginatively describes a scene; there are few technical directions and no editing notes, scene numbers, markups, or breakdown annotations. All the technical and artistic information will be implied through creative writing to be interpreted by a director, actors, and a production team. The conventions of the spec script are more literary. It is relatively easy for an active imagination to visualize the movie by simply reading it.

A shooting script is one that has been converted from the master scene format to include scene numbers next to scene headers, modifications for production, and any other helpful pre-production information a director may want to include. Scene numbers help the team breakdown the script and prepare it for scheduling. A shooting script is then "locked" for production; the scene numbers won't change, though scenes might be omitted or altered when production begins.

Even if you are writing a short script for a film you intend to produce yourself, I recommend thinking of it as a "spec" script and writing it in the master scene format. The more literary style of the master scene format better supports the fluid process of story and character discovery before becoming too involved in deliberating specific production questions. Trying to write a shooting script before the project is really at that stage of its development may ultimately be restricting and frustrating. It may drive writers to think too much about script's production, than the development of an emerging story and its characters.

Basics of the Master Scene Screenplay

The screenplay consists of five major elements. These are

- The *Scene Heading* (the label at the beginning of every new scene)
- *Action* or *Visualization* (narrative description of the setting, characters, and action in a scene)

- The *Dialogue Block*, which consists of a *Character Name* (the capitalized name of a character) and *Dialogue* (the words that character says)
- *Transitions* (fades, dissolves, and wipes that move action between scenes)
- *Parentheticals* (which provide context or brief instructions for actors or production).

Using a dedicated software program for screenwriting can make formatting easier. The writer won't have to think about such things as margins and spacing, the font and size (Courier, 12-point), and capitalization of scene headings and character names. Though new writers may be working with dedicated software, it helps to know what a screenplay looks like, why it looks the way it does, and which elements serve which purpose. If a writer doesn't have dedicated software, it is important to manually create the standard margins, which vary on the page for a screenplay. A page is a standard 8.5 by 11 inch size. For scene headings and visualization or action descriptions, the margins are 1.5 inches on the left with a 1-inch ragged right margin. The margins change again for the dialogue block. Character names (IN ALL CAPITALS) are 4.2 inches from the left side of the page. The dialogue that follows the character name is indented 2.9 inches from the left side of the page with a ragged 2.5-inch right margin. Actor directions within the dialogue block or the parentheticals have 3.6-inch margins. Margins from the top and bottom of the page are both 1 inch. Pages are sequentially numbered in the upper right-hand corner. Descriptions and dialogue are single-spaced. Different elements of the script are separated with double line spacing. Longer descriptions of visualization in the action element can be separated into blocks with an extra line between them to make the page less dense and more inviting for the reader. The examples in this book mimic screenplay formatting as closely as possible, however the constraints of publishing may alter the measurements of margins for readability.

Writing software makes paying attention to these details less necessary, allowing a writer to concentrate on characters and story. Writing software will also automatically number the pages in the top right corner, a half inch from the top of the page. With these traditional margins and spacing and consistent use of Courier 12-point font, one page of a screenplay can be estimated to run about one minute of screen time. A 30-page script in screenplay format can be estimated to run about 30 minutes. A 120-page script will be a two-hour feature film. A five-page script will be about five minutes long.

Scene Headings

The scene is the primary building block of the screenplay and scene headings are critical to signaling the start of each new scene. Every scene begins with a scene heading to immediately orient the reader to the position inside or outside of a location, the place where the action happens, and time of the scene about to follow. The scene heading contains these three elements: INT. (Interior) or EXT. (Exterior) to explain whether the location is indoors or outside, the LOCATION or the setting, which is followed by the time, usually the choice between DAY and NIGHT. A dash with a space on either side separates the time from the location. The scene heading puts these three elements on one line in all capitals. Every location change or a significant time lapse within the same location is an indication of a new scene and the need for a new scene heading. The scene heading for action that takes place in the evening just outside of Frank's bar would look like this:

EXT. FRANK'S BAR - NIGHT

If the action moves to another location, writers will need to insert a new scene heading, even if the action is uninterrupted. In this case, the new scene heading might use the word CONTINUOUS in parentheses after DAY or NIGHT to indicate the unbroken quality of the action. If characters walk uninterrupted from the parking lot or the exterior of Frank's Bar to the interior of the bar, the scene heading for the new location might look like this.

INT. FRANK'S BAR - NIGHT (CONTINUOUS)

Some writers have substituted CONTINUOUS for DAY or NIGHT but leaving out "day" or "night" might be confusing once the script goes to production and scenes are shot out of order. The goal is to be clear but maintain the brevity the scene heading demands. If action takes place in the same setting as the one preceding it, only at a later time, it's necessary to break out the new scene with its own heading and a time-of-day modifier in parentheses.

INT. FRANK'S BAR - NIGHT (LATER)

One common error I've encountered is when writers include visualization or extra details in the scene heading. A scene heading generally has only three elements: indication of whether the scene is indoors or outdoors, the location of that scene, whether the scene occurs during the night or day. On rare occasions, a scene heading might include additional elements for more explanation. If a writer is dealing with historical settings or a nonlinear script moves quickly among several different time periods, an additional time notation or modifier may be necessary for clarity. Sometimes such modifiers also appear as text superimposed over the scene. If superimposed text for scenes moving aggressively among time periods seems awkward or unnecessary, the writer might follow DAY or NIGHT with a date in parentheses. No other material belongs in a scene heading.

INT. NANCY'S DORM ROOM - DAY (FALL 1901)

If a writer has a situation where one character is inside a space and speaks to another character who is standing just outside that space, the scene can be written with INT./EXT. in the scene heading. The slash indicates that the scene mixes the interior and exterior locations in the same scene. For example, imagine a scene where once character leans against a car and another character sits in the driver's seat with the window open, and these two characters converse with each other. In this situation a new scene heading each time a character spoke would make for awkward reading. The scene heading for a situation where two soldiers have a conversation through the open window of a Humvee would look like this.

INT./EXT. MILITARY HUMVEE - DAY

If a location has many parts or sublocations, moving the action to another one of these areas requires a new scene heading. For example, a primary setting might be Amy's house, but inside Amy's house are several different rooms. If action moves from one room to another, the script needs a new scene heading. Some writers might refer to this as a secondary scene heading. A secondary scene heading has the same three elements but adds specificity to the location.

INT. AMY'S HOUSE - BEDROOM - NIGHT

Some writers might refer to scene headings as slugs. However, this can make for confusion when others use the terms slug or slugline to refer to specifics within the visualization. A slug is a capitalized line that is separated within the action to call attention to some element such as a FLASHBACK, a MONTAGE, or some odd new thing in the visualization that needs special attention. Because of this potential for confusion, it's better not to refer to a scene heading as a slug. However, it is important to be aware that when some writers or producers discuss a slugline, they might be referring to a scene heading.

Consider which of the three options below would be the better choice for a scene heading.

- The camera slowly opens up on a long shot of Bob's messy bedroom.
- INT. BOB'S BEDROOM - DAY

- ```
  We see the inside of Bob's bedroom as daylight
  winks through the curtains.
  ```

If you chose the middle example, congratulations. And, to be clear, screenwriters wouldn't have a bullet point at the beginning of a scene heading.

Writing Action or Visualization

Directly following the scene heading is the action element, the narrative description of the setting, or what many writers refer to as the visualization. Some media professionals describe the successful writing of this action element as writing that is analogous to poetry. It is concise, clear, and brings an image or an action to vivid life in the imagination. It has a rhythm and flow that is seductive to readers. It is crisp creative writing with a mission.

All actions in a screenplay are happening now. When screenwriters provide description of the physical space, the characters in the scene, and any important activities, they use the present tense. The action element can also describe what audiences hear in the form of sounds and music but not conversations. Anything characters say to each other must be scripted as dialogue.

For lean, active writing in the visualization, writers might omit helping verbs. A list of helping verbs include forms of "be," "have," and "do." Helping verbs purportedly provide support for action verbs but make for stodgy reading in scripts. So, instead of writing, "`Martha is taking the dog for a walk,`" screenwriters will choose to write "`Martha takes the dog for a walk,`" or even "`Martha walks the dog.`" This shortens the sentence and clears the action verb of unnecessary "help."

Scripts additionally stay active, steering clear of passive voice, which usually involves a verb sandwiched between the words "is" and "by." For example, "`Martha is hit by Jared again and again,`" is an example of passive voice. Active voice would acknowledge that Jared is doing the hitting so he should be the subject of the sentence. "`Jared hits Martha again and again.`" Generally, the noun doing the action should be the subject of the sentence. "`Amy eats all of the pie,`" not, "`All of the pie is eaten by Amy.`" "`The car hits the dog,`" not, "`The dog is hit by the car.`" Active voice means that the subject of the sentence is the person or thing doing the action.

The writing in a screenplay is less formal than in essays or other documents. A complete sentence with a subject and a verb may not be necessary. However, descriptions of action generally follow accepted grammar rules. For example, verbs should agree with subjects. Adjectives usually come before the noun they
  ```

> **Example 6.1 Comparison of Action Elements in Two Scene Visualizations**
>
> EXT. OLDE DESERT INNE - DAY
>
> In a long shot we see the dusty Buick being driven into the gravel parking lot of the run-down Arizona motel. The sun is beating down mercilessly on everything. The audience can hear the CRUNCH of the car on the gravel and the WHINE of a neon light. We watch as the camera zooms in on a close up of the motel's sign, which reads OLDE DESERT INNE - VISIT OUR LOUNGE. The camera is quickly tilted down and zoomed in so we see a hand-written poster that has been taped in the hotel window. The close-up shot is showing us that this hotel is FOR SALE. The writing on the poster is fading, and the sign is insecure and twisting in the hot breezes.
>
> EXT. OLDE DESERT INNE - DAY
>
> A bright, hot Arizona day.
>
> A dusty Buick CRUNCHES across the gravel parking lot of the run-down motel. WHINING neon flashes 'OLDE DESERT INNE - VISIT OUR LOUNGE.' Breezes tug at a faded, hand-written poster taped to the hotel window. The sign reads FOR SALE.

describe. Proper nouns have an initial capital letter with a few exceptions (e.g bell hooks or e.e. cummings). A period generally follows the end of a sentence, thought, or phrase.

Because screenwriters will write only what an audience will be able to see or hear, it is unnecessary to include phrases like "we see" or "we hear." You will encounter produced screenplays that use these phrases, but their use of was not likely the reason a studio selected the script for production or why it made an award-winning movie. Example 6.1 shows two differently written action elements for the same script. The preferred writing is the second version, which eliminates camera directions, "we see or hear" phrases, and passive voice.

Notice how in the first example the technical cues also tend to make a reader consider production issues rather than imagining and enjoying the story as it unfolds on the page. The phrases "we see" and "we hear" are just unnecessary. Rather than allowing words to excite a mental movie, technical directions and "we see" or "we hear" phrases tend to jolt readers out of story, reminding them that they are reading a screenplay. They take up space on the page and create a barrier to the literary experience of getting swept away in the story. If you are an avid reader of screenplays, you will notice that the "we see" and "we hear" phrases occasionally crop up in produced scripts that were made into really good, even superior movies. New writers see these phrases in the scripts of produced films and think they are the signals of professional writing. Those phrases are not responsible for the screen experience. When you come across these phrases in the scripts you read, consider if the action might be more concise or descriptive without them. Instead of, "We hear the EXPLOSION of bombs in the distance," simply write, "Bombs EXPLODE in the distance." The phrases "we see" and "we hear" or their counterparts "the audience sees" or "the audience hears" are not wrong, just not necessary for vivid writing.

A master scene screenplay or spec script considers camera angles and shot sizes to be those technical decisions the director will make in pre-production planning. Visualization in a master scene screenplay makes clear what is important to the story without detailed technical directions. A writer who includes a lot of detailed technical cues in a master scene film script might be accused of "over-directing." A writer with a background in advertising might be tempted to include camera directions and other technical cues in a screenplay, indicating camera movements like ZOOM, PAN, and TILT and shot sizes like ECU or XCU for an extreme close-up or MS and XLS for a medium shot or extreme long shot. Audiovisual advertising copy is much less literary in form. It generally doesn't have to be shopped around to advertisers and producers in script form. Pre-production schedules are tighter for commercials. Ad copy is essentially a shooting script, usually with a quick deadline and often written as split-page television copy rather than in the screenplay form, though some advertising companies may use a modified version of screenplay format for their scripts. Decisions about shot sizes are directorial decisions. Different directors might have different interpretations of the line in script visualization that reads, "A bright, hot Arizona day in the desert." It's the prerogative of one director to envision a vast desert horizon, blistering in the sun, while another might imagine a brittle, scraggly brown weed clearly losing in the battle against heat and drought. For a writer to get caught up in production details such as shot sizes and camera movements while writing a spec script takes the focus away from the characters and their story.

It used to be a traditional production practice to open a scene with a wide shot or establishing shot before moving to closer shots within a scene. Although the practice of moving inward from the wide establishing shot may not be *de rigueur* for production anymore, it is helpful for writers to think about establishing the scene in the visualization, particularly in a new location, to consider what readers need to know about that location and the characters so the scene will make narrative sense. Help the reader understand where they are before describing details or specifics of action. A director might open the scene with a puzzling extreme close up of some strange object to involve audience curiosity before revealing the scene location. However, I've read too many scripts where writers make this directorial choice in a screenplay and the result was just confusing, particularly if the visualization of that detail seems irrelevant to the scene's purpose or what a reader needs to know about the location.

The writing of an action element in a screenplay is generally single spaced. If it is necessary for descriptions to be substantial, writers can break action elements into blocks, putting a space between them. Consider the logical place to break up a block of visualization. It may be that one sentence of description can stand alone. It may also make sense to add space before a new character enters the scene, when the description of a location changes to become the description of an action, or when a block of text otherwise calls for a visual breather for the reader. For the example scene, a new block of action might describe the driver and passengers of the dusty Buick as they exit the car. If visualization seems long and especially dense on the page, it may also be a clue that the action is over-written.

Though screenwriters don't include explicit technical directions in their scripts, everything in a screenplay must be producible. A script will be translated into picture and sound and must be described in those terms. Audiences must be able to see or hear what a character feels. A character's internal thoughts must be expressed verbally or in some manner that visually reveals her thoughts through her actions. Scene descriptions loaded with comments on a character's backstory and character's internal thoughts are not producible. If narrative descriptions have details that cannot be revealed through dialogue or action, a development executive may reject the script as "too expository." The problem of being able to externally realize a character's internal backstory quickly becomes apparent in the following example visualization, which is too expository.

How would a director produce the action element in example 6.2? What would the actor cast in the role of Amy do in that scene after she got a beer from the refrigerator? How would a production convey the important information about Amy's backstory the way it is written in this scene? One solution to

> **Example 6.2 Expository Writing**
>
> INT. AMY'S KITCHEN - DAY
>
> AMY (21) enters the shabby kitchen of her apartment and grabs a beer from the fridge. She is haggard from the many trials of her life and glad to finally be alone and in her own kitchen where she feels safe and sheltered. She doesn't know how to act around Tom. She doesn't know how to act around anybody. It's all so confusing for her. It is no wonder Amy has a difficult time with relationships. Amy had been an abused child, in and out of foster care and a revolving door of group homes. She never fit in. She was considered "a behavioral problem." The system gave up trying to make Amy part of any family. Finally, when she turned sixteen, the social worker told Amy she was close enough to adulthood to be on her own, to find a job, have an apartment, and figure out her own life. And now she is twenty-one and legally drinking, but after five years on her own, she still hasn't figured out her life.

this problem might be to insert a series of flashbacks, showing Amy's unhappy experiences in a succession of foster and group homes. Amy could also reveal her unhappy backstory in conversation with another character. Regardless of the chosen solution, the script would need to be rewritten if it was to be produced in a way that audiences can watch it on a screen and understand the information about Amy's background and motivations.

The first time a character appears in a screenplay and is described in visualization, writers will use upper case for the character's name to call attention to a new character that casting will need to consider. After this initial introduction, screenwriters generally use standard capitalization for character names. The use of ALL CAPS in visualization is usually for those characters that have not previously entered the script. Music and sound effects can also be capitalized in a screenplay to draw attention to these audio elements. Some writers will only use ALL CAPS for those sound effects they consider to be especially important. Slugs or sluglines are used to bring attention to an element in the visualization of a scene. A slug is written in ALL CAPITALS on its own line. If the name of a previously introduced character appears in a slugline it will also be ALL CAPS. These cues for production aren't really directions that interrupt the flow of the text, unless a writer gets carried away and overuses sluglines and music cues. Producers expect this and even novice script readers become accustomed to the different use of capitalization pretty quickly. The question to ask is whether the sluglines and the number of capitalized audio cues help to clarify the scene visualization or clutter it.

One problem I've encountered as a judge for screenplay competitions is the tendency some writers have to skip any narrative description and plunge from the scene heading directly into dialogue without letting the reader know which characters are in the scene, what they are doing, or giving the reader some brief idea of what the setting looks like. While long, overwritten visualization can be tedious, omitting visualization entirely is likely to leave the reader confused about the scene. Another common complaint I have about narrative description is choppy writing. In this case, scene descriptions seem like brief lists that don't really help create a mood for the scene. It's possible that these screenwriters have heard that production companies like "lean, mean" scripts. However, brusque, bumpy writing is not likely to create narrative flow. It intrudes on that lovely, literary experience of being seduced into the story. Likewise, long, dense paragraphs in a script may indicate too much specificity and not help to move the story forward. The writer was possibly caught up in elaborate descriptions or trivial particulars about the location. The question to ask is whether a particular element of description is necessary for understanding the characters, location, and actions or if it is a nuance better left to the director, costumer, stylist, or set designer. Writers will want to balance the tendency to omit the narrative description or severely truncate it in an attempt to be "lean" with the opposite temptation to overwhelm narrative description with unnecessary details.

Another common problem with visualization is simple confusion. Sometimes this is a problem with many characters in a scene and the overuse of pronouns, so it becomes unclear who is doing what. The visualization in the example could be fixed by simply using the proper name of characters instead of a pronoun.

A different pronoun issue deals with references to gender-nonconforming or non-binary characters. In 2017, the Associated Press adopted the use of "they" as a singular pronoun and several writers' websites recommend the use of plural pronouns (they, their, them) for nonbinary characters. The problem with plural pronouns is that for many readers, "they" still conjures the idea of multiple characters. Other readers may be insulted thinking that a plural pronoun suggests multiple personality disorder or mental illness for the nonbinary

> **Example 6.3 Overuse of Pronouns**
>
> ```
> INT. ABANDONED SALOON - DAY
>
> Tony, Joey, and Mike enter through the swinging
> doors of the old saloon. The place is grimy and
> neglected, but still fully stocked with dusty
> bottles. He laughs and goes to the bar. He wipes
> the dust off some glasses. As he reaches for the
> whiskey, he sees a snake on the shelf. He screams
> a warning. The snake draws back. He hisses. As
> he rushes to help, the snake seems to retreat
> momentarily. Then suddenly he strikes, biting
> deep into his arm.
> ```

character. Clarity is the top priority and the gender-neutral use of a singular "they" could confuse some readers. At this writing, the queering of the English language is still a work in progress. Some websites list multiple options for singular, nonbinary pronouns. These include pronouns such as co, ey, per, sie, ve, and ze (Kutson, Koch, and Goldbach, 2019). Unfamiliar pronouns can create new confusion for readers not accustomed to seeing one of these new pronouns in use, and some predictions are that these pronouns won't survive the test of time. At this writing, I won't make predictions. Until one or more of these pronouns become widely adopted, it may be simpler to try and avoid pronouns for nonbinary characters and use the character's name instead. If the nonbinary character is the protagonist and it would be awkward not to use a singular pronoun, a little research may suggest which pronouns seem to have the most current, widespread use. Select a pronoun and use it consistently. The reader will eventually become accustomed to seeing it. If the widespread adoption of "they" means using a plural pronoun for the nonbinary character, the context needs to make it clear that the pronoun refers to a singular character.

Other common problems with visualization include writing that is awkward or stilted with words and phrases that intrude on the flow. Good screenwriting avoids clichés. Instead of describing a character as "dressed to kill," perhaps a character looks "stylish" or "elegant clothes" flatter the character. If the character is about to commit murder, that should be made clear. Instead of writing that a character "gets her ducks in a row," describe what the character does to prepare. Instead of writing that a character has "`nerves of steel`," consider how the character's actions can show the character's fearless confidence. Instead of describing a character as a "`diamond in the rough`," consider describing those visual elements or actions that suggest the character's potential.

In addition to being selective with phrases and word choices, writers will want to be cautious with homophones. A homophone is a word that is pronounced the same way as another word but differs in meaning. It may even be spelled the same, such as pipe (a musical instrument) or pipe (a long cylindrical tube used in plumbing). Among the most problematic are homophones that are spelled differently, such as their (a possessive plural pronoun), there (an adverb indicating a place), and they're (the contraction of they are). Writers want to be sure they are not writing the word "air" when they mean to write "heir," or "ant" when they mean to write "aunt." Substituting the word "prey" for "pray," "cell" for "sell," "die" for "dye," "steel" for "steal" and "weather for whether" can create confusion for the reader, even though the words sound alike. A homophone mistake can be intentionally funny. During the 2020 presidential election and the frantic final vote count, a television reporter kept referencing the surge of "mail ballots" that were "finally getting counted." One voter shouted at the television screen, "I want to hear about the female ballots, too."

Be careful not to confuse a plural with a possessive. An apostrophe before an "s" can indicate a possessive, as in "`The boy's dog runs into the road.`" The ending "s" without an apostrophe indicates a plural, as in "`The boys play a vigorous game of basketball.`" The apostrophe can also indicate a contraction for "it is" as in, "`It's obvious the boys aren't paying any attention to the dog.`" In the following case, the possessive pronoun will not use an apostrophe. "`A squirrel roots in the grass and the dog quickly spots its prey.`"

A computer spell check may not catch homophone or word usage errors. If writers are at all uncertain about the word choice, they shouldn't be ashamed to consult a dictionary. A dictionary and thesaurus are among the writer's most useful tools, and most scripting software will have both built into the program. Finally, writers want to avoid redundancies and repetitions in visualization. The advice is to be clear, concise, and colorful.

Formatting the Dialogue Block

The third element of the screenplay is the *dialogue block*, which is composed of a character name in upper case followed by what that character says written in standard capitalization. Because the character name has

> **Example 6.4 The Dialogue Block**
>
> ```
> INT. SHED - NIGHT
> ```
>
> The shed door GROANS open on rusty hinges. Amy enters the dark, cramped space, shining her flashlight over mounds of abandoned stuff. John follows behind her, repeatedly slapping his flashlight with his hand and shaking it. The flashlight won't work.
>
> > JOHN
> > Damn.
>
> > AMY
> > Like the proverb says, it's better to check the batteries than curse the darkness.
>
> > JOHN
> > Darkness always finds us, Amy.
>
> > AMY
> > Next time just check the batteries.
>
> > JOHN
> > Where's the fun in that?

different margins from the dialogue that always follows it, dedicated screenwriting software will consider the dialogue block as two separate elements. However, there is never dialogue without a character name in all caps preceding it and never a character name floating in all caps in the middle of a page without at least one word of dialogue following the character's name. Chapter 7 goes into more detail about considering how to script the way characters talk. For now, know that a character's dialogue has bigger margins on the page than action and falls flush left but somewhat centered under the name of the character speaking those words. Because ALL CAPITALS have special uses in media scripts, it isn't recommended to use them for emphasis in dialogue. Screenwriters might underline a word if it is absolutely essential that this word be emphasized in dialogue and its context doesn't make that reading clear. Again, you will likely find produced screenplays that used ALL CAPS for emphasis in dialogue, even though it is not recommended.

> **Example 6.5 Dialogue Block with V.O. Parenthetical**
>
> ```
>                JOHN (V.O.)
>      The winter of 1963 was not a
>      happy time in my life. And
>      things were about to get worse.
> ```

Using Parentheticals

Parentheses have special uses in the screenplay. Unlike a novel or short story, screenwriters won't use parentheses for asides in dialogue or digressions in the script. Parentheticals have other important uses. They may follow a character name on the same line with the character name if that character's speech isn't dialogue but a voice-over (V.O.). In this case, the character isn't on the screen speaking to another character but acts as a narrator for the action.

The voice-over is an example of non-diegetic sound, where the source of the sound does not come from within the world of the film. It is a narrator's commentary on the scene. Other examples of non-diegetic sound might include music added to create a mood or sound effects the characters in the scene do not hear but the writer adds for dramatic effect or commentary. If the character John is visible in the scene where the example dialogue occurs, he might be trudging alone across a snowy landscape, but not speaking to another character or even aloud to himself. With voice over dialogue, John might not even appear in the scene but is a narrating voice, setting the scene for action between other characters who will create the conditions of John's misery. A voice-over is one way writers are permitted to get inside a character's mind and actually verbalize those thoughts.

If a character speaks and is present in the scene but not visible, that character is considered to be "off set" or in theatrical terminology, "off stage." A character who speaks "off set" will have (O.S.) in parentheses after the character name to indicate that the character is not in visual range but near enough to be clearly heard. The character is present but not visible in the scene. The difference between a voice over and off set dialogue is that other characters in the scene can hear O.S. dialogue, while the voice-over is the distinct privilege of audiences to hear. The O.S. is diegetic. Some screenwriter's Internet sites recommend using the voice-over designation for characters in telephone conversations, where one of the characters is not on-screen. However, since these are diegetic conversations, using the off-set or O.S. designation may have more clarity for readers. The unseen character on the other end of the phone conversation is diegetic, characters in the scene can hear that speech.

> **Example 6.6 O.S. in a Dialogue Block**
>
> INT. THE FOYER OF RAY'S APARTMENT - NIGHT
>
> Jack and Ray are wild-eyed, crouched among the boxes piled near the front door of Ray's cluttered foyer. They listen to thumping of heavy boots and CLATTER of weaponry from the hallway.
>
>   DETECTIVE EARL (O.S.)
>   Open up! Police!
>
>   DETECTIVE JOE (O.S.)
>   We know you're in there, Jack.
>   Open the door.
>
> Jack draws his gun.
>
>   RAY
>   (quietly)
>   Should we—
>
>   JACK
>   (interrupting)
>   —Keep still.
>
>   DETECTIVE EARL (O.S.)
>   We're coming in, Jack, so you might as well open up and save us all some grief. I hate unnecessary force, but I will break this door down.

Suppose we wanted to write a scene about fugitives hiding from police inside an apartment. To create tension, we wanted the fugitives and the audience to hear the police but not be able to see them. In this scene, the brief dialogue of the police detectives stays in the hallway just outside the apartment door.

The storyboard in Figures 6.1a–6.1c shows how such a scene might be visualized.

Parentheticals used within a dialogue block can explain the quality of the following line of dialogue, providing a clue to the actor about how to convey the line. It can also let actors and producers know if the dialogue

THE TRUTHS OF STYLE AND FORMAT

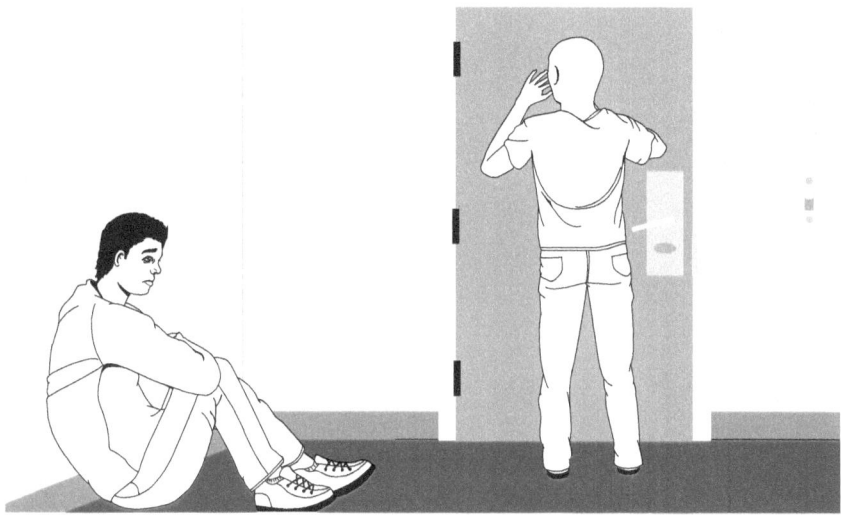

```
INT. RAY'S APARTMENT-DAY
JACK and RAY listen to the THUMPING of heavy boots and CLATTER of
weaponry from the hallway.
DETECTIVE EARL (OS) : Open up! Police!
DETECTIVE JOE (OS) : We know you're in there, Jack! Open the door
```

```
JACK draws his gun.
RAY: Should we--
JACK: --Keep still.
```

Figures 6.1a–6.1c Police are in the hall

DETECTIVE EARL (OS) : We're coming in, Jack, so you might as well open up and save us all some grief. I hate unnecessary force, but I will break this door down.

Figures 6.1a–6.1c (continued)

should be a different language than what is scripted, if it has a particular tone or attitude, or if it is dialogue the character is reading or singing. If the subtext of the dialogue isn't clear, a parenthetical description is helpful. A character's use of sarcasm is one instance where actors may need an additional clue, because with some forms of sarcasm, the character will say the exact opposite of the intended meaning. The parenthetical will help an actor correctly interpret the delivery of that line. Sarcasm may seem pretty obvious if a character performs a perfect overhead smash technique in a game of tennis to make the winning point and tells her opponent with a grin, "I suck at tennis," but a parenthetical prior to that line will remove any doubt. Writers try to avoid too many of these parenthetical directions. If the written dialogue is authentic to a character who has an established perspective and unique patterns of expression, an actor won't need many special dialogue directions. Another use for parentheticals is in a scene with several characters. If one character speaks specifically to Nancy and it isn't clear from the dialogue that Nancy is singled out, the parenthetical (to Nancy) makes this clear.

> **Example 6.7 Misuse of the Parenthetical**
>
> INT. WAREHOUSE -DAY
>
> Jones enters the warehouse with Amy following closely behind him. They walk to the table where Edward and Larry are still packing boxes. Edward looks up in annoyance.
>
>   EDWARD
>   (to Jones)
>   What's been keeping you?
>
>   JONES
>   (sullenly)
>   Don't start with me. Talk to your girlfriend if you want to know why we're late.
>
> Jones glares at Amy. There is no love lost between these two. Amy stalks to the table to help Larry finish packing.
>
>   JONES (CONT.)
>   So we get to the car but then she's gotta go back inside. She says it's to feed the cat, only I don't ever see no damn cat. She goes in her bedroom and locks the door. Twenty minutes later and she's finally ready to go. What do you suppose she was doing for twenty minutes?

If action interrupts character dialogue, a parenthetical after the character's name lets the actor know that the character's speech has resumed. Dedicated screenwriting software will usually automatically generate this continued status for interrupted dialogue. Dedicated screenwriting software will also automatically generate parentheses in footers for page breaks as (CONT'D) and (MORE). If the page break occurs in the middle of dialogue, these let an actor know there is more of the character's speech on the next page. Some screenwriting software will automatically generate a CONTINUED when a scene extends through multiple pages. These aren't really necessary. Some script consultants believe these page CONTINUED notations are annoying and clutter a script. Some recommendations are to turn these off in the software or document preferences.

Another note on parentheticals is to avoid writing extended character actions in a parenthetical. Lengthy character business and scene visualization misplaced under the character's name within the parenthetical throws off the timing and flow of a script. Extremely short business that effects a specific character during specific bit of dialogue might be included in a parenthetical, unless it needs more than a couple words of explanation. Parentheticals should be short; one or two words and not several sentences. Descriptions of character business or visualization that belong to the entire scene should go in the action element.
Making a practice of putting action or extensive character business in a parenthetical can overinflate a script's page count and the estimation of the running time of the film. The contradiction between Uncle Murphey's dialogue and the character's attitude are clear with the use of a one-word parenthetical. The actor knows not to yell the line. Actors generally like the opportunity to interpret their characters without a lot of detailed and unnecessary guidance. Writers are advised not to overdirect a screenplay with too many parentheticals.

Using Transitions

Writers may choose to indicate a transition between scenes. Transitions appear in upper case on the right hand of the page after the last element of the previous scene and followed by a colon. In some screenwriting software, the colon typed in a transition element will automatically prompt the insertion of a new scene heading.

Transitions between scenes include "FADE IN," "FADE OUT," "WIPE TO, "DISSOLVE," and "CUT TO." Because most transitions between scenes are cuts, writers can eliminate the "CUT TO" transition because it is really unnecessary. With every new scene heading, the reader knows the old scene has ended. The recommended style is to just follow the last element of the previous scene with a new scene heading and leave out the transition unless there is a specific reason to include one. For example, writers might choose to include a transition like "DISSOLVE TO" when they want to slow down the reader or indicate a passage of time. Some writers combine "FADE OUT" and "FADE IN" transitions between scenes as "FADE TO," leaving "FADE OUT" for the end of the script.

THE TRUTHS OF STYLE AND FORMAT

Example 6.8 Misuse of the Parenthetical

INT. LIMOUSINE - DAY

Everyone in the limo wears formal dress. All snazzy. Uncle Murphey is a .007 stand-in.

Susan crawls in wearing rumpled army fatigues. Hair in a mess. She closes the limo door and grins smugly at her uncle.

                SUSAN
     Are you mad?

            UNCLE MURPHEY
     (Straightens his bowtie and
     lights a cigarette before
     sipping from his bourbon.
     Then he winks at Susan
     calmly.)
     You're damn straight I'm mad.

Corrected Parenthetical

INT. LIMOUSINE - DAY

Everyone in the limo wears formal dress. All snazzy. Uncle Murphey is a .007 stand-in.

Susan crawls in wearing rumpled army fatigues. Hair in a mess. She closes the limo door and grins smugly at her uncle.

                SUSAN
     Are you mad?

Uncle Murphey straightens his tie, lights a cigarette, sips his bourbon. Then winks.

            UNCLE MURPHEY
     (calmly)
     You're damn straight I'm mad.

Other Script Formats

Television Scripts

Because writers tend to crossover from one medium to another, it is useful to be able to adapt to the script conventions of different media. Often the changes in script formats are minor enough that adjusting to a new style is not difficult and screenwriting software that provides television templates makes the adaptation even easier.

The formats for dramatic television series are largely borrowed from film and have many things in common with screenplays, but the realities of time and economic constraints in the production of episodic programs for television create some differences. If the show is a one-hour drama series shot single-camera style, the script will typically follow the screenplay format. Television limited series and miniseries, which are dramas written for television and have a predefined number of episodes, also look like film scripts. However, if the show is a half-hour comedy or sitcom shot with multiple cameras in a studio with a live audience, or even filmed on location with canned laughter added, there are several differences in the script formatting and these differences occur both in the formatting of the script and in the writing style. Once a showrunner's sitcom series has been greenlit or accepted for production, the season is often produced very quickly. For these reasons, episodic television scripts might have a much more specific, technical form and a less literary style of writing.

In formatting a script for a half-hour episodic television series (a teleplay), the acts and scenes are usually identified, capitalized, and underlined in the center top of the page. Characters appearing in the scene are identified under the scene heading in parentheses before the scene begins. The scene headings are underlined, but otherwise look like film scene headings. The action element or visualization in many sitcoms is written flush left, single-spaced, and in ALL CAPS. This is similar to split-page advertising copy, where descriptions, actions, and video cues are written in ALL CAPS. Because all the visualization is capitalized, writers of television sitcoms will underline the character name on the first introduction to call attention to the new character. Episodic television visualization tends to be quick, based on familiar sets and locations. Visualization may also have more technical details, describing shots and angles that a master scene script for a film would avoid. Once the pilot has already established settings and the general tone for the series, it may be unnecessary to repeat these familiar descriptions and instructions in subsequent scripts. It is worth noting that over a period of multiple seasons a particular sitcom may develop unique elements in its script formatting, even evolving a distinctive shorthand that is familiar to staff writers, cast, and production crew.

The dialogue block in a television sitcom is similar to film, written in standard capitalization, but dialogue will be double-spaced. Margins are wide, so directors, actors, and crew can mark them up with notes to facilitate cold readings or rehearsal. Because of wider margins, double-spacing, and a tendency for more dialogue than action, estimating the runtime on the page count for television sitcom script differs. A 22-minute show may have a script that's 40 pages or longer. Screenwriting programs will often provide example templates from various shows to assist formatting for writers who want to demonstrate their abilities to write in the tone of a specific show.

Television sitcoms tend to be multiple story structures, A, B, and sometimes a C or even a D story within two evenly divided acts. The series episode might start with a teaser or cold open, which is a quick scene with an opening joke. An episode might end with a curtain line or that last quick joke, sometimes referred to as a tag or wraparound. Like the cold open, the curtain is quick, about a minute long, and offers that last joke that buttons up the episode. The sitcom episode that could stand on its own works especially well for broadcast and cable syndication, where audiences might happen upon an episode out of context from the season. An audience member stumbling across an isolated episode could still enjoy the story without having to understand the longer story arcs of an established season or even know what happened in earlier seasons. However, as more people began to binge-watch entire seasons of television on streaming services, executive producers of television series began to think of their work as 13-hour movies.

Because hour-long episodes in a TV series use the same formatting as film, running time is estimated at one minute a page. However, the script for an hour-long episode on commercial television should be less than 60 pages to accommodate advertising. An hour-long episode in a television drama series might begin with a short *teaser* two or three pages long, followed by four or sometimes five acts that run from 11 to 14 pages each. Because half-hour television sitcoms double-space character dialogue, the estimation of running time based on page count will be double, about 30 seconds per page. In television sitcom format, a half-hour slot will likely accommodate a 40-page script with commercial breaks. For a sitcom, there is a short *teaser* or *cold open*, followed by two acts, buttoned up with a *tag*, or final joke.

The writing environments between single-camera film productions and television series also differ. The culture of the television writer's room is intense, with as many as eight to twelve writers under the guidance of the show's executive producer or showrunner. The showrunner is the person who has created the concept behind the series and developed the characters. This person has the power. The showrunner develops story lines, writes scripts, controls the budget, determines the sets, and is in charge of hiring and firing the writing team. Showrunner Ligiah Villalobos asserts that staff writers are the lowest level of writers on a television show. The large number of staff writers in the writers' room of a sitcom is necessary because of the jokes. "You want diversity in the writers' room to help keep the joke count high. The variety of different perspectives adds to the joke possibilities. The revolving door of the writers' room is all about power structures and personalities. People are hired because of their talent as writers and not because of their talent as leaders" (2019). The script for a television episode goes through five steps: story, outline, first draft, second draft with revisions, and then the polish. "It's important for writers to be able to adapt their original voice to fit existing characters and when you're producing one show per week, you can't be precious with your own work." Though the director is in control of a film production, a television showrunner will outrank the directors of episodes. One frustrated television director described his experience as the director for a sitcom as similar to hosting a major party, where someone else gets to invite the guests, choose the music, and decide which refreshments will be served.

A spec script in television can be a spec script for an existing show or a spec pilot for an original show, where the writer hopes to become the showrunner. Writing a spec script for an existing show demonstrates a writer's ability to adapt original ideas to an existing story and preexisting characters. A showrunner might hire a staff writer who can successfully match the existing tone of the show but also bring in a fresh story idea or a new perspective to consider. At this writing, professional advice suggests it is more likely that a showrunner will want to see a spec pilot, even if the showrunner is hiring staff for an existing series. The current advice is to have a diverse writer's portfolio that demonstrates the ability to work with an existing series or develop something completely new. It doesn't hurt to have a portfolio that demonstrates the ability to adapt to different writing conditions. Scene headings, visualization/action, the dialogue block, parentheticals, and transitions are those basic elements that shape the writing of a scene for a screenplay. Other types of media scripts will use these fundamental elements with some differences. Writers who decide that their short film is actually the pilot episode for an episodic television series or webisode will want to adapt what they've written to fit those expectations.

Written Documents for Fictional Multimedia and Interactive Stories

Emerging technologies and the immersive renaissance have impacted storytelling and the way scripts are crafted for these new experiences. However, story and characters are still key, and emerging templates for virtual reality (VR), augmented reality (AR), and extended reality (XR) media scripts have familiar screenplay elements while emphasizing such things as sound effects and the player's point of view (POV) as separate elements. These scripts might utilize slugs within a scene to enrich the visual perception of the immersive world though not necessarily to drive the story forward as they do in a film. The ability of audiences to react to and interact with stories rather than simply perceive screen events propel the story content. Reading a script for an interactive story is not the literary experience of reading a screenplay for a film. Many of these come in the preliminary form of walkthroughs, which might include *cutscenes* that resemble screenplays in formatting; however, walkthroughs will also include charts and detailed visual descriptions for conceptual design documents. The ultimate document prepared for production is often some form of storyboard.

The production of every project tends to have its unique path, but interactive stories and games don't generally start with a writer who seduces potential producers with a literary experience. The writer usually comes to an interactive project after a project director has secured the funding, the concept, and perhaps has acquired some initial flow charts for the project's design. The job of writers will be to make sure players have the adventure they seek with compelling choices, complex N-P-C (or NPC) personalities with believable dialogue, and side quests or assignments that add to the interest and urgency of the story's main mission. Though it is more technical than a screenplay, writers will need to bring their understanding of characters and narrative structure to interactive stories.

The flow charts for interactive stories are basic diagrams of a story's potential movement from the start of the action to its conclusion. These charts use shapes and arrows to demonstrate where a player will encounter a cutscene, how players change locations, what choices a player has in a location, and results of those choices. Writers may also be involved in developing design documents, which are detailed accounts of the story's elements from the biographies and descriptions of the characters to the descriptions of locations, player choices, outcomes of choices, and how the menus will work. Writers might begin with a high-level narrative summary, which explains the interactive narrative just as a synopsis or treatment describes a potential film. Writers sometimes create the descriptive lists of all the story's branch targets or locations to guide designers. There might be a detailed story outline, including the number of cutscenes for production.

Just like a film script, the scene is the basic block of an interactive story. Scenes are either playable scenes, where players make decisions and take actions; cutscenes, which players tend to simply watch as other N-P-Cs interact; or hybrid scenes, which includes elements to watch and elements to play. The scripts for cutscenes are typically formatted like a screenplay. Playable scenes will typically use the branch target or location like a scene heading followed by a description of the space. These descriptions tend to look similar to the visualization of screenplays and include explanations about audio elements in the scene. The details of the if/then player options and variable selections in the scene, as well as the consequences of each choice will follow the description of the location or branch target. At this writing, the documents created for interactive stories are evolving and different production groups may have unique preferences. Though interactive scripts include cutscenes that look like screenplays, scripts also include flow charts, lists, and even design documents. The final storyboards for interactive narratives also tend to resemble those created for film production, and like storyboarding for film there are few fixed rules for how they must look.

Transmedia storytelling is content with a common thread in which audiences might play an active role. A transmedia story involves multiple media forms, such as movies, blogs, videos, podcasts, e-books, social networks, and webisodes, engaging the strength in each of these forms for its narrative. A fictional character from a popular movie or TV show might interact with audience members through a social media platform like Facebook. Videogames, podcasts, or other media may then extend and deepen the narrative.

Media technologies will continue to evolve and overlap, but production professionals will always have the expectation that scripts are easily understood, that writers recognize the current practices and needs of production for a particular project, and that writers will take those abstract rules of grammar and language to inspire the media artists that will bring a project to life. The current fascination with franchises only emphasizes the potential of strong narratives with compelling characters to successfully migrate across media platforms and the need for writers to understand the ways screen technologies merge and impact story.

References

Associated Press (2017). *Associated Press Stylebook 2017: And Briefing on Media Law*. P. Froke, O. Garcia, D. Minthorn, and K. Ritter. eds. New York: Basic Books.

Knutson, Douglas, Koch, Julie M., and Goldbach, Chloe (2019). "Recommended Terminology, Pronouns, and Documentation for Work with Transgender and Non-Binary Populations." *Practice Innovations* 4(4): 214–24.

Villalobos, L., and Hackel, K. (2019). "The Television Writers Room: The Organization of Long from Storytelling." In *Write Now: Screenwriting Trends and Tips in the 21st Century*. University Film and Video Association Conference, July 30–August 2, 2019. Minneapolis, MN: Augsburg University.

Chapter 7

GUARDED DIALOGUE AND CANDID SILENCE

> It is always the best policy to speak the truth, unless of course, you are an exceptionally good liar.
> —Jerome K. Jerome, author and humorist (1859–1927)

There are two primary ways of understanding a visual story: watching what the characters do as a response to a problem or situation and hearing what they say to each other. This chapter focuses on dialog that follows from a character's intentions, including the ways a few characters might use dialogue to slant, reframe, lie, misinterpret, distort, and evaluate their situations.

Some media critics have admired the majestic imagery of film but seem to disparage film dialogue. They consider dialogue to be the principal element of television or theater, sometimes expressing an attitude that makes it seem as if they believe television and theater to be inferior art forms because of their heavy reliance on dialogue. This denigration of dialogue is perhaps vestiges from the early days of silent film, when intertitles flashed on the screen interrupted the action to explain something elusive or reveal what the characters said. Audiences had to read these intertitles to understand the dialogue. Or perhaps the scorn for film dialogue is residue from that period during film's conversion to sound, when awkward technical requirements for sound recording hampered visual possibilities and made the staging of actors seem stiff and unnatural (O'Brian, 2005). Perhaps it is also a frustration with how difficult it is even in a new millennium to get clean, effective audio recordings on location, making it necessary to use A-D-R or automated dialogue replacement to fix the sound qualities of recorded dialogue. Perhaps it is simply a preference those critics have for the visual over the verbal, the longing to see rather than hear a story unfold.

It's true that dialogue is an essential element of live theater, where locations are limited to a single physical stage and quickly changing the sets and locations needs creative ingenuity and capable stagehands who understand their job. When it is impractical or too expensive to visually stage an action for a live theatrical performance, it becomes necessary for dialogue to reveal what audiences cannot see. With similar limitations, early television programs tended to be produced indoors on studio sets. The situation comedies and soap operas of early television had limited action, relying on funny or emotional dialogue to reveal events that happened off camera. When film transitioned to include sound, technical requirements for dialogue hindered and confined the action. Silent film projects didn't have those same limitations. Even with a modest budget, a silent film project could show many events and locations in rapid succession. With an adequate budget, early films could deliver a superb visual experience, such as the physical stunts from the silent films of Buster Keaton (1895–1966) and Charlie Chaplin (1889–1977), which were accomplished without the need for computer-generated imagery (CGI). After recovering from the technical restrictions of sound, film projects once again tended to prioritize action.

By the new millennium, a stunning visual experience had become routine for moving image media. Audiences in the late twentieth and early twenty-first centuries could see spectacular wars fought in outer space, watch wizards cast astounding magical spells, experience the stunning beauty of an alien world, and observe stories from distant history awash in fresh, vivid spectacle. The visual experience in twenty-first- century media can be breathtaking. Because it is generally more satisfying to see events happen rather than hear a character describe them, a primary wisdom about writing scripts for moving image media remains, "show don't tell." Even so, well-written dialogue has its purpose. Dialogue can be witty, astounding, revealing, and deeply engaging in its own right.

Although the dialogue block is the emphasis of this chapter, it's important to stress that dialogue doesn't happen in isolation. The environment and the actions in a scene frame, motivate, and sustain the conversations between characters, even for those conversations happening in a nebulous void. This is why it is not a good idea to directly follow a scene heading with dialogue. Action or a scene's visualization reveals which characters are in the scene, what they are doing, and their relationship to the setting and each other. While it is possible to have an effective scene without dialogue, it is difficult to create an effective scene without any visualization. This doesn't mean that dialogue doesn't perform key dramatic functions, but that often the location and actions cue the dialogue for the characters in that scene.

The Functions of Dialogue

In moving image storytelling, character dialogue has two primary missions: It should feed or explain the action and help to expose the personality, attitude, mood, or motives of the character speaking. Dialogue that doesn't fulfill the functions of supporting the plot or revealing a character can be cut.

Exposing the Character

Before dialogue can support a plot, it must first reflect the character speaking. Whatever a character says that moves the story forward must also be consistently true to the character's personality. Dialogue is a critical element in character development, working to help reveal a character's perspective, dramatic need, and intentions. What a character chooses to say reveals how the character interprets events. In the case of a deceitful character, dialogue might become an attempt to hide what the character has done and what the character actually wants. What a character asserts, what is held back, and what slips out can be among the most important clues to understanding who that character is. Characters commenting on the behaviors of other characters or events in the story reveal how and why they feel the way they do.

When balanced characters open their mouths to speak, the dialogue focuses their intent and defines their reality. Balanced characters will generally speak the truth they understand but may not always speak out. Sometimes it is the disturbed, dishonest, or distraught characters who inspire the more interesting stories and challenging dialogue.

In the 1990 Academy Award–winning screenplay, *Dances with Wolves*, screenwriter Michael Blake describes several peculiar events as Lieutenant John J. Dunbar leaves the madness of the Civil War for an outpost on the frontier. One character that Dunbar meets on his westward journey is Major Fambrough, a mentally unhinged army lifer stationed at Fort Hayes. Fambrough speaks pretentiously, as if he is a king from the Middle Ages, calling Dunbar "Sir Knight" and referring to the frontier as the "realm." Concluding a disturbing encounter in which the Major's behavior and dialogue are decidedly peculiar, Fambrough tells Dunbar, "I just pissed in my pants and nobody can do anything about it." After Dunbar leaves for Fort Sedgewick, a crazed Fambrough commits suicide inside his office. In the screenplay, Blake continued to emphasize Fambrough's madness with scenes describing the major wearing a ridiculous, plumed hat and running naked onto the parade grounds of Fort Hayes with his sword and pistol. In the script Major Fambrough finally commits suicide with the announcement, "The king is dead ... long live the king." These naked parade ground scenes were cut from the film. Blake had already made it obvious from the dialogue in the previous battleground sequence and the dialogue in Fambrough's office that Civil War military culture was infused with an ominous insanity. It wasn't necessary to have Fambrough streak nude across the parade grounds.

Dialogue can also expose traces of the potential that a flawed character might have, hinting at a broken character's ability to change, suggesting that a character may have the skills needed to restore the internal stability that backstory, plot, and other characters may have broken. In the 1992 comedy film *Hero*, Bernie LaPlante is an id-driven character who steals from the survivors of an airplane crash even as he saves their lives. After another character, John Bubber, takes credit for the heroic rescue to claim the reward, Bernie confronts him. Though both men are flawed, Bernie will acknowledge his own weaknesses and consider John Bubber to be the better public face of heroism. Bernie's conversations with John reveal Bernie's reluctant capacity for valor as he attempts to convince a despondent John Bubber that Bubber is actually the man with a natural "gift" for heroism, whereas for Bernie, any heroic action is a momentary loss of sanity. "`If I was gonna be saved I wouldn't wanna see Bernie LaPlante comin' outta the goddamn smoke an' darkness an' fear an' stuff. I'd wanna see John_God_Damn_Bubber!`" This dialogue reveals the character's capacity for humility and a balance he did not previously possess.

Dishonest characters might outright lie, slant, or intentionally withhold information that doesn't support the dishonest character's goals. The 2017 film *Lady Bird* shows the coming of age struggles of Christine "Lady Bird" McPherson, a high school senior whose family struggles with financial issues. Her mother Marion works double shifts as a nurse; her father has been laid off, something that had been withheld from Lady Bird until Marion becomes angry enough to tell her. Many of the characters in this film lie to each other. Lady Bird lies to a popular classmate about where she lives to impress the girl with a more affluent address. Lady Bird's boyfriend withholds the fact that he is gay, too afraid to confront his own truth. Her next boyfriend, Kyle, lies to Lady Bird about his sexual experience, letting her believe he is a virgin. When Lady Bird tells him ecstatically that "`We deflowered each other. We have each other's flowers,`" he denies that he lied to her, explaining bluntly that he has probably had sex with six other people but doesn't keep a list. Lady Bird complains, "`I just had a whole experience that was wrong.`" Lady Bird's father withholds from his wife that he helped Lady Bird fill out financial aid applications for prestigious colleges on the east coast. When she learns that Lady Bird has been accepted at New York University, Marion stops speaking to her daughter. The film shows how Lady Bird navigates a world filled with characters who can't bring themselves to explain or face their truths and how she contributes to this deceptive world.

Supporting the Plot

By revealing elements of backstory, current circumstances, and other information audiences need to understand events on screen, dialogue works to assist the plot. Characters use dialogue to explain an issue, describe what has been done, and clarify what still needs to be done to resolve a situation. A police detective can review the clues uncovered at a crime scene with her partner. The captain of a space mission might discuss the atmospheric challenges of an alien planet with his science officer. A high school principal might assess the problem of gang interference at the school with some of the faculty and staff. Dialogue serves to explain the major conflicts, supplementing actions with important, perhaps missed details, and helps set the parameters of a dispute or struggle. Even as it fulfills these missions for the plot, dialogue should appear naturally from a character and the situation. The obligatory plot support that dialogue provides should not seem obvious or forced, unless the narrative is attempting to deliberately interrupt realism or naturalism in its storytelling, or it is in a character's nature to be awkward.

If dialogue is important for explaining a complicated backstory, it helps when a character hearing about that past, like the audience, has not been privy to it. In Guillermo del Toro's award-winning, controversial film *The Shape of Water* (2017), Zelda Fuller is on the janitorial staff at a government laboratory and must interpret for her coworker Elisa Esposito, who is mute but not deaf. Zelda explains Elisa's puzzling circumstances and the scars on her neck to both the audience and Colonel Strickland, the man in charge of a secret government study of a curious amphibian man held prisoner in the lab. Because Strickland is ignorant about Elisa's backstory, it's plausible that Zelda would need to explain it to him. Conversations between two characters who lived a backstory together and intimately know that history can seem stiffly forced, when one character asks another, "remember when …" and then goes on to relate the details of a past event that the other character should already know. The challenge is to find ways to make such a conversation seem necessary for the characters. Perhaps there are bits of that history one character forgot or intentionally tried to forget. The other character feels compelled to review that uncomfortable shared history, offer a different perspective on it, or argue about what those events actually mean. If all characters remember the shared history, jokes, teasing, or other banter can reveal parts of the backstory to the audience without a direct and unnatural recitation of it.

The same holds true for other information audiences might expect all characters to know. For example, the pilot and copilot of an interstellar spaceship shouldn't need to review the instrument panel with each other when it is the audience that needs to understand the particular functions of the wormhole gauge and the tesseract calculator because these figure prominently in the plot. That information will need to slip into a conversation that seems to be about something else, perhaps the captain's complaint that another crew member has spilled food on the panel or the copilot's concerns that the instrument doesn't appear to be functioning properly. In *Star Wars Episode IV: A New Hope* (1977), even though Luke Skywalker and Han Solo are both presumably capable pilots of space crafts, it is helpful that Luke may not fully appreciate the concept of hyperspace and the dangers behind a jump to lightspeed. Luke's relative inexperience allows Han Solo to explain to both the character Luke and the watching audience that `"Traveling through hyperspace ain't like dusting crops, Boy. Without precise calculations we could fly right through a star or bounce too close to a supernova"` (Johnson, 2017).

Recapping or *recapitulation* is dialogue in which characters restate what has already happened, but recapitulation also functions to remind audiences and other characters of important incidents. Recapitulation not only summarizes those events important to the plot, but it can also create anticipation, telegraphing expectations. In *The Shape of Water*, Col. Strickland, Dr. Hoffstetler, and General Hoyt discuss what they all know, why the amphibian man is a government asset. What makes the conversation seem natural rather than a maneuver to reveal to audiences the backstory about the creature's discovery and the government's interest in him are the different perspectives each of the characters have about how to study the creature, the potential he represents, and whether he should be dissected for closer analysis. It also helps that General Hoyt doesn't have all the information and wants an update on some events.

The Verbal and the Nonverbal

Dialogue is verbal communication. Scholars describe verbal communication as those interactions exchanged through language, the words that people write, speak, and sign. People absorb language from infancy as they acquire speech and learn to exchange ideas with friends and family. Language is specific to a group or culture. Communication scholars refer to those elements such as body language, attitude, gestures, tone of voice, pitch, volume, and similar cues as the nonverbal elements of communication. Such things as frowns, grunts, squeals, and smiles may be able to communicate across cultures that use different languages. Some nonverbal expressions, such as certain gestures, can have explicit meanings for different groups, making these gestures a form of learned symbolic behavior like language. For example, the signal for white supremacy among some extremist groups is similar to the sign for asshole in American Sign Language, but simply means "okay" for other groups.

Because authentic dialogue includes both verbal and nonverbal forms of communication, writers will want to consider how the action element motivates the dialogue that follows and how a nonverbal gesture influences the meaning of spoken words. Though screenwriters often describe dialogue and action as the separate elements of a script, they are the interwoven threads of one garment. Dialogue relies on the actions that precede it just as the meaning of those actions is often explained through dialogue.

When the verbal meaning of a character's statement contradicts the nonverbal, audiences will usually trust the nonverbal meaning. One good reason to give a character some business or action in a scene heavy with dialogue is that attitudes expressed in those nonverbal actions can be extremely revealing. A character setting a table for dinner doesn't have to say he is outraged if he slams cutlery down on the table in a visible show of anger. If the character declares through dialogue that he is, "Just fine. Nothing's wrong," most audiences won't trust that claim; it contradicts the nonverbal irritation demonstrated with the banging of forks and spoons. A character who tells her lover that she can't abide the taste of chocolate after she has gobbled all of a candy bar and is licking every bit of the chocolate from between her fingers, is really declaring her approval of it. There may also be other, more intimate meanings in a character's announcement that she hates chocolate that may have nothing to do with the chocolate and everything to do with the lover who gave her the candy. Nonverbal communication in a scene is important to its *subtext*, or what a character means but doesn't directly express. Subtext is often the character's truth, but the character may be too proud, ashamed, shy, afraid, cunning, guilt-ridden, or oblivious to say that truth openly.

In season one of the television series, *Breaking Bad* (2008–13), chemistry teacher Walter White writes the word "chiral" on the blackboard and lectures to his high school chemistry class about the concept of chirality. Like the right and left hand, organic compounds can exist as "mirror image forms of one another other all the way down at the molecular level. But, although they may look the same, they don't always behave the same." White goes on to explain how the right-handed isomer of the drug Thalidomide is perfectly good medicine for morning sickness in pregnancy, but the left-handed isomer of Thalidomide can cause terrible birth defects. The good drug and its mirror image, the bad drug, behave differently. This monologue explicitly establishes White as a chemistry teacher who knows his subject, but the subtext of this speech and White's stammering confusion when a student asks if chirality will be on the midterm, suggests that White also struggles with chirality in the complex compound of his own moral integrity. Subtext of the speech is revealed in both the nonverbal and in the implicit meanings within White's verbal lecture. The subtext in Walter White's chemistry lesson is not only about his own moral struggle but it also telegraphs a major theme of the entire series. When White tells his students, "`Technically, chemistry is the study of matter, but I prefer to see it as the study of change. It's growth, then decay, then transformation,`" he is announcing the broad strokes of a journey audiences can expect to see. Dialogue provides a foreshadowing of events, telegraphing what audiences should expect.

When Lieutenant Dunbar tells Major Fambrough that he requested a post in the western hinterlands because, "`I want to see the frontier ...[...] before it's gone,`" he telegraphs the film's larger message about the fragility of the natural world and Native American culture under the destructive onslaught of a powerful European American expansion with its prejudiced perspective. Dunbar's concern for a lost frontier was clearly Michael Blake's broader message to honor a simple, natural life. Dialogue can also falsely telegraph expectations for events. When Major Fambrough declares that a frontier post means that Dunbar must be an Indian fighter, he falsely telegraphs expectations for Dunbar's future at Fort Sedgewick and reinforces typical expectations for the Western as a genre: brave white men defending the westward migration of wagon trains and settlements against the ruthless attack of Indian warriors. However, the only Indian warriors Dunbar will eventually fight in this Western are the Pawnee, which he confronts in defense of the Sioux tribe and not as vindication for their assaults on white pioneer culture.

If all the characters in a script continually and bluntly say what they want or what they think, the dialogue can have an emotional directness that feels unnatural. Critics will sometimes refer to this as *on-the-nose* dialogue. Because people in our life experience are rarely so direct, on-the-nose dialogue may not feel genuine. In a game of poker, a player learns to "breast her cards" or hold them near the chest so other players can't see them and be tempted to cheat. Similarly, people learn not to blurt out everything on their minds, because in the game of life this directness can be detrimental to a personal goal. There may be one prominently outspoken personality in a group where others will be more circumspect, but even blunt characters may not always wear their hearts on their sleeves or be candid about longings and ambitions. People will withhold their truth out of guile, shyness, politeness, or perhaps because it's just no one's damn business. Though dialogue has a mission to serve the story, it serves the character first.

Scripting a Different Language

The dialogue block of a character who speaks a foreign language is written in English if the production of the script is intended for English-speaking audiences. A parenthetical under the character's name reveals the language the character will actually speak, even though the dialogue block is written in English. Italicizing the foreign dialogue further emphasizes that the written dialogue in the script is essentially English subtitles rather than the actual language the character speaks. In *Dances with Wolves*, Michael Blake chose to insert a parenthetical in ALL CAPS in the action to indicate how Native American language should be treated rather than have a parenthetical in each dialogue block indicating the language of each speaker. Much of the script after page 22 is in the Lakota language, so the screenplay makes the following announcement. `PLEASE NOTE: ALL INDIAN DIALOGUE WILL BE IN NATIVE DIALECT AS INDICATED BY TRIBE. SUBTITLES WILL BE USED.` Readers can assume that dialogue blocks written in English for Native American characters will be performed in the Lakota language with English subtitles in the film. Later in the script after Stands with a Fist has been using the "white man talk" with Lieutenant Dunbar, her dialogue block has a parenthetical with the word "translating," to indicate that she is not speaking Sioux but explaining something in English for Dunbar. Because Dunbar and Stands with a Fist eventually speak two languages, the script uses a parenthetical to make it clear which language they speak.

A writer might choose to write that character's dialogue block in the actual foreign language if the meaning of the foreign-language speech is clear in context or if other characters will be interpreting for a character who does not speak the language. For example, I had a former student writing a script about a young man from an immigrant family. His protagonist had become so immersed in American culture that he no longer understood his family's native language or its culture and actively resisted both. While the protagonist was visiting his uncle's family, he relied on his grandfather or other family members to translate the Spanish language for him. The use of the foreign language in the dialogue without any subtitle translation was intentional to show the protagonist's estrangement from his native culture and his separation from his family's roots. Subtitles were also unnecessary because other characters were either translating for the protagonist or the meaning of the dialogue was obvious from the context. The writer wanted his English-speaking audiences to feel his protagonist's cultural isolation. If most members of the English-speaking audience couldn't understand the Spanish, the absence of subtitles emphasizes what the audience has in common with the protagonist. Nothing is more excluding than not even being able to comprehend or "get" the family jokes.

Even though sign language is not spoken, it is a form of verbal communication. Deaf communities in different countries will use different sign languages and some deaf groups will develop unique signs within a subculture. The screenplay by Patrick Sheane Duncan for the film *Mr. Holland's Opus* (1995) features dialogue in sign language formatted as dialogue but with a parenthetical to reveal that this dialogue is signed rather than spoken conversation. On page 60 of the screenplay, protagonist and music teacher Herrick (director Stephen Herek changed the name to Holland) learns that his infant son Cole is deaf and will never hear or appreciate the music that is so important to Herrick. Page 97 of the script reveals that Herrick can't communicate with his teenage son because he never learned to sign properly. Throughout the script any time the deaf character Cole speaks, a parenthetical explains that his dialogue is actually signed.

In *The Shape of Water*, Elisa is mute, not deaf, but when she uses sign language, the script does not use a dialogue block for the English subtitles of what she says. Instead the visualization will indicate, "Elisa signs." Elisa's friends translate for her, often repeating what she signed, or the context of the scene makes it clear what Elisa wants to communicate without translation.

Listening as Dialogue Research

One way to acquire an ear for the rhythm and flow of dialogue is to develop the habit of truly paying attention when other people talk. Researching real-life conversations includes listening for ways a person might have made a point more quickly or more clearly, hearing what was successful in the funny story someone told but also listening for the surplus that could have been cut to make the story funnier, more compelling, or more efficient. The biggest difference between real-life conversations and media dialogue is the script's necessity for efficiency. Real-world conversations can be full of stilted, artificial, repetitive, and sometimes nonsensical rituals people invent to fill up a void in social situations. Conversations in life can be disconnected, tedious, and pointless. If there was a goal, real-life conversations can drown that goal in needless words. When this happens onscreen, audiences can get bored with characters and the media story. Conversations in moving image storytelling need to serve the missions to move the story forward and expose personalities. There is no social contract between the characters on a screen and the audiences watching them. People who might not walk out on each other will happily walk away from a screen, turn the channel, or fast forward through boring character dialogue. The trick is to reproduce just enough of human ritual to seem authentic without slowing down the story with unnecessary baggage.

Characters in a moving image story may also want to avoid painful or embarrassing conversations just as people do in real life. I have encountered screenwriters who will have implausible events happen to solve issues between their characters rather than write a challenging conversation. However, media stories are often better served when scripts confront and embrace these difficult conversations. Somewhere between on-the-nose and avoidance is a conversation that reveals a character truth and shifts the story forward.

My experience listening to people talk comes from years working in radio and television newsrooms. Journalists are privy to listen to a lot of different conversations: those that happen formally during meetings or press conferences, less formal conversations initiated through interviews, conversations that happen in moments of tragedy or disaster, off-camera conversations where people might change their demeanor because the camera has been put away, and those truly off-the-record moments when people might divulge information or "leak" something they want known without letting the public realize where the information originated or who leaked it. All of these conversations, both on and off the record, can help journalists better understand a situation and reveal something about the personalities and perspectives of those sources willing to tell them things.

Reporters learn to listen to what people say in a particular way. Journalists listen for the *soundbite*, or those moments in an interview that seem to best capture or encapsulate how a person feels, clearly summarize the circumstance, or expose that person's opinion and personality. The soundbite is the most understandable explanation an expert gives for a situation. A soundbite is that shaken response from a victim that reveals the depth of a tragedy. A soundbite is the angry response of a politician caught out in a harmful distortion. Soundbites include eyewitness accounts, opinions, justifications, descriptions, and confessions. Effective dialogue in fictional scripts might be considered ongoing character soundbites with enough conversational fat to soften the sharp edges.

Writers don't have to work in a newsroom to listen to people talk or—more importantly—hear what people have to say. One way to develop an ear for dialogue is to engage in the practice of eavesdropping. Discussions in digital meeting spaces may not have the same spontaneity or the randomness of those face-to-face encounters in public environments. Still, any unscripted conversation is worth a careful listen. There are several things to consider while observing other conversations or participating in your own discussions. Note the speaker's assertions. What are the speaker's claims about a situation? Observe the speaker's attitudes. What does a person profess to feel? Recognize the speaker's knowledge. Can the speaker's understanding of the situation be trusted? Why or why not? Consider any nonverbal cues. What do those nonverbal messages suggest about the speaker's claims, emotional state, or understanding? Do the verbal and nonverbal contradict each other? These observations of real-life conversations can provide the fodder for scripted dialogue.

Transcribing a lived conversation and then transforming it into scripted dialogue with redundancies and extraneous material removed, and rewriting it to be more poignant, clever, or humorous can be a useful exercise.

When it's difficult to overhear dialogue in public spaces, news, documentary, and reality programming can also offer opportunities to study unscripted speech, to listen for unique expressions and get a feel for the general movement of conversations. It is also useful to compare unscripted conversations to the scripted dialogues encountered in popular media, looking for where in the action dialogue seems necessary, examining the story function the dialogue serves, and assessing what it is that makes these scripted exchanges engaging, funny, or moving.

Dialogue research isn't necessarily something that must happen prior to writing but might become a customary practice of intentional listening whenever the opportunity surfaces. Carefully listening to what other people have to say has attractive secondary benefits, particularly if you are involved rather than eavesdropping on someone else's conversation. There's less of a chance of misunderstanding what someone has told you if you are really paying attention, and other people tend to appreciate a good listener.

Reading produced scripts with strong, clever, and insightful dialogue is another way to get a feel for how dialogue flows between characters. There are many screenplay collections available for study. Some Internet collection are available for free. Study produced scripts that have received awards for writing. Examine the media product produced from these award-winning scripts and study how actors interpreted dialogue passages. Question what makes the dialogue work.

Regional Phrases and Dialect

Like people, characters reflect the environment that created them. Characters speak their native language, use dialects and regional phrases, and have distinctive expressions developed from their unique experiences. The grammar might be incorrect and littered with colloquialisms.

Critics consider Billy Bob Thornton's Academy Award–winning screenplay, *Sling Blade* (1996), to be a prize of Southern storytelling. The narrative takes place in Arkansas in a location ripe with a particular southern dialect. The protagonist is an intellectually challenged man named Karl who spent much of his life in a mental institution because as a 12-year-old boy he murdered his mother and her lover with a "`sling blade`." Authorities locked Karl in a mental institution rather than jail because they didn't think he was "right in the head." In Thornton's script, Karl's speech identifies him as a southern character. For example, Karl will refer to laundry as "`warshing`" and the mental institution where he lived as the "nervous hospital." Thornton spelled out certain words in character dialogue in the way he wanted them pronounced. Even if all the main characters in the script come from the same region, like those in Thornton's script, each character will have a unique way of speaking. All the characters may have Southern accents, but each one will have word choices, attitudes of expression, and motivations for speaking that are unique.

Phrases are another way to identify a character's background or attitude. The phrase, "Have a blessed day," continues to be popular in some parts of the United States, especially the south. It is most often used as an exaggerated form of "Have a good day." A person who tells another person, "have a blessed day," appears to invoke a day sanctified with divine approval for someone they barely know or don't really know at all. In some situations, the phrase has come to have the contradictory meaning, "Get bent." It's a curse, even though it might be offered with the sweetest smile and an exaggerated sugary tone. Similarly, the Southern phrase, "Bless your heart," has multiple meanings. Traditionally it was a sincere expression of sympathy, usually spoken after hearing some bad news. More recently, the phrase is used in combination with an insult, such as, "Bless his heart, he's smart as a stump" or "Bless her heart, she has all the charms of a zit." Pretending to bless someone's heart sounds like concern, but in this case, it becomes a sarcastic expression of endearment for someone the speaker doesn't like or respect. It is one of many southern expressions that developed because people are not supposed to "act ugly." More recently, the offering of "thoughts and prayers" has come to mean "I don't care," as the public recognizes that too many people, politicians in particular, are quick to offer "thoughts and prayers" for citizens facing tragedy but refuse to offer useful policy or tangible help.

One of many reasons why writers are advised to "write what you know" is that attempting to develop characters that come from a region or culture that is unfamiliar can result in stiff and unnatural dialogue unless the writer does careful research, understands how people use their regional phrases, when they would naturally use them, and what those phrases mean.

Just as every person has a way of speaking, all characters will have their own vernacular. The teacher will talk about student assessments and lesson plans, the mechanic might argue about the engines and oil changes of life, a new mother's dialogue is besieged with bottles, diapers, and desires for a moment's nap. Each character has life circumstances, views, conflicts, and needs that are the fodder for their dialogue. Where the character grew up, the character's friends, parents, education, the character's drives, and perspectives all converge to influence a character's speech patterns. It is important to listen to your own characters. Knowing a character really well, knowing all her motivations, understanding her disappointments, and realizing what she thinks about the world is the best way to predict and script what that character will say in any circumstance of any scene.

Punctuation: A Writer's "Directing" Tool

I never enjoyed learning punctuation rules in English classes any more than I enjoyed diagramming sentences. However, in screenwriting, punctuation becomes less about rigid grammatical rules and more about the way that writers can shrewdly "direct" their scripts. Punctuation is the tool that gives writing movement, rhythm, and emphasis. In developing scripts for moving image media, the main "rule" of punctuation is to help a reader interpret the story, to help the producer find the narrative flow, and to help an actor deliver the dialogue. It is punctuation that manages the progress of the story within your narrative descriptions. Any use of punctuation that will help the understanding of a story—or help the reader find its pulse—is a correct use. For that reason, punctuation is handled a tad differently in writing for moving image media than it is in the formal writing of books and magazine articles. Punctuation is important to the clarity of writing action, but punctuation is critical for guiding the flow and emotion of dialogue. This discussion about specific punctuation is not a set of rules so much as a way to think about using punctuation as an interpretative strategy for revealing the attitudes and intentions, the pace and emphasis of a character's dialogue.

Writing Full Stops, Beats, and Pauses

Perhaps the most common punctuation mark is the *period*. We learned in English classes that writers use a period to indicate the end of a complete sentence. In formal writing a complete sentence begins with a capital letter and includes both a subject and verb. But it is perfectly acceptable for a screenwriter to insert a period after a phrase that is grammatically incomplete if it enhances the sense and rhythm of the dialogue. Sometimes a phrase or a single word in isolation makes a dramatic point. In conversations, authentic characters are like people; they rarely speak in complete sentences. A period tells the actor to come to a full stop. When a period signals the full stop, the parenthetical directions (a beat) and (a pause) are unnecessary. An actor may choose to insert a longer pause if the dialogue suggests this might be effective without being told to do so in parenthetical direction. If a pause needs more significant time than a period suggests, interrupt the dialogue block with a bit of quiet business or action, such as a character's raised eyebrow, a shift in the character's posture, or a change in the character's expression to provide a natural reason for the longer pause with the business that fills it.

One mistake I noticed in both student and competition scripts is the complete elimination of periods in dialogue altogether and sometimes in the writing of action elements as well. The writers making this mistake will have a character say a phrase or even a complete sentence without a period to bring the character's speech to a full stop. This puzzled me because the period seems like the simplest punctuation to understand and use. I finally realized that these writers weren't using periods when they sent short text messages to friends. Instead of a period, they hit the return key. The full stop or the completion of the thought is implied in the confined space of the text on a screen. That expressive conclusion of a thought gets experienced when an author hits the return. It feels like a period. This tendency to omit periods has also become a trend in e-mails and social media posts. While the lack of a period may not create profound confusion in a text message, omitting periods in character speeches disturbs the flow of the speech and the meaning of the character's dialogue. When a character's speech must come to a full stop at the end of a sentence or after a word or phrase, a period is necessary.

A comma also tells the actor to interject a pause, just not as long a pause as the period. The comma separates words or phrases. It allows a short breathing space for actors and gathers words into effective rhythmic groups. A comma that supports the pacing of words in speeches or narrative descriptions is a properly placed comma.

Exclamation Marks, Questions, and Ellipsis

Emphasis in character dialogue should seem natural, the excitement should be evident from context even without exclamation marks. It is a character's choice of words and the descriptive situation that gives a speech the sense of urgency. A long string of exclamation marks does not add tension. If anything, a succession of exclamation marks seems like a humorous comic book effect rather than a declaration of real danger. If an exclamation mark is truly necessary for clarity, one exclamation mark should do the trick. In the example, substituting a simple period for excessive exclamation marks in Helen's dialogue leaves more options open to the actor, ranging from screaming the line with veins popping to delivering the line with a cold, quiet rage. Depending upon the context, Helen may not really want Mark to shut-the-hell-up at all. Underlining a word tells an actor to emphasize the word, though general advice is to avoid doing this. If a character has distinct and consistent forms of expression or the context suggests emphasis, it may be obvious to the actor when a particular word should be stressed. Because capitalization has special uses in writing media scripts, it's better to avoid using all caps to emphasize a certain word in the dialogue block. *Question marks* appear in dialogue blocks to indicate that the character has a query. For the actor the question mark indicates a rising vocal inflection. It's

> **Example 7.1 Using Periods and Commas**
>
> MADELYNN
> I will not. Eat. Meat. I will not eat beef, chicken, pork, mutton, or fish. I will not eat any animal that people make into pets. I certainly won't eat any baby animals with cute faces.
> (considering)
> Now, I might eat a snake just to try it. Just to see what it tastes like. I mean, if the occasion to eat snake meat should ever arise, I'll give it a go. Once. I won't go out of my way or anything. But I will taste a tiny bite of snake meat out of curiosity. Generally, I won't eat meat.

a good idea to keep questions short. If the character is not really asking a question, don't use a question mark. Notice in the example dialogue block, a question mark in Helen's line could change the way the line might be delivered. Similarly, removing question marks can change the delivery and meaning of a line of dialogue. Unless the setting is a situation like a police interrogation, a courtroom, or a seminar, dialogue that is a series of questions from one character followed with answers from another can seem like an unnatural setup for the purpose of delivering backstory information.

The ellipsis is that sequence of three periods in a row. Writers of formal articles and books will use an ellipsis to indicate an omission of words within a sentence. This often happens in a long quotation where part of the quoted material is not relevant to the point the author is making, so the author substitutes an ellipsis and readers will understand that this is not a verbatim quote. Sometimes writers will use a string of dots as a substitute for other punctuation, such as commas or periods. Nothing litters a dialogue block (or an action element) more than words and phrases continually strung together with ellipses. A script with a breakout of "ellipsis acne" can be awkward to read and seem immature. Ellipsis used this way can also become habit-forming.

Example 7.2 Misuse of Exclamations, Question Marks, and Ellipsis

INT. HELEN'S OFFICE - DAY

Mark leans over Helen's stylish office desk, his large hands flat on the glassy surface. Helen is not intimidated.

> MARK
> I didn't come in here to talk about the way things were, Helen … I'm here to talk about … the way things are going to be. You want to hear about the way things … will be?

> HELEN
> Shut the <u>hell up</u>!!!!!!!!!!!!

> MARK
> You've been holding out on me, Helen?

Mark stands and smugly adjusts the sleeve of his jacket. Helen reaches for a box of tissues, removes one, and wipes Mark's fingerprints off the glass top of her desk.

> HELEN
> You expect me to pay you today.

> MARK
> I expect … to get paid.

> HELEN
> Remind me what you've done for me lately, Mark.

> MARK
> This conversation is not about the past … this is about our … contract for the future.

> HELEN
> I don't see a future for us, Mark.

Some writers will use ellipsis in a character's speech, to indicate where the character is hesitant to speak or has incomplete thoughts. If the character doesn't know what to say, it may serve a screenplay better if the character didn't have dialogue at that particular moment. Writers ... who find themselves ... consistently headed ... for the three dots ... in a character's speech ... might stop ... to consider ... whether it is the character who is hesitant ... or the writer. Sometimes ellipsis legitimately serves a purpose for a character who stutters or stammers. If ellipsis is a feature in the dialogue blocks of multiple characters, the writer is likely searching for clarity or purpose for those characters. Individual characters haven't found their voices. If multiple characters have "ellipsis acne" in their dialogue blocks, it's time for a good scrub and peel.

In the example dialogue (Example 7.2), the ellipsis is not really helping the flow of Mark's speech, which might be better off with a full stop or by simply removing the ellipsis.

Hyphens and Dashes

Hyphens are one dash used to connect related letters or words. For example, writers can assist acting talent by writing large numbers as a smaller number and word connected by a hyphen, such as 12-thousand instead of twelve thousand or 12,000. The dash is also useful punctuation for a hesitant or interrupted character. Dashes can indicate where one character intrudes on another character's dialogue or where a bit of action disrupts the dialogue. Dashes demonstrate the abruptness of that interruption.

Dashes, like commas and semicolons, help the rhythm of the script by introducing a pause. Dashes can also replace words with a more effective pause. In in dialogue in Example 7.3, the words "it is" in Sonja's speech have been replaced with a dash. In this way the dash helps mimic human speech, which often leaves out some words. Two dashes in Sonja's dialogue followed by two dashes in Jack's dialogue indicate that, not wanting to hear Sonja preach about the First Amendment, Jack has cut her off. If there is a concern that the dashes on their own are not clear, a writer can also add a parenthetical indicating the interruption. Hyphens are additionally useful to separate or emphasize a character's aside, or a quick digression in a speech that interrupts the main thought. Hyphens isolate, express, and perhaps stress the point made between the hyphens.

Quotations and Apostrophes

Because they use dialogue blocks, scriptwriters rarely need quotation marks. However, this punctuation may come in useful if one character is mimicking or directly quoting another.

Example 7.3 Using Hyphens and Dashes

```
EXT. LAKESIDE - DAY
```

Trees along the shore cast shadows on the water. Sonja and Jack sit on the pier together in their business clothes, shoes off. Bare feet dangling in the water. A breeze plays with hair that has come loose from Sonja's barrette.

>   SONJA
> Censorship is political poison gas - a nasty weapon when the wind shifts.

>   JACK
> And you think the wind has shifted?

>   SONJA
> I know it has. If we don't respect --

>   JACK
>   (interrupting)
> -- Look. The Internet is a vile place. The instinct to want standards -to crave some tiny bit of decency- is not wrong. I don't want to take away your First Amendment rights, but rights come with obligations. For one, a lie is not protected speech.

A bird CALLS shrilly from a branch overhead. Jack looks up, spotting it in the sunlit tree.

>   JACK (CONT.)
> How does it protect anyone's rights to let a crazy man advocate murder on the Internet?

The apostrophe, which looks like half a quotation mark, is welcomed in the dialogue block, because it often indicates a contraction or words such as don't, couldn't, wouldn't, and shouldn't. Contracted verbs are the type most people use in ordinary speech. Contractions seem authentic, less stilted, and formal. The apostrophe is also used to indicate possession, as in the title of the 1982 film *Sophie's Choice*. Screenwriters can additionally use the apostrophe to set off sarcastic or ironic comments, though this might also be indicated through parenthetical directions prior to the sarcastic dialogue, if it isn't clear through punctuation alone.

Colons and Semicolons

The colon has specific uses in writing media scripts. It's often found most directly after a transition, where it may prompt a new scene heading in some scriptwriting software. In some forms of radio and television writing, the colon separates a character name from dialogue or a sound source from the description of the sound. Because the colon has other standard uses in writing scripts, it might be more confusing than helpful for an actor seeing it in a dialogue block.

Some screenwriters might use semicolons between clauses, doing away with the need for some connectives like *and, but, for, or*. It is not punctuation frequently found in the dialogue block, but it's not forbidden. If a semicolon does appear in a dialogue block, the actor might give it a longer pause than a comma but not the full stop of a period.

Numbers and Keyboard Symbols

Signs and symbols ought to be avoided in the dialogue block altogether. Write the word "hashtag" or "number" rather than use the symbol # in a character's dialogue. Write out the word dollar rather than use the sign. Use the word percent rather than the symbol; use the word "and" rather than an ampersand. If numbers appear in character dialogue, write them out. The idea is to help talent easily read and understand the dialogue and its intent.

Abbreviations. Periods That Aren't Pauses

Screenwriters abbreviate the words "interior" and "exterior" in a scene heading. Within parentheticals, the abbreviation O.S. substitutes for "Off Set" and V.O. substitutes for "voice-over." You may encounter scripts that omit periods, using OS and VO, though many screenwriting software programs still use these. While media writers use abbreviations in technical directions, the general rule for dialogue is to avoid any abbreviations. There are four abbreviations that are so well recognized in the English language that to use the word each one represents would be more confusing than using the abbreviation. These are Mr., Mrs., Ms., and Dr. (for doctor, not drive). The period after these abbreviations is unlikely to bring the actor to a full stop because these four abbreviations are so customary that we've learned to ignore the period they use. Avoid most other abbreviations in character dialogue. Instead, write out the word the actor is supposed to say.

Avoiding periods in acronyms will also avoid confusion. *Acronyms* are the initial letters of long words and phrases that are spoken aloud as words or initial letters. Within a dialogue block, acronyms should be written in such a way as not to confuse actors. For example, the acronym for Young Men's Christian Association, which the Village People famously made into a disco song in 1978, might be written as Y-M-C-A, to indicate that each letter is to be spoken as an individual letter. The same would go for the acronyms for the Federal Bureau of Investigation (F-B-I), missing in action (M-I-A), or unidentifiable flying object (U-F-O). Separating the letters of the acronym is especially helpful if the acronym is not particularly familiar. For acronyms to be spoken aloud as words, write them in all caps but without the hyphen or dash between letters. Examples such as AIDS (Acquired Immune Deficiency Syndrome), MADD (Mothers Against Drunk Driving), SADD (Students Against Destructive Decisions), and DARE (Drug Abuse Resistance Education) are fairly common and not likely to cause confusion. Because script dialogue tends to avoid ALL CAPS for emphasis of a word, the actor will understand that this is an acronym.

Less common acronyms used in dialogue will need some explanation so audiences will understand what characters are talking about. Acronyms like PAWS (Progressive Animal Welfare Society), CAPER (conspiracy against professors evading reality), and KISS (keep it simple, stupid) may be familiar to some audiences, less so to others. If other characters, like members of the audience, don't understand the unfamiliar acronym, it seems natural for the character using it to offer an explanation. Clarification might also be offered visually, such as with a sign on a door. Acronyms that have become so familiar that they have developed into words are actually treated like words and use normal capitalization. Zip code (zone improvement code), CARE package (cooperative for assistance and relief everywhere), scuba diving (self-contained underwater breathing apparatus), radar (radio detection and ranging), and snafu (the original army acronym for "situation normal, all fucked up") are all examples of acronyms that have entered the English language as regular words. If an acronym is also a proper name, it will need to be capitalized on the first letter. Other acronyms that have become regular nouns will use all lower case unless they appear at the beginning of a sentence. For example, capitalize Spam for the brand name of the canned food (shoulder, pork, and ham) but use lower case for the unsolicited messages or "spam" that litter e-mail and social media.

> **Example 7.4 Alternate Ways to Curse**
>
> Traditional:
>
> ```
>             MAMIE
>     You're a bitch and everything
>     that comes outta your mouth
>     is shit.
> ```
>
> Alternate:
>
> ```
>             MAMIE
>     You're the rosy red hole on a
>     sorry dog's backside and every
>     single thing that comes outta
>     your mouth is the reek of that
>     dog's rosy red hole.
> ```

Cursing and Dialogue

In some comics, writers indicate that a character is cursing by using a string of punctuation and other "top of the keyboard" symbols instead of the actual word in the dialogue bubble. But an actor has to speak scripted dialogue out loud, so writers can't be shy about writing the actual curse words if actors need to say them. If it is part of a character's personality to curse, writers must actually type what the character says in the dialogue and not write in a parenthetical (the character curses) or use a string of comic book style "top-of-the-keyboard" symbols in a character's speech.

Cursing or swearing uses taboo words that are stigmatized topics in polite conversation. These usually refer to sexual or bodily functions or are expressions that reference religious beliefs in a rude or negative way. Very often the use of taboo words instantly communicates frustration or anger. Research shows that swearing is more likely for an extraverted person (Jay, 2009). Though it might seem effective for characters to swear, littering all character dialogue with curse words, in a belief that dialogue sounds edgier or more authentic if characters curse, can be a problem if the characters start sounding alike and don't develop unique voices. Cursing might be warranted if a character is experiencing a period of pain or bad luck, if the character is trying to draw attention to a situation, if the character is abusive and trying to inflict psychological violence on another character, if the character is trying to stress a point in an argument, or if the character is that super extraverted person who habitually swears.

Some curse words may limit distribution possibilities for the produced script. If cursing in a script is confined to those moments where it feels necessary and allotted to characters most likely to curse, then a produced movie will have less dubbing or bleeping when it gets to the point of broadcast television distribution or other venues where profanity is restricted. Unusual forms of euphemistic profanity have comic possibilities to make a character seem uniquely lewd.

Dialogue and Devices

Just like people, characters watch television, use computers, tablets, and phones. Digital devices have become a significant part of contemporary life and have taken on important functions in storytelling, particularly in dialogue. As with spoken conversations between characters, dialogue on devices should support the plot or reveal the character.

Texting on a phone may have usurped talking on a phone in contemporary communication. When there is only one text message, the text can be described in visualization as a cellphone display with the exact words of the message in quotations. But if the text is part of an ongoing conversation, as it so often is, the messages can be scripted like dialogue with the words (TEXT) in a parenthetical next to the character's name with the words of the message underneath like dialogue but italicized. Other options are to keep the text conversations in the visualization and use formatting similar to radio dialogue. The character's name in all caps followed by a colon with the exact words of the message all on the same line afterward. When another character responds, formatting moves to a new line, just as radio dialogue does. If the text needs multiple lines, the message may not be suitable for texting, which tends to be brief. As with any script formatting, clarity and consistency are important. Choose a style and stay with it.

While it is best to avoid symbols and text speak in actual dialogue actors will say, text that audiences will read on a screen can and should mimic the way people use devices for conversations. Symbols and shorthand acronyms like "LOL" for "Laugh Out Loud" or "IDK" for "I don't Know" can appear in texts, where they would be avoided in the dialogue an actor speaks. If the initials "L-O-L" appear in actual dialogue, treat them like an abbreviation.

If a character interacts with another character through a screen, as in an online meeting, script the conversation like normal dialogue. Visualization prior to the dialogue can indicate that one character is on a screen, while the other is in the location. A parenthetical next to the character's name (ON SCREEN) helps clarify. The parenthetical (O.S.) in this instance is confusing, since the character is actually in the scene and visible to other characters though on a screen.

> **Example 7.5 Character on a Device**
>
> INT. SUE'S KITCHEN - DAY
>
> The kitchen is a magnificent mess. Dirty pots, spices, measuring cups, spills strewn across countertops.
>
> At the stovetop, a haggard, flour-smudged Sue struggles to follow along as she watches a CHEF JENNY video on her IPad. Amy lounges on a kitchen bar stool, sipping white wine and watching with a cool, critical eye.
>
>   AMY
>   Bob would probably be just as happy if you ordered out.
>
>   SUE
>   I'm doing this.
>
>   CHEF JENNY (ON SCEEEN)
>   The filling is key to a successful turkey pie. Once you've melted the butter over medium high heat, add the onions, carrots, celery and garlic, stirring occasionally. Then you'll whisk in a half teaspoon of black pepper, and one teaspoon of salt...
>
> Sue is quickly behind and confused.
>
>   SUE
>   How much black pepper?
>
>   CHEF JENNY (ON SCEEEN)
>   Then we stir in one tablespoon of minced, fresh Italian parsley, one and a half teaspoons of thyme, a third cup of flour, two cups of chicken broth, and a half cup of heavy cream.

There may be good reasons to use devices to introduce, explain, and reveal elements of a story. News and documentary footage and characters such as television journalists, documentarians, and media personalities can quickly explain a backstory and a larger story conflict in their reporting. For example, in Brad Bird's script for the 2004 animated film *The Incredibles*, the interviewer on faded documentary footage asks Mr. Incredible, Frozone, and Elastigirl questions about the superhero life, and the documentary goes on to reveal a mash-up of their answers, introducing the principal players in a story about superheroes. Later in the script news reports highlight and summarize why some citizens sued superheroes and why the government created a Superhero Relocation Program, where superheroes must act like average citizens and their "secret identities become their only identity." The speeches of these characters on a screen are generally treated like any dialogue. Visualization will use a slug to call attention to the device, followed by the character's dialogue block scripted in the familiar style but with a parenthetical such as (ON SCREEN) or (ON CELL) next to the character's name to indicate the device on which the character appears.

Dialogue and Ad-lib

I have encountered screenplays describing in visualization that two characters "quarrel" with each other or "disagree" about what to do without bothering to script the argument as dialogue. Actors encountering that script would have to imagine and ad-lib the dialogue for themselves.

Ad-lib is short for *Ad libitum*; it is extemporaneous, unrehearsed, unscripted dialogue. The Latin phrase means "as you desire," providing the actor the freedom to speak as the character without following the written text of the screenplay. When entire scenes of a film are ad-lib, it becomes a form of improvisational filmmaking. Directors may encourage actors to improvise on the scripted dialogue or even ad-lib entire scenes, avoiding the necessity for a script. The dangers of relying on ad-lib and improvisation is potential loss of control over the objectives of a scene or the ambitions of the movie as a whole. The advantage of experimenting with ad-lib for a director is potentially capturing the spontaneity of a reality media performance. Relying on ad-lib is not recommended for the writer, whose job is to provide a script to the director complete with authentically clever and meaningful dialogue that seems spontaneous but supports the plot and exposes the characters. If a director has the time and budget to experiment with ad-lib in a scene, that is a completely different matter. It is a director's prerogative and not a writer's decision. If it is important that two characters disagree, discuss, or debate something, these conversations must be scripted as dialogue.

Writing meaningful dialogue is an aptitude that develops from watching other people, listening carefully to how people talk, and absorbing the natural ebb and flow that are the rhythms of conversation. Just like real people, anytime characters speak, they are projecting from their own perspective and experience. Their dialogue may not reflect the larger truth of a story but signals what a specific character believes to be truth—unless the character lies. Dialogue serves the character first and the plot second. Writing authentic dialogue means understanding the characters and their intensions, appreciating the mission of the dialogue for the scene, and knowing how that conversation serves the larger story.

References

Jay, T. (2009). "The Utility and Ubiquity of Taboo Words." *Perspectives on Psychological Science* 4(2): 153–61.

Johnson, P. (2017). *The Physics of Star Wars: The Science Behind a Galaxy Far, Far Away*. Avon, MA: Adams Media.

O'Brian, C. (2005). *Cinema's Conversion to Sound: Technology and Film Style in France and the U.S.* Bloomington: Indiana University Press.

Chapter 8

THE SCENE AND THE STORY

The pure and simple truth is rarely pure and never simple.
—Oscar Wilde

One of the pleasures of watching stories unfold on a screen is the discovery of meaning in them, finding a purpose in the characters' actions and noting the consequences of their choices. A fundamental difference between what we experience in life and the screen stories that reflect those human experiences is the clarity and simplicity that often seems apparent in a world created for a screen. Even when writers demand tough work from their audiences in that quest for meaning, finding meaning in screen stories is typically less arduous than finding it in life. When an author asserts that there is no meaning to stories or life, that position is generally obvious, too. It can be nice to see the truths in our fictional stories so vividly, even if their counterparts in life experience are rarely easy to see, much less understand. When the truths we live are complex, difficult, and incomprehensible, clarity in storytelling offers audiences some existential relief. A large part of that clarity in a narrative screenplay comes in the work each individual scene does for that bigger story.

We know the scene is the basic unit of a script, a significant thread in the larger fabric of narrative. Scenes can be as short as a single shot or as long as 20 pages, or more. What defines a scene is time and location. Theoretically, an entire script could be composed of one scene, so that rather than a thread, a scene becomes the entire fabric. This would be a story confined to one location and one period of time. The risk of designing a one-scene movie, game, or TV episode is finishing with a project that feels visually static and cramped. Generally, if the project is substantially longer than a skit, it takes many scenes knitted together to fully reveal the conflicts, characters, and plots. And, just as writers answer questions about who, what, when, where, why, how, and how much for their larger story, writers will also want to know the answers to these questions for each specific scene. *Who* is in the scene? *What* is the scene about? *What* do the characters want and *what* will they get, if anything? *When* does this scene occur? *Where* does this scene take place? *Why* is this action happening now? *How* does the scene progress and *how* is it related to other scenes? And *how much* will this particular scene reveal of the answers to those larger story questions?

The Length of a Scene

The shortest scenes in a script are very often the description of a physical locale that launches audiences into the specific time and place where the story occurs. For example, in the 1997 science fiction action film *The Fifth Element*, the very first scene consists of the scene heading followed by a description "Somewhere in the Nile at the edge of the desert." There is the superimposed text, "EGYPT 1913," a character, and an action, "OMAR and his mule zigzag along the bottom of sun scorched dunes." That's it for this scene. Later in the script when time advances hundreds of years, there is another extremely short scene. The scene heading is simply EXT. EARTH ORBIT. This scene heading establishes Earth in its revolutions in space, but because it is impossible to distinguish between DAY or NIGHT in outer space, the scene heading omits this usual information. The following action line describes a passing spaceship disappearing into "the star-spattered cosmos" at "unbelievable speed," while another space craft, a warship, moves in, eclipsing Earth's orbit. The purpose of both of these short scenes is establishing, helping audiences understand the time and place that are the setting for the important actions and odd results that will ultimately enlist a former Special Forces soldier turned cab driver in an adventure to save all humanity. Most scenes in the script are longer than these two examples.

On the other extreme, the first scene in the space film *Gravity* (2013) unfolds in outer space, drifting weightlessly page after page after page, describing a view of Earth from space as objects and characters float through this spectacular panorama and weightless astronauts banter with Mission Control via radio. Most scenes in most scripts are shorter. This extremely long, 20-page scene is a script anomaly, and its length requires that this scene do more work than simply establish a location. It also sets up the film's characters, catastrophes, and themes, doing much of the heavy lifting of act 1. Typically scenes in a screenplay run an average of about one to three pages, but there are no rules and no absolute page count for the length of a scene.

Regardless of their length, all scenes have a mission. Every scene should tell an essential part of the larger story, answer a question, create new problems and questions for future scenes to grapple with, or highlight continuing struggles in an ongoing conflict, challenge, or obstacle for a principle character to overcome. An extremely short scene might simply establish the time and venue, relying on a subsequent scene to reveal the personalities and needs of key characters, though a short scene can also do important work in revealing a character. Even the shortest scenes might develop or reinforce character relationships, adding new intimacies, difficulties, or liaisons for the protagonist. In one example, a short scene toward the end of the screenplay for *The Florida Project* (2017) consists of a scene heading and one line of visualization:

```
EXT. FIELD - RAIN - DAY
Halley and Moonee run and frolic in the rain.
```

In the context of other scenes, this short scene reinforces the relationship that 6-year-old Moonee has with her very young, single mother, Halley. We already know they are undisciplined companions in cons and crimes, responding to events and opportunities rather than planning for a future. This short scene is an important reminder that Halley and Moonee live in the moment and effusively enjoy those that offer some fun. It will be the work of another scene to introduce a new conflict and the fraught responses of these children living on the dysfunctional edges of extreme poverty. This particular scene simply strengthens understanding about the close, impulsive relationship between a girl and her young mother. For Halley and Moonee, subsequent scenes will bring the tension of an investigation from the Department of Children and Families and potential separation, which the work of this short scene in the rain renders even more poignant.

Each scene has a primary job to do, though a carefully crafted scene can carry a heavy load, providing answers to many questions, creating reversals in action, or adding new conflicts and tensions. What defines a scene is not length, action, or questions answered, but time and place. In a screenplay, every change in a location or significant change in time requires a new scene heading and becomes a new scene.

The Development of a Scene

The scene heading that begins every new scene offers at least partial answers to two questions, explaining *when* and *where* the scene takes place. Descriptive action or visualization is the next element following the scene heading. A scene needs some minimal visualization to describe a space, an action, and characters if there are any characters in the scene. It's a good idea to set the stage, particularly if this is the first time a particular location appears in the script. The visualization might offer concise explanations to establish the setting in the reader's imagination, helping the reader to envision what should appear on the screen. Location descriptions need not be long or extremely detailed, but if there is something unusual about the space, that unusual element would be described when it's first noticed. The beauty of a snow-capped mountain range, the rubble of a war-torn neighborhood, the extensive taxidermy collection hanging on dingy walls inside a bar, the significant things that make a location noteworthy or unique deserve a quick mention. Effective descriptions are kinetic, visual, and succinct. It's best to avoid expressing personal reactions to a space, such as calling it "hideous," "amazing," or "incredible" and instead describe what makes that place "hideous," "amazing," or "incredible," so readers can imagine the space and have their own personal reactions to it.

If written text, such as a locale or a date, needs to be superimposed on a scene, the superimposed text should come after at least one sentence of description that reveals the backdrop for that text, even if it's just to indicate that the backdrop is a black screen. If text on a screen is necessary, standard formatting suggests that the text should be placed within quotes and preceded by the word SUPERIMPOSE in all capitals, followed with a colon, and then followed the exact wording that should appear on the screen. Words on a screen are not necessary for establishing a story but are sometimes helpful for clarity. Texts on a screen are not relegated to the opening of a story. They can appear anywhere in the script.

If text on a black screen opens the film, there won't be a scene heading and such texts on black screens are not technically a scene. The Star Wars franchise is famous for its scrolling text that opens each movie with words crawling upward over a black screen with a written narrative summary that introduces the movie's actions. Many other screen stories have copied, mimicked, and parodied this opening. It's not unusual to have some establishing text at the beginning of a screen story. In Suzan-Lori Parks script for *The United States Vs. Billie Holiday* (2021), text over a black screen also opens the movie, revealing that "IN 1937, A BILL TO FINALLY BAN THE LYNCHING OF AFRICAN AMERICANS WAS CONSIDERED BY THE SENATE. IT DID NOT PASS. BILLIE HOLIDAY ROSE TO FAME IN PART DUE TO HER STRANGE SONG 'STRANGE FRUIT,' A LYRICAL, HORRIFYING DESCRIPTION OF A LYNCHING." The scene that follows this establishing text describes the famous blues singer in 1957, already well into her successful music career and already strung out as she is about to do a radio interview.

After the scene heading and after visualization has provided important details about the location, a scene might then answer *who* questions, indicating which characters are present in this scene. Both of these things can happen in one sentence, as in, "OMAR and his mule zigzag along the bottom of sun scorched dunes." The goal is to create in the reader's mind the experience of watching a movie by describing images, sounds, and actions in such a way that a scene unspools in the mind as it would on a screen. Dialogue comes after this visualization, at the point where dialogue would naturally occur, if there is any dialogue. A scene doesn't need to have dialogue. Many don't.

There are no rules about where a scene should start once the scene heading is established. Historically, live theater began action with the entrances of characters and ended with their exits. But some film and television scenes don't even have characters. A scene in which a house burns, a storm rolls across a field, or an avalanche begins its destructive journey can be significant to the story without any human or animal character appearing in it. Other scenes might commence with characters already in place and deeply involved in an action. Understanding where a scene should start means understanding the mission that particular scene has in the overall story and knowing what actions are significant to that mission. What larger story questions will this particular scene answer? An introductory scene might answer some of the *who* questions about the protagonist or main characters. *Who* are these characters? *What* do these characters look like? *Why* should an audience care about them?

When a character enters the script for the first time, the character's name appears in all capitals with a brief description. Specific details about a character's clothes and other minutia are unnecessary, unless those items help identify the character or are important to the plot in some way. For example, if a character wears a scarf that later becomes central to the action in a scene, this scarf should be mentioned when it first appears around the character's neck and before it is actively used. If the scarf becomes a murder weapon, a protective face covering, or features someway in an elaborate seduction, the scarf would be mentioned the first time it surfaces. It shouldn't seem as if the scarf miraculously appears in the action when a character needs to use it. Once a character has been established, the character's name appears in the script visualization with normal capitalization and additional character descriptions may not be necessary unless something happens to change the character's attitude or appearance. As discussed in Chapter 2, it isn't essential for the script to describe details about a character's height, weight, hair color, eye color, or manicure unless these physical details are important to how the character will function in the story. The script would want to mention the clubfoot of a competitive skateboarder or the height of an extremely short but gifted basketball player, especially if her height is a major theme in a story where she will always be challenged to stand tall, both emotionally and physically.

An example of a lean but effective character description appears in the 2018 Academy Award–winning script for the film, *BlacKkKlansman*. The script is based on the memoir of the real Ron Stallworth, the first black police detective in Colorado Springs who engineered an undercover investigation into the local chapter of the Ku Klux Klan (KKK) (Stallworth, 2014). The title of the script is an obvious statement about the protagonist and his situation, but protagonist Ron Stallworth won't enter the script until page four. The first three pages offer partial answers to the bigger story questions "what" and "why," describing an unfolding media collage of damaging stereotypes and prejudiced attitudes. These first pages summarize various clips from *Gone with the Wind* (1939), D. W. Griffith's *Birth of a Nation* (1915), notable civil rights footage, news clips, and KKK propaganda–style films that deride people of color and warn that America has entered an era of miscegenation and integration that has put the country on the path to becoming a "Mongrel Nation." When the protagonist does enter the story for the first time, the script offers partial answers to the "who" question, introducing Stallworth as "Black, 21, Handsome, Intelligent, sporting a good-sized Afro, rebellious but straight laced by most 1970s standards." Unless some consider an Afro as a sign of rebellion, the descriptive phrase "rebellious but straight laced" is not visually evident in this opening scene but are qualities that will be revealed as more scenes progress. Then the script gives Stallworth an action; "He gets out of his Ford Pinto, staring at the cavernous opening to Norad."

A key bit of information about Stallworth comes not in the script's description of him and what he does, but in dialogue. The character himself explains in a brief V.O. that he never really thought about racial justice or political controversies before moving to Colorado Springs. "I never thought much about all these Racial, Political things ... " Instead, Stallworth describes himself as " ... asleep ... not woke, but that would soon change." Stallworth's voice over reinforces the central conflict and the specific relationship of that conflict to the protagonist. Until he begins his journey in Colorado Springs, Stallworth was largely oblivious to how deeply racism corrupts America's grand ambition to enable all Americans to achieve their potential.

This introductory scene in *BlacKkKlansman* does many important things. It describes the rugged beauty of the mountain setting in Colorado Springs, where US army troops are marching near Fort Carson and NORAD (the North American Air Defense Command). The graphics "1972" superimposed on the scene confirms the time period. The scene then describes the protagonist. The phrase, "a good-sized Afro" is a further clue to the time period and suggests that the protagonist is young, progressive, and has a self-confident perspective. The Ford Pinto that Stallworth drives also reinforces the 1970s time period and because it was an economy vehicle of that time period, Stallworth is likely a man of modest means. The voice over telegraphs the change or the "character arc" Stallworth will experience on his journey to get "woke." The entire scene is only a half a page long and ends when the location changes.

Though a scene may not directly reveal *what* the main characters want, the writer should understand those character dynamics and how they might bubble under the subtext of a scene. Other questions to ask about a scene involve *why, how* and *how much. Why* is this happening? *How* will the action unfold? *How* will the scene progress? *How much* of the action is necessary? And, *how much* information will the scene reveal or withhold? Notice that the screenplay for *BlacKkKlansman* doesn't introduce Stallworth as he travels to Colorado Springs or before the drive as he packs for his move but begins with his arrival in a new place. We don't know exactly *why* Stallworth came to Colorado Springs. The scene isn't explicit about whether Stallworth came looking for opportunity, though that is implied.

In the next scene, Stallworth is inside the Colorado Springs' City Offices, staring at an ad attached to a bulletin board. The ad encourages minority applications to join the Colorado Springs Police Department, the CSPD. Without dialogue or voice-over, audiences learn that Stallworth needs a job. When he rips the ad from the bulletin board, it's clear that Stallworth wants this specific job. There's no obvious conflict in this scene, though the ad's specifically worded encouragement for minority applicants hints at the possibility for racial tension at a time when America is just beginning to open the doors of employment for people of color. Race continues to be a thematic thread in this scene.

By the end of page four, Stallworth is already in the personnel office of the police department, applying for the job and answering questions like "Would you call yourself a womanizer," "Do you frequent night clubs," "Do you drink," "Have you ever done any drugs," and "What would you do if another cop calls you a Nigger?" The assistant chief of personnel, a middle-aged Black man named Mr. Woods, and the 50-year-old white Chief of Police, Chief Taggert, both grill Stallworth in the job interview. Mr. Woods, warns Stallworth that he will be the Jackie Robinson of the Colorado Springs Police Force, or the only Black officer. Breaking a barrier like this one cannot happen without pain. This scene is largely dialogue and suggests that this police department is one ready for change with a white police chief who claims he will have Stallworth's back but also warns that any racial tensions will be Stallworth's to balance. In two pages, the scene does the job of setting up potential conflicts and revealing more information about the background of the protagonist. The scene ends when, "Ron weighs The Journey ahead," then a new scene heading follows.

After a brief scene showing Stallworth as a uniformed police officer happily walking the streets of Colorado Springs (success; he got the job), a subsequent scene shows that Stallworth has ended up working in the Records Room of the CSPD. Already fellow officers are testing him. One will show him a magazine photo of Faye Dunaway, while making suggestive comments. Stallworth responds carefully, not taking the bait. The officer then comments that he is disgusted when he sees a white woman and a Black man. Another officer will call for the file on a Black suspect, which he refers to as a "toad," the officer's unflattering term for a man of color. This short scene is less than two pages but fulfills Mr. Black's predictions about how Stallworth's fellow officers will behave, demonstrating how misogyny and stereotypes dominate the thinking of these men. Stallworth's colleagues are comfortable in their beliefs that Black men are sexual criminals and "toads." Eight pages into the script, Stallworth voices his dramatic need: Stallworth wants to be an undercover detective, but he will be stuck in the records room until a unique opportunity gives him that chance to go undercover.

When writers have used an outline of their complete narrative to summon when and how the answers to their story questions are discovered, they have a better understanding of what a particular scene should reveal—reviewing a list of important story events, when and where these moments happen, and how they relate to each other is helpful.

The Scene and the Montage

A montage is one way to compress time, visually answer important story questions, and quickly advance the narrative. A montage is a series of story moments that can happen within a scene and single location, compressing time into a series of quick actions, or the montage can be a succession of shots in various locations. These multilocation shots work together like a scene to introduce conflict, provide exposition, and add tension. Perhaps one of the most famous examples of a montage is the 1976 training montage from the movie *Rocky*. The script describes multiple short moments from fighter Rocky Balboa's workouts in the gym, jogging the streets, getting encouragement from neighbors and fans. The montage has a triumphant ending with the sequence at the exterior of the art museum where

```
the huge flight of stairs seems to reach to the
heavens. Rocky takes a deep breath and sprints
up the never-ending stairs. Halfway up, his body
shows the strain. Nearing the top, Rocky pumps
with all his strength and arrives at the very
```

```
top. He looks down the steep stairs and swells
with pride. He is ready.
```

When it was produced, this montage played with a musical bed, compressing Rocky's months of arduous training into a few moments with the mission to show how hard Rocky works toward his goal. In a more recent montage example, the screenplay for *The Shape of Water* has a montage that reveals the developing relationship between Elisa and the amphibian man as she boils eggs, selects records, plays music, and uses sign language to communicate with the creature. Like a scene, a montage can have many different missions.

The first three pages of *BlacKkKlansman* is a medley of media images that emphasize the theme of historical injustice. These images don't reveal anything about the protagonist or his story but instead emphasize the history behind the core theme of the movie. Director Spike Lee reprises a similar use of news and historical footage montages in his 2020 film, *Da 5 Bloods*. He takes this idea a step further in the newer film. When characters have discussions about African American history, non-diegetic photos and news clippings illustrate the conversation, visually pausing the narrative action for an educational moment.

Based on the 1983 novel by Walter Tevis, Scott Frank's 2020 adaptation of *The Queen's Gambit* became a limited-series television drama streamed on Netflix. It tells the story of a young chess genius growing up in a Kentucky state orphanage for girls in the 1950s, which sedated the girls to keep them docile. Taught to play chess by the school's janitor, the character of young Beth Harmon develops into a formidable chess player with an equally formidable addiction to drugs and alcohol. Montages do the work of showing Harmon's developing chess skills as well as her developing addictions.

The 2020 Netflix film *The Life Ahead* tells the story of an elderly Holocaust survivor and retired prostitute nearing the end of her life. Madam Rosa has been raising the children of other prostitutes and now in her 80s she's asked to take in one last troubled child, a Muslim boy from Senegal. Two montages do the work of establishing the young teen's character. One establishes Momo as a tough street kid, who successfully makes a substantial amount of money selling drugs in an Italian port city. Another music video–style montage condenses events of an outdoor party on evening streets colorfully awash in neon reflections. Momo dances happily, as if he has found his home and family among the drug dealers, prostitutes, migrants, and refugees who gather in the city's social margins. The montage ends in the morning when Momo returns to Madam Rosa's apartment and sees the elderly woman on a stretcher taken away by an ambulance.

The writing goal for a montage sequence is to understand its mission, decide what series of visuals will best fulfill this mission, and then describe each visual clearly and succinctly. There is no format that all professionals agree is the standard for the writing of a montage. The visual progression is easy to see on the page when writers choose a format where each moment is flush left on its own line with a bulleted or numbered description concise enough to be expressed in a single sentence or two. If the montage is its own scene, happening in a single location, some writers will add the word MONTAGE to the scene heading. The visualization that follows this scene heading is a list of significant moments in that location. Each event in this list might be numbered, bulleted, identified alphabetically, or be set off with a dash. If the montage does not begin the scene but happens further down in a scene's action, writers will use a standard scene heading. The place in the scene where the montage starts might have a flush left slug BEGIN MONTAGE or SERIES OF SHOTS, which is then followed with a list of those montage moments. The flush left notification BACK TO SCENE or END MONTAGE indicates when the montage is over. If there will be more action and dialogue within this same scene location, BACK TO SCENE is helpful. If the scene ends when the montage ends, some writers will just follow it with a new scene heading. A montage happening in multiple locations might have the designation MONTAGE – VARIOUS followed with a flush left list of scene headings and a brief description of the moment or what's happening in that location. The flush left END MONTAGE notifies the reader when the montage is over. The montage mentioned earlier from the *Shape of Water* is set off with the word MONTAGE and includes various locations in the descriptive list with dashes to designate a new shot. The montage is over when the dashes disappear and the music ends. Most montages are presented as lists, but there are also some examples of montages where the key moments are not formatted as a list but run together in a paragraph style separated only by commas. Whatever the style preference, if there is more than one montage in a script, the style should be consistent.

Instead of a backdrop of music or sound, a montage sequence might need voice over narration to provide additional explanation or some insight from the narrator in contrast to what the visuals show. The question for writers is where to position the voice-over to make the most sense for the script. As with much of screenwriting "rules," the main point to consider is clarity. If the voice-over functions to introduce the montage, it might logically precede the montage series. If the voice over continues, functioning as a bed under the montage, the action element could include a note to further explain that the voice-over continues throughout the montage. The actual voice over is formatted the way a dialogue block is usually formatted, with the parenthetical (V.O.) beside the narrating character's name. Follow the dialogue block with the series of shots flush left. If the voice over is not introductory but adds new insight or creates a verbal argument in contrast with the montage, it might seem more logical to place it at key points within the series or even at the end of the montage list.

Some writers consider the montage as the "poetry" of moving images, intercutting actions in the film to create metaphors and emphasize themes as well as condensing action (Reid, 2005). In the 1972 musical *Cabaret*, a wickedly sexualized Bavarian slap dance with an exuberantly high-kicking chorus line is intercut with shots of a group of Nazi thugs violently beating a man in a back alley. By intercutting two distinctly separate but comparative actions, the sequence shows how life inside the Cabaret is hilarious fun for the patrons, while the streets are subject to the steady corruption and brutality of the Nazi party. Sometimes a montage is the poetry of editors; many times it is the poetry of writers.

Scenes as Flashbacks, Dream Sequences, and Hallucinations

Scenes that are flashbacks interrupt the narrative flow of a chronological story; consequently, flashback scenes work best if relaying a verbal description of that back history through dialogue feels awkward or unnatural, or when a flashback adds visual excitement that compliments rather than derails the chronological tension. If it is essential for audiences to know a specific history in order to understand a character's decisions, a flashback into a character's memory may be necessary. In *The Perks of Being a Wallflower* (2012) the protagonist Charlie suffers from depression and has flashbacks or brief, boyhood memories of his Aunt Helen, which are clearly labeled in the script as flashbacks. Aunt Helen is dead, and Charlie suffers considerable guilt associated with her death. When the flashbacks and present-day scenes intercut, `flashback` or `present day` will be indicated in the scene heading. The flashbacks in this film are not long, detailed backstories but very brief, acute memories that have contributed to Charlie's deteriorating mental health.

Before the scene heading for a flashback scene, insert the flush left notation or slug, "`BEGIN FLASHBACK`." The notation "`END FLASHBACK`" announces when the flashback is over. If an entire scene is a flashback, an alternate way to indicate this is to attach the word [`FLASHBACK`] in brackets to the end of the scene heading.

Dreams are not flashbacks, but an experience happening when characters are asleep. A dream sequence invites audiences into the interior psychological space of a sleeping character as wishes or fears take form inside a character's mind. Because they are emotional distortions emerging in sleep, dreams are not reliable story sources. Dorothy's technicolor adventure in Oz is a dream sequence, though it isn't identified as such until toward the end of the film. Until then, Dorothy's adventures are a fantasy adventure that waits to be dismissed as a dream in the hard black and white, diegetic "reality" of act 3. Sharon Packer's examination of dreams explains that Dorothy's adventures in Oz turn out to be "the day residue of a dream, to use Freud's term, where both the significant and insignificant events of the preceding day are described and disguised in the dream" (2002, p. 57). Packer believes these psychological dimensions are partly responsible for the movie's extremely long shelf life. The dream tells Dorothy that her instincts to love and protect her friends will save her from the Wicked Witch of her nightmares and the troubles in her Kansas life. Dorothy doesn't really need a wizard's help; those instincts are already hers.

Movies themselves are like public dreams, offering audiences a hypnotic relationship with the screen and an opportunity to dream with eyes wide open. The 1924 Buster Keaton silent film *Sherlock Jr.* maybe one of the earliest to make this claim. Keaton plays a movie projectionist who admires detective work. When the father of a woman he loves wrongly accuses him of theft, the projectionist dreams he is a crime-solving detective. The projectionist falls asleep while showing a film and his dream-self jumps into the movie projected on the screen. Like dreams, the film environment illogically cuts between various bizarre locations taking the surprised projectionist to each new location. Ultimately, Keaton's dream-self becomes the detective he admires, able to frustrate thieves in the film's dream world, solve the crime, and rescue the girl. When he wakes, the projectionist learns he has been absolved of all wrongdoing. A little sleuthing from someone else had detected the real thief. The projectionist then looks to the film world for instructions about romantic behavior.

If a screenwriter wants readers to know they are about to enter the dream life of a character, the same logic applies to formatting, attaching the notification [DREAM SEQUENCE] to the scene heading or leading the sequence with the flush left announcement "BEGIN DREAM SEQUENCE" and closing it with "END DREAM SEQUENCE."

Hallucinations serve similar purposes, allowing audiences to slip inside the psychological theater of a character's mind. Hallucinations are the outcome of a condition, such as sickness, deprivation, or ingesting drugs, alcohol, or poison. Hallucinations might also indicate that a character is mentally unstable. The screenplay for *Black Swan* (2010) does not identify scenes as dreams or hallucinations in the scene headings but allows visualization in subsequent scenes to clarify what happened when the protagonist Nina awakes in bed from a dream or when events in the next scenes clarify that what Nina thought had happened couldn't have occurred. In the film based on her novel, *How to Build a Girl* (2019), Caitlin Moran's protagonist has anxiety and infatuation-induced hallucinations that are more attributed to an over-active imagination and teenager angst than mental illness. In the screenplay for *The Hunger Games* (2013), poisonous Tracker-Jacker wasps sting protagonist Katniss Everdeen, who is already sleep deprived, "Katniss is at a loss. Maybe hallucinating ..." Katniss can no longer trust her own perceptions. The script's visualization tells us that "The woods are still until they start to move in a hallucinogenic way, swaying." This kind of delirium can bring new tension to the scene. Though Katniss's hallucinations include distorted memories, they also endanger a character who needs her wits to survive in the deadly games of a post-apocalyptic world.

Released in 1980, not too far removed from a period of American cultural fear and fascination with hallucinogenic drugs, the movie *Altered States* suggests that bizarre perceptions induced through sensory deprivation or psychoactive drugs are legitimate states of being and are as real as the usual perceptions of someone awake and experiencing the familiar world. This movie argues that delirium is real, too. The protagonist is a scientist, Edward Jessup, who goes on a quest to discover his original self by venturing into a chemically transformed consciousness. As his mind expands, Jessup's body de-evolves, reverting to earlier and earlier stages of human development. A similar fate befalls the character Lucy from the 2014 science fiction film of the same name, but rather than hallucinations, the drugs in Lucy's system give her special powers, which ultimately take her on a journey backward in time and space to the great chaos and the origins of life.

A difficulty with hallucinations and dream sequences is the temptation to use them to excuse script issues (Cornish, 2010). Audiences drawn to the bizarre visualization of dreams and hallucinations can be repulsed by the story excuse, "it was all a dream." The questions to ask are why is this character dreaming? What is the dream's subconscious message for the character? For the audience? Similarly, if a character is hallucinating, what does the confused fantasy reveal? How does the hallucination bring new tensions to the story? Consider if the hallucination is necessary. Maybe the hallucination is a convenient excuse for a character who can justify behaviors with, "I was really bonkers."

Connecting Scenes

Even if the structure of the story is not linear or chronological, finding a logical connection between scenes with a through line audiences can follow helps build satisfying stories. When scenes violate temporal, chronological order, they can have causal, character, visual, and thematic relationships. The screenplay for *United States vs. Billie Holiday* (2021) is a thinly linear account of events from 1947 to 1949 thickly bookended with events from the early and late 1950s and includes flashback scenes from Holiday's childhood. In the last pivotal scenes in the screenplay, Holiday is with her band on a bus tour of the South in 1949. In a short scene, "the bus rides along the countryside, then pulls over to the side. Billie gets off to pee." The two scenes that follow this one happen "moments later" as Holiday walks deeper into the woods and comes upon the aftermath of a lynching, sobbing children, a burned house, and a father trying to "undo his wife's dangling body from a nearby tree." Holiday walks backward in shock, bumping into her lover and FBI agent Jimmy. Then she runs into an abandoned shack, where in the next scene a montage shows Holiday having an emotional breakdown. Shots connected in a paragraph style describe Holiday in various rooms with characters who appear from "nowhere" and her drummer Carl reflected in a mirror as he is preparing works for her to shoot up. Viewing these scenes in the produced film, it is unclear if Holiday actually witnessed the aftermath of a lynching, is having a drug-induced hallucination, or an emotional reaction to her tour of the South and its cruel relationship to a song she had been repeatedly warned not to sing. The series ends with Holiday walking down a hallway toward a bright light, which becomes a new scene when she steps into the light of the stage at Carnegie Hall. The script visually and emotionally connects scenes that happen in different times, places, and perhaps inside a character's head.

The chronological connective tissue is obvious in the first scenes examined from *BlacKkKlansman*. In an America with a long history of racial injustice, young Ron Stallworth arrives in Colorado Springs. He needs a job. He sees an opportunity for a Black applicant to get a job as a cop. He interviews for the job and is warned that he will be breaking racial barriers on his own. He gets the job. His fellow officers taunt him. The actions in one scene become the destiny of the next. Each scene in *BlacKkKlansman* also has racial tension heating, simmering, boiling, or at least evident in the cooler waters. Consider what happens in the previous scene that can motivate the current one, then ask what happens in the current scene that can activate the next. For example, a scene that mentions a character's name might invite a new scene in which that character appears.

The Intercut Sequence

When quick, simultaneous actions happen in two different locations, calling for an intercut scene allows writers to avoid having to continuously repeat the scene heading for each location. After the notation NOTE: INTERCUT SEQUENCE flush left, establish the first scene in the sequence with its scene heading and visualization. Then establish the second scene with its slug and visualization. Proceed with scene visualization or dialogue for both scenes. At the point where the intercut sequence ends, simply END INTERCUT SEQUENCE. The beauty of the intercut sequence is that it efficiently handles a situation like a phone call between characters in two locations, contrasting the situations of two different characters, and comparing simultaneous actions of different situations.

Example 8.1 Intercut Sequence

```
INTERCUT SEQUENCE

INT. MIKE'S OFFICE - DAY
Mike strides into his office, tossing his coat on
the desk. The phone RINGS.

EXT. THE HARRIS DRIVEWAY - DAY

On her cell phone, Sara frowns. Worried. Beside
her is the new Prius. Large scrapes gouge the
side of the vehicle. The windows are smashed.

                    SARA
          Mike. Mike. Pick up.
                    MIKE
             (into phone)
          Hello.
                    SARA
          It's me. I'm at the house in
          the driveway. It's been keyed.
                    MIKE
          What?
                    SARA
          The new car. Someone's keyed
          the new car. Windows are
          smashed, too.
                    MIKE
          Stay where you are. I'll be
          right there.
                    SARA
          We know who did this.
                    MIKE
          Do nothing. I mean this. Do
          nothing.

Mike grabs his coat and is out the door.

END INTERCUT SEQUENCE.
```

Stylized Scenes

Breaking the Fourth Wall

Some scenes might incorporate specific techniques that would seem to violate traditional ideas about the expected or traditional presentation of media characters in a scene. *Breaking the fourth wall* is a moving image media convention borrowed from theater in which actors remind audiences that they are not really omniscient, godlike observers who can voyeuristically peer into the intimate, emotional moments of characters' lives but are in actuality the spectators of a theatrical production. A theater's proscenium stage has three solid walls and an invisible "fourth wall" between the audience and the action. Sets will be constructed with three walls, but actors pretend there is also a solid fourth wall and no audience watching. In realism, this pretense of a fourth wall is maintained from the beginning to the end of the play. A dramatic script breaks the fourth wall when an actor steps away from the action to acknowledge the audience and speak directly to them. Some of William Shakespeare's monologues do this, as when Robin Goodfellow at the end of *Midsummer Night's Dream* apologizes to the audience for any offenses they might have suffered while watching the performance.

Though the theatrical fourth wall is very literal in a television sitcom shot in front of a live audience, in much of moving image media, the fourth wall is the camera itself or that ever-moving space between characters' actions and the camera's eye. An actor breaks the fourth wall by turning to look at the camera, acknowledging the audience's gaze via the camera lens, and letting the audience know exactly what the character thinks. In the American version of the television series *House of Cards* (2013–18), the character of Congressman Frank Underwood (Kevin Spacey) often turns to address the camera directly. Within the first minute of the very first episode, Underwood and his driver Steve Jones are witnesses when a car hits a neighbor's dog. Underwood sends Steve to see if the neighbors are home, and then crouches near the whining animal at first comforting it before explaining directly to the audience, "There are two kinds of pain. The sort of pain that makes you strong, or useless pain, the sort of pain that's only suffering. I have no patience for useless things." Underwood then uses his bare hands to put the dog out of its agony, telling the audience, "Moments like this require someone who will act, who will do the unpleasant thing, and the necessary thing." Later in the same episode Underwood attends a 2013 New Year's Eve party with his wife and introduces the audience to key political players and their weaknesses, revealing that Underwood is cynical and ruthlessly pragmatic, but also establishing the audience as an invisible companion on Underwood's journey, as he tells audiences directly, "Welcome to Washington." From that first episode onward, Underwood makes the audience his confidant with the breaking of the fourth wall a regular feature of Underwood's dialogue as he explains from his callous perspective all the alleyway negotiations and unseen levers of power lurking behind the operations of American government. Even though audiences become Underwood's invisible confidant, the series does not sacrifice the audience's omniscient perspective. Audiences will observe exchanges that Underwood will never know about, maintaining dramatic irony as a feature of the series. Breaking of the fourth wall is generally non-diegetic so that other characters are usually oblivious when it happens. However, we learn in season five of *House of Cards* that Frank's wife Claire Underwood has been aware of a viewing audience and also breaks the fourth wall.

In the 2020 period comedy film *Enola Holmes*, the title character is Sherlock Holmes's younger sister, who appears to have inherited a genetic propensity for solving mystery. As she goes on a search for her missing mother, Enola will turn to the camera from time-to-time to comment on the ridiculousness of her situation. By breaking the fourth wall, the script intentionally destroys the realism that moving image media often attempts maintain. Usually breaking the fourth wall is a feature of dialogue, though it doesn't have to be confined to dialogue. In Mel Brooks's 1974 film *Blazing Saddles*, a fight among railroad workers, cowboys, and the citizens of the town knocks down the set of their Western film, rolls into the set of a musical to disrupt the action of an extravagant number, and then continues to expand, invading the studio commissary where the action becomes a food fight. Fighting then ventures off the studio lot and onto the streets of Burbank. Anytime a camera, which represents the spectator's gaze, allows the audience to see and hear the artifices of the production process, a fourth wall has been broken.

The Voice-Over Scene

Like breaking the fourth wall, a character voice over lets characters express their thoughts directly to an audience. The audience is not only privileged to omnisciently peer at significant moments of a character's life but also has access to that character's inner thoughts. The voice over is non-diegetic, meaning that these inner thoughts are not part of the action of the media story and other characters in the scene won't hear them. There have been periods when critics were highly disparaging of voice-over narration, usually because the voice-over told a story rather than showed it. Because the voice-over was often used at the beginning of the script, some critics considered it a cheap expository trick. That stigma seems to have been lifted from more contemporary use and the voice-over as a technique has become more prevalent. When a voice-over provides insights into qualities of a character or elements of the plot too complex for action, it can be a useful script device.

Joel Goldberg, the protagonist of the psychological television thriller series, *You* (2018-), opens the premier episode with a voice over as the beautiful Guinevere Beck opens the door of his bookstore and enters. "Well, hello there. Who are you?" He then continues to inspect and analyze her, while the voice over lets the audience hear his thoughts. "Your blouse is loose. You aren't here to be ogled but those bracelets; they jangle. You like a little attention. Okay, I bite. You search the fiction, 'F' through 'K.' Hmm, you're not the standard insecure nymph hunting for Faulkner you'll never finish. Too sun-kissed for Steven King. Who will you buy?" Goldberg does not address the camera or acknowledge the audience directly, instead audiences hear Goldberg's inner thoughts as he observes that Beck does not wear a bra and interprets her reach for a book as a sexual signal. From the earliest scenes of the first episode, Goldberg establishes himself as a creepy stalker, and yet he also feeds a neighbor's son when he discovers the young boy sitting alone in the apartment stairwell while his mother and her boyfriend have a shouting match inside. Goldberg's voice over monologue continues throughout the series, allowing audiences to hear directly the blunt expressions of Goldberg's perspective.

The 2020 psychological thriller, *The Devil All the Time* uses a narrator voice over to introduce the characters and explain how their various stories intersect. The film's narrator, Donald Ray Pollock, is not a character in the film but the author of the book on which the film is based. Pollock's V.O. provides a transition between stories, connects scenes together, reflects on important actions of an earlier sequence that inspire the actions in a new scene, and adds backstory about the setting, the Ohio town of Knockemstiff. The V.O. also explores thematic contexts and even explains character motivations. Pollock offers a new twist on the "Voice of God" narration, which was a documentary technique that employed a deep, disembodied male voice over artist who seemed to have the power to know and speak an objective truth (Wolfe, 1997). Pollock's narration is folksy, but it is also the creator's voice with the unpretentious authority to explain why his character Arvin returns to his childhood home rather than make a clean getaway to a different future. "But in this moment, he felt a sudden force pulling him back towards Knockemstiff. No matter what else happened, he had to try to set right those things about his father that still ate at his heart."

Lampshading

Writers practice lampshading when they create scenes that openly acknowledge the weaknesses in their scripts and admit that their choices make it difficult for audiences to suspend disbelief. Lampshading is principally achieved through dialogue, when characters comment that the action they are about to undertake is a cliché or when they notice that very thing needed to save the day improbably and miraculously appears. The lampshade salutes the story holes in the script, the lack of character development, or the implausible devices a writer uses to solve a story problem. When authors use a lampshade to embrace and highlight the flaws in the script, they suggest it is silly for viewing audiences to accept a proposition that they could become omniscient spirits voyeuristically peering into a genuine world. By hanging a lampshade on a ridiculous plot point, by confessing to the most awkward and obvious *deus ex machina*, writers announce that they've painted the plot into a corner but are going to let characters walk across the wet paint anyway. When this happens, the script hangs a lampshade that directly illuminates the tracks on the floor and celebrates the mess.

The 1999 comedy film *Galaxy Quest* derives much of its humor by hanging lampshades on the improbable plots and exaggerated characters in a parody of a defunct television science fiction series similar to *Star Trek* (1966–69) and the continuing devotion of their overly enthusiastic fans. The movie asks what would happen if the cast of a canceled television sci-fi series had to survive a genuine space adventure by relying on the overblown writing of old episodes for guidance. Scenes in act 1 reveal that even though the show is long cancelled, the cast of *Galaxy Quest* is a persistent presence at science fiction conventions because of the show's cult status. The star of the series, Jason Nesmith, glories in the attention, while the rest of the cast resent Nesmith and the sad state of acting careers that have been reduced to roles in commercial advertising and fan conventions. Early scenes stoke that tension between Nesmith and the other actors. In particular, the character Alex, who had been a Shakespearian actor before the TV series, begrudges the alien makeup and prosthetics he must wear as the character Dr. Lazarus and the catch phrase that devout fans wait breathlessly to hear, "By Grabthar's hammer, you shall be avenged." Scenes contrast the foul mood of the cast with Nesmith wallowing in his star spotlight as he shouts his own catch phrase, "Never give up ... Never surrender." When "actual" space aliens receive interstellar transmissions from the canceled TV show, these aliens believe the episodes are historical footage. They have no concept of fiction. The aliens closely study the series for its wisdom, develop a functioning model of the fictional starship, and believe that the actors from the series are wise, heroic leaders, who can help them defeat an aggressive reptilian warlord who seems ruthlessly determined to conquer the galaxy. Throughout the movie, the characters comment on the bad writing of the canceled television series. The lampshades include commenting on unknown functions of set decorations on their space craft, a female crewmember whose job is to repeat the computer while looking sexy, the predictability of implausible plots, and the likely death of a series extra. This aggressive lampshading does not pretend that the scene offers a reality for audiences to believe but invites playful skeptics to enjoy the script's overt self-criticism and by extension, to critique the media experience in general.

Less overt but still lampshading, Alfred Hitchcock's 1954 thriller, *Rear Window*, has more than one character comment that a killer attempting to cover up the murder of his wife should have closed the blinds. Of course, with the blinds closed, there wouldn't have been a movie.

Techniques like breaking the fourth wall and lampshading tend to be functions of dialogue and the tropes of comedy and satire. Using lampshades and breaking the fourth wall in a scene can seem gimmicky unless these techniques genuinely support the mission of the scene and the style of the script as a whole.

Gaslighting

The opposite of lampshading is gaslighting, a psychological term taken from the 1940 film *Gaslight*, in which a man manipulates his wife into questioning her own reality and sanity. Gaslighting is not a technique writers apply to violate the naturalism of a scene but what characters do when they violate the trust of other characters, manipulating the gullible characters into believing something that isn't true. Gaslighting often serves as the backbone of an entire script.

In *The Devil All the Time*, the Reverend Preston Teagarden seduces an underage Lenora, convincing her to expose herself to him by using her religious faith and his position as someone with special understanding of the Lord's desires to make the girl his willing victim. He tells Lenora, "To show yourself as the Lord made his first children … truly turn yourself to him … and his witnessing of it." Once she becomes pregnant, Preston denies responsibility and gaslights her into accepting all the shame. "How … could I be the daddy … when all we done is spend time with the Lord?" A character who attempts to gaslight another character will lie outright, withhold information, project their personal faults and liabilities onto their victims, and deny what is in plain sight so convincingly that victims might doubt their own judgment. Like the original 1944 film for which it is named, the technique of one character's gaslighting of another can become the narrative spine for an entire movie in which each new scene is a continuing manipulation. The 2020 version of *The Invisible Man* shows how the villain uses science innovation to have other characters question the protagonist's sanity.

The Work of a Scene

Writers should be able to find at least one answer to an important story question in the work of a scene. William Akers provides a helpful detailed checklist for discovering whether each scene in a script has been "pounded" enough in his textbook *Your Screenplay Sucks* (2008). A scene needs to reveal something about the characters, add tension or conflict to the story, or move the plot forward. A scene should be cohesive, resolved in its moment, and reflect the vitality of the narrative as a whole. If a scene uses techniques like lampshading or breaking the fourth wall, that technique should support the style of the story, not perform like a singular gimmick. Every scene is a necessary fact in the story's argument until the narrative premise has finally been proved and the story's truth is revealed. In the writing of the first draft, it may not be evident if a scene is doing its share of the work. The review and revision process following that completed first draft is the obvious time to test, trim, tighten, connect a script's scenes, and decide if it contributes a necessary fact in to help reveal a story's truth.

References

Akers, W. M. (2008). *Your Screenplay Sucks! 100 Ways to Make It Great*. Studio City, CA: Michael Wise Productions.
Cornish, A. (2010). "Originality in Dream Sequences, a Challenge for Films. All Things Considered." NPR. July 24, 2010, 3:00 p.m. ET.
Packer, S. 2002. *Dreams in Myth, Medicine, and Movies*. Westport: Greenwood.
Reid, M. (2005). "Cinema, Poetry, Pedagogy: Montage as Metaphor." *English Teaching: Practice and Critique* 4(1): pp. 60–69.
Stallworth, R. (2014). *Black Klansman: Race, Hate, and the Undercover Investigation of a Lifetime*. Spartanburg, SC: Police and Fire.
Tevis, W. (1983). *The Queen's Gambit*. New York: Random House.
Wolfe, C. (1997). "Historicising the 'Voice of God': The Place of Vocal Narration in Classical Documentary." *Film History* 9(2): 149–67.

Chapter 9

HONEST REVISIONS

> History is strewn thick with evidence that a truth is not hard to kill, but a lie, well told, is immortal.
> —Mark Twain

I met Billy Bob Thornton at a film festival in Alabama, where he bragged that his award-winning screenplay *Swing Blade* (1997) was a one-draft miracle, materializing on the page in its perfect, Academy Award–winning form without revision. I remember the astonishment I felt on hearing that boast because it was so contrary to my own experience and what I knew about the project development processes of other writers. A significant part of writing for most of us comes in revision, taking an early draft and honing it into the best version of the story we can make, which often takes multiple drafts before feeling the satisfaction of knowing a story has found its best form. A short time after Thornton boasted about his one-draft phenomenon, I learned that he neglected to mention that his award-winning feature had been adapted from *Some Folks Call It a Sling Blade* (1994), a short film Thornton wrote and produced that includes the same mentally handicapped character who killed his mother and her lover as well as some of the exact same dialogue that Thornton made famous in *Sling Blade*. Many years later, I discovered that Thornton had preceded the short script with a monologue for a one-man show, "Swine Before Pearls," which featured some of this same material. Thornton wrote and performed his monologue at the Tiffany Theater, West Coast Ensemble, and other venues starting in the mid-1980s (Collins, 1997). It's a little easier to believe that *Sling Blade* was a one-draft wonder knowing that this was material Thornton had been revising for a decade or more before he adapted it into a feature script. The mentally challenged Carl was a character Thornton knew intimately. What's a little harder to understand is the notion that a truly phenomenal, award-winning script might materialize directly from a gifted writer's mind in its finished form like Athena from Zeus's forehead. The notion that a script should arrive like Athena, fully grown, captivating, exquisite, and clothed in impressively shining armor without any awkward spots is mythological. The idea that a sincerely talented writer should find revision unnecessary and that only an imposter or a hack would resort to revision is both harmful and wrong.

For most of us, there is no shame in revision. In fact, one of the joys of writing is to take that first draft and challenge yourself to make it better. If creative excitement is the natural order of life, it is as much a part of the revision process as it is in the writing of that initial draft. What is especially fun about revision is finding that unexpected joke in the dialogue, that new twist in the existing plot that makes the next reversal even better, and the many surprising ways to polish a story with characters who can have a genuine impact. The revision process attempts to balance that impulsive drive to create with the control needed to help audiences understand the creation. It is about finding the clarity critical to every element of a script from its concept and characters to its structure, formatting, word choices, and punctuation.

One of my saddest experiences as a teacher is watching a young writer give up on an interesting concept because the very first attempt at the first few pages didn't sizzle as he predicted or expected it should. So the young writer discards the entire concept as "pure crap" and goes on a restless, disappointing conceptual hunt with a fierce Athena fixation for that idea that will deliver full-blown beauty in the very first draft of that very first scene. When his trove of loglines and story concepts doesn't produce the immediate and expected excellence, he wails, "All my ideas are garbage."

Creative blocks happen in the shadow of the Athena fixation, or the obsession on the finished script and the unrealistic expectation that the final draft will be the first. It is sometimes challenging to rid writers of the notion that a worthy script should happen instantaneously. A ticking deadline added to this Athena fixation makes the ingredients for writer's block. When I've suspected that young writers put unrealistic demands on their creative processes, I sometimes challenge them to take their crappiest concept, the idea they think has the least potential, and keep reworking it. The outcome can be ridiculously silly, but results can also be surprisingly interesting. It's also fun to see "crap" become the enriched soil of a gripping story. The way to bust through a block is to reject Athena fixations and acknowledge that revision is a vital part of the creative process. Give revision the time and attention it deserves. Also, acknowledge that magic can happen during revisions.

It helps to approach revision as a genuine pleasure now that the hard work of that first draft is complete.

The Readable Text and Cold Table Readings

A *table reading* is closely associated with production. It is that recommended preproduction step after casting and before setting the shooting schedule, when a director assembles the writers, cast, and crew to read through the full script out loud and discuss it. It is that important social occasion when the cast and production team meet, get to know one another, and begin to understand the story they are about to create for the screen. However, a cold reading of a script is also a valuable writing tool long before the script is even close to a production contract. Writers' groups and screenwriting classes employ the cold table readings of scripts as a way to identify story problems, unnatural or awkward dialogue, boring bits, unnecessary scenes, structural issues, and characters that don't seem authentic. The table reading and workshop are also where writers see how their ideas, stories, and characters fit into the larger cultural landscape and how audiences might respond to them.

For writers who don't belong to a group or who aren't involved in a writing class, achieving a cold reading of that first draft might mean convincing family and friends to participate but it can happen, often for the price of a pizza. Cold table readings during the pandemic were more awkward and necessitated using an Internet application, but they were still valuable regardless of the technological issues that inevitably intruded, and participants who were forced to provide their own snacks. One upside of a remote table reading is the ability to assemble a group of far-flung friends and supporters and the opportunity to introduce generous, resourceful people from other states and countries to each other without concern about the expenses of travel or finding a hospitable location, though organizing around time zones can be a bit of a bear. One of the genuine needs writers have is for this kind of support that a community of creative people can offer.

Try to assemble a group large enough to cast someone in each of the major speaking roles, someone to read minor roles (one-liners), and have an extra person as the action reader to deliver aloud all those elements that aren't dialogue. It's important to keep in mind that your sister, classmate, or members of your writers group are not likely to be professional actors. Don't set expectations for a cold reading too high. Even with amateur readers, sharing an early draft of a script at a table reading not only shines a light on a script's successes and weaknesses, but it can also nurture the creative spirit, motivating the imagination for the revision process that lies ahead.

Once you've pulled together your group and assigned roles, clear your mind and listen carefully as the script progresses. Refrain from directing participants so you can actually hear the reading. This advice also stands for those writers who intend to produce and direct their own scripts. At this stage of development, the workshop focus is on the script and not the performance of it. Listen to the way the action reader describes actions, settings, and characters. Are you able to visualize the scene that the action reader describes? Were important details left out? Did descriptions become a quagmire of unnecessary minutia, hampering the progression of the story? Were action descriptions producible or were there long, expositional passages? Were the readers cast as characters able to bring some life to your dialogue? Did punctuation appropriately lead interpretations of the dialogue? Did any characters have monologues that need cutting? Did each character sound different? Where did readers stumble or labor over the material? Was the dialogue believable?

Take notes.

Workshopping after the Read

Table readings are valuable not only for hearing the work come alive but also because the readers can offer useful feedback in a *workshop* after their cold reading of the script is finished. When the cold reading is over, ask questions of your participants. What did they like about the story? What did they understand about the characters? If there are elements they were confused about, can your friends, family, or classmates articulate where and why they struggled? You'll find it more constructive to just listen to this feedback and avoid attempts to defend the work. The point of a table reading and workshop is to inspire the revision process, not justify the current draft. Listen for those consensus opinions. If there is an outlier judgment about a character, a bit of action, or the story as a whole, take note of that as well. There may be something useful to you in that unique opinion.

Finding Meaning—What Readers Understand

One thing a workshop experience will reveal is how others understand or assign meaning to your story. There are different ways to examine a script for meaning (Bordwell, 1989). The simplest or most obvious is the script's *referential meaning* or the concrete, bare bones plot summary. Understanding a referential meaning requires that workshop readers are able to answer the basic who, what, when, where, and how questions about the script just as audiences watching the story on the screen should be able to do. For example, the referential meaning for *BlacKkKlansman* might be, "In 1970s America, an African American cop manages to infiltrate a local branch of the Ku Klux Klan with the help of a Jewish surrogate." Reverential meanings can sound like a logline.

The workshop should tell authors whether or not their readers can identify the referential meaning in this early draft of the script. Can your readers answer the basic questions about your story? If not, revisions will need to address and clarify omissions and confusions at this very basic story level. It may mean returning to the logline that initially inspired the story concept. If the referential meaning is obvious in that conceptual logline, the confusion in the script likely reflects changes that happened during the writing process, places where the story strayed. Sometimes new discoveries and character developments that emerge while writing can profoundly alter a story. For example, if writers change their minds about who their protagonists are after they're well into the writing of act 2, that switch can make for a puzzling script. A protagonist might have a delayed entrance, arriving late to clean up the mess other characters made, as Police Chief Marge Gunderson arrives late in *Fargo* (1996) to solve the crime, but a writer's uncertainty about a character's role can make for a muddled plot. If attempts at innovations in the writing or modifications from the original concept have confused things, it's worth reconsidering the original logline as a guide for creative revisions or at least carefully examining those places where significant changes to the concept occurred and consider ways of fixing awkwardness and correcting misperceptions.

The *explicit meaning* is the purpose of this story and its truth, explaining what the main characters learn from their experiences. It answers the big 'why' questions. The explicit meaning is often expressed in the dialogue or is easy to see in the choices characters make, leaving nothing to inference or suggestion. The explicit meaning is the clearest message behind the narrative and what an author hopes will be the audience takeaway. In *BlacKkKlansman*, the explicit meaning or takeaway deals with Ron Stallworth's journey to become "woke" to the reality that racism is a historical, dangerous, and continuing American custom, infesting both citizens and institutions with harmful ideas and practices. Yet, as Ron Stallworth feeds his investigation's documents into a shredder, he observes that helping others get "woke" is a daunting challenge. "The Truth is erased, so no one can learn from it." The stubborn hold racism has on America is explicit, obvious from the script's opening media montage to the last moments in the screenplay when the protagonist sees a burning cross, "its Flames dancing, sending embers into the BLACK, Colorado Sky."

Workshopping a script in a cold table reading and discussing it afterward can reveal if the readers "get it," if they understood what the main characters learned or refused to learn from the actions that unfolded on the page.

The *implicit meaning* is less tangible, going beyond what is explicitly stated in the film. Audiences understand the literal implications of a story's action, when a heroic protagonist defeats a villain and "good triumphs over evil," but there may be other, less obvious meanings woven into the heroic layers of the protagonist's journey. For some audiences a hero's triumphant defeat of the villain may seem secondary to the costs of that victory, the hardships of the journey, and what the protagonist might never say aloud about the anxieties of the battle and the wounds that scar the soul.

One thing to remember about your readers and your ultimate audiences is that they are creative people, too. Ultimately, audiences decide what the story means. They apply their own experience and understanding about the world to the adventures they see on screen. Someone might decide that *BlacKkKlansman* implies that however much people may yearn to escape or ignore the problems of a racist culture, these attitudes are too deeply imbedded in the American psyche to be easily overlooked or uprooted. Because *BlacKkKlansman* is a comedy with comical scenes and exaggerated characters, other audience members may conclude that racism and the people who think that way are a joke. Someone else may decide that a smart, determined person can find a way to accomplish anything, even something as difficult or outrageous as a Black person going undercover inside a white supremacist group. Another audience member might decide that *BlacKkKlansman* shows how a Black police officer is psychologically incapable of being sent undercover to infiltrate a traitorous civil rights rally featuring the dangerous ideas of a man like Kwame Ture (Stokely Carmichael) and return with useful police intelligence against his own racial group but will instead take any opportunity to spy on white people. Another person might decide that the politics of race is not likely to help a serious romance move forward.

There can be many different implicit meanings in one script as workshop readers discover for themselves a relevant message that an author perhaps never intended to send. Some of these may be eye-opening for an author to hear but are not necessarily important to the revision process unless there is a consensus opinion that an implied meaning is explicit. If enough people at a table reading are coming away from the story with an idea that the author never planned, this unexpected interpretation is something to keep in mind for revisions, especially if the author objects to this unintended meaning. What things led to this interpretation? If the implicit meaning was inadvertent but agreeable, it may mean that audiences perceived an unconscious purpose. Writers will want to consider whether the story is understated and layered enough to invite audience creativity, even if the writer won't be able to fully control the direction that creativity takes. It is a celebratory event when a script provokes interesting or unexpected workshop discussions. This suggests that audiences are finding their own truths in the implied meanings of your narrative.

I should note here that *obstinate audience* members may fully understand the author's intentions but will deliberately choose an alternate reading that better fits with their personal beliefs about the world. Audiences generally select stories that support their values, "but if they happen upon unsupportive stories, they can interpret, remember, and act on that content in tenacious ways producers never intended" (Edwards, 2020, p. 88). You might encounter this kind of pigheadedness in a workshop, a reader who understands an author's intentions but refuses to acknowledge them and deliberately inserts extreme ideas. If this happens at your workshop, applaud the reader for this unique insight and move on. Implied meanings can be beyond an author's control.

The *symptomatic meaning* treats an explicit meaning as the expression of a wider set of values characteristic of a whole society at the time period in which the story was written and produced. The symptomatic meaning is the result of economic, political, or ideological conditions in the larger social world during the period in which the work emerged. Workshop readers might find symptomatic meanings in a script, though referential and explicit meanings are the more important concerns of writers, because these are more directly connected to the story's clarity and those deliberate choices the author made while writing.

Symptomatic meanings arise naturally because authors are a product of their experiences at the time in which they live. Even scripts with historical settings will carry the residue of an author's contemporary concerns. Michael Blake's screenplay for *Dances with Wolves* (1990) is about a Union soldier's desire to see the West "before it disappears." The Industrial Revolution was well underway by the time of the American Civil War, but the fear that the natural West might disappear feels less like the anxiety of a Civil War soldier and more like a concern of the 1990s, as environments became polluted, habitats disappeared, animal species went extinct, and Native Americans' cultures that once thrived had vanished. Values that honored a simple, natural way of living and rejected the acquisition of wealth as the path to a rewarding life also had more prominence in the 1990s. In an intentional push back against decades of Westerns in which Native Americans had been cast as villains, it was Blake's mission to show that Sioux customs, language, beliefs, and habits were not dangerous or threatening. A growing part of American culture in the nineties wanted an antidote to the historical view that cultural difference signaled the inferiority of a group. Some Americans were ready to recognize the importance of other cultures and accept an advancing multicultural world.

Although *BlacKkKlansman* is about events that take place in the 1970s, the story about a Black police officer hoping to root out a dangerous, local branch of the Ku Klux Klan emerged in American theaters in 2018, at a time when white supremacist groups had already reemerged on the national scene, galvanized with new determinism to "take back our country" (Nelson, 2017). This was also a time when Black Lives Matter (BLM) had become a widely recognized movement with international support. Concern about police violence against people of color inspired international protests. The script for *BlacKkKlansman* ends with a burning cross, but the produced film added news footage from the 'Unite the Right' rally in 2017 that brought neo-fascists, neo-Confederates, neo-Nazis, Klansmen, and other far right groups to Charlottesville, Virginia with the purpose to unify the American white nationalist movement. That rally ended in violence when people opposed to the ideas behind white nationalism arrived in counterprotest and a man deliberately rammed his car into these counterprotestors, killing a young woman. The symptomatic meaning of *BlacKkKlansman* with this final news footage emphasized that America has more work ahead before realizing its ideal of a culture where all citizens can pursue happiness and achieve their potential.

While writers might have an intentional mission, they cannot help the cultural imprint of their own time period. It will find its way into the work, sometimes in support of the explicit meaning and sometimes in contradiction of it. If your script inspired workshop readers to talk about contemporary events in relation to the incidents in your story, this is another potentially celebratory moment. Symptomatic meanings remind us that the practice of writing can never be fully separated from the values and concerns currently present in the author's cultural tradition even if the script is set in the distant past or light-years in the future.

When the cold reading and workshopping event is over, thank everyone for the valuable time they gifted you, their reading efforts, and their opinions, even if those judgments were negative. The next step is to apply what you've learned from the workshop to the revision.

The Missions of Stories in Revision

During the writing of the script, the creative process is more an act of surrender to creative impulses than control. The revision process is more about logical control than surrender, but it's still a creative process. Revision is the time to consider if a scene fully connects to the story, if it does the work it needs to do or if it can be cut. If a scene reveals important character information, answers basic story questions, and connects to other scenes, it's likely a keeper. The revision process will consider the details, the small textures and nuances of writing, asking if a particular word used in a description truly visualizes that action, that place, or that character. It should go without saying that revision is also a time for writers to carefully consider such practical details as grammar, style, and format and whether the punctuation supports the flow of the story for a reader. Along with the small details, revision also considers the bigger mission of the story as a whole and whether the goals for the script have been satisfied.

The three prime goals of any story are *to inform, to entertain,* and *to persuade.* While one mission might dominate others in a particular story, it's impossible to fully separate these objectives. This means that to be successful, a story cannot simply and only entertain. A story must inform to entertain. Audiences must understand and be willing to accept the world a writer has created in order to be swept away by it. Audiences must be convinced that this particular narrative is worth the investment of their time. As audiences begin to appreciate the outcomes of a character's choices and actions, successful stories that primarily want to entertain cannot avoid traces of persuasion. For example, audiences lured into rooting for the young girl Mulan to succeed as a soldier might also be persuaded to reconsider what any resolute girl can achieve (*Mulan*, 1998, 2020). Audiences who become concerned about Woody's potential plight as a neglected toy might be persuaded to realize that shared play and friendship have more benefits than being the dominant toy in the room (*Toy Story*, 1995). A film like *Nomadland* (2021) might convince audiences to reevaluate their attitudes toward those hardworking individuals who chase low-wage jobs from one town to another and perhaps consider that a houseless person is not necessarily homeless.

Audiences who were entertained by Topher Grace's comedic portrayal of the Grand Wizard David Duke in *BlacKkKlansman* might be sobered to see the final news footage in the film, which shows footage of the real David Duke as the national director of the Ku Klux Klan and a featured speaker in the 2017 Unite the Right rally. The real David Duke is not clowning when he vows that Charlottesville is "the first step toward taking America back." It was a particularly disquieting bit of footage on which to end a rollicking crime comedy, but a script that hammers its explicit meaning mercilessly has not seduced its audiences with entertainment. A script that is too on the nose with its referential story and its explicit truth has not found the compelling subtext in the narrative or the powerful personalities within the characters that lure the audience inside. The three goals of informing, entertaining, and persuading continually overlap and augment each other.

The derivative story pattern can be persuasive even if it isn't original or particularly engaging. The most banal and predictable stories cannot escape informative or persuasive impact if an explicit meaning is so frequently repeated that it saturates a culture. Too often the explicit meanings in these hackneyed stories are both harmful and wrong. The lie that is so often repeated and so universally recurring can eventually seem like a truth. For example, a common "truth" in romantic stories crafted for heterosexual girls and women has been that only the most beautiful protagonist can live happily ever after and in her pursuit of that happiness, other women are the protagonist's worst enemies. A common "truth" in action adventure stories crafted for heterosexual males has been that only a protagonist who looks tough and acts aggressive can be triumphant. Familiar "truths" in stories with nonbinary characters are that these characters are wretched oddballs to be pitied, jokes for the amusement of straight characters, or monsters deserving of a hero's violence (Russo, 1981; Epstein and Friedman, 1995).

Decades of media research suggests that all these explicit "truths" are not only inaccurate but they are also psychologically damaging. They are persuasive simply because the explicit meaning in these stories is so often repeated. The message is hard to escape. Audiences may be unaware of how mired they've become in derivative storytelling until a fresh perspective emerges to challenge their thinking. As new voices bring more diversity and authenticity to public storytelling, audience perspectives also develop.

The Finished Script

If it's usual to have multiple drafts of a script, writers might wonder if they will even realize when the revision process is over. A writer's satisfaction with the characters and the story is an important determinant. However, the revision process is not always over when a writer's intuition says it is. Even an award-winning script optioned by a potential film producer may need revisions if the optioning group is not fully satisfied. Realities of production may keep a writer in the revision process even after the script has been greenlit, transformed to a shooting script, and gone to production. Impositions of a sudden budget cut, location restrictions, casting problems, insurance issues, time constraints, artistic disputes, stunt complications—there can be a long list of things that might intrude on a script, requiring an author to continue revising and rewriting scenes until they are shot and in the can. After principal photography is complete, a director might decide to lose a scene or move it from its location in the script to another part of the story. These decisions may not involve a writer unless a scene needs to be rewritten and reshot to satisfy the director's vision.

If a writer feels the script is finished and intends to send it out for evaluation, most readers now accept finished scripts in digital formats whether it's a screenplay competition, studio reader, production company, or editor of the literary magazine that publishes scripts. If a finished screenplay needs to be submitted as a paper copy, it should be printed on one side of white paper and three-hole punched for binding with brads. Most long-form scripts have title pages. The title page has the name of the screenplay and the important contact information for the author or agent. If the reader needs to do a blind assessment of the script as often happens in script competitions, writers may be asked to submit two title pages: one with and one without identifying information. Dedicated screenwriting software will prompt writers for the title page with boxes to fill in the standard information. Extremely short scripts may need identifying material at the top of each page.

Pay attention to requirements before submitting scripts to a producer, competition, or reader. Most are pretty clear about what they will accept, what they expect to see with a submission, and whether an agent is necessary. If a production company wants to see a logline and synopsis included with a script, not sending them risks rejection. Many times all a production company is willing to read are a logline and a synopsis, so these should be intriguing and polished to accurately reflect the script they represent.

Any act of speculative writing is writing for a client you do not know, whose needs are continually shifting, who may be more interested in a sure thing than a risk, or who may not even know what they want. What is not helpful to the revision process is an observation that truly awful scripts are continually produced in mainstream media, and the writer knows their script is better than the garbage that constantly clogs the cultural landfill. That sort of thinking suggests that if garbage scripts find production, a revision is unnecessary because that first draft is "good enough." The revision process is about writers putting their focus on their own work, making sure the work tells a clear story with captivating characters and that it satisfies its mission. The finished script should represent your proficiency as a writer for moving image media.

Scripts in Competition

Some script competitions promise to connect winning writers to producers. In this role some competitions are more useful than others. However, it may be more realistic to consider the script competition as a review. Screenplay competitions involve judges who read a script and then provide the competition management with numerical scores. The competition then averages those scores to determine winners. There is not a uniform template that all competitions use for judging; however, most competitions score a script based on some version or combination of the following elements:

1. Concept: The idea behind the story is engaging or unusual.
2. Plot: The story has energy, feeling, and a sense of momentum and connection.

3. Structure: If the script has a traditional structure, it flows naturally, carrying and reinforcing the important moments of the story. If the script uses an alternate structural form, that form supports rather than detracts from the narrative.
4. Character: Characters are well developed, with clear motivations and unique voices.
5. Conflict: Tensions in the story are effective.
6. Dialogue: The dialogue works to effectively reveal character and move the story forward. If the script is without dialogue, the story moved effectively without it.
7. Warmth: The quality of emotional content in the story drives reader's concern for the characters and their actions.
8. Resolution: The resolution is satisfying or if the ending is unresolved, the story resonates with interesting questions.
9. Format: The script follows the current formatting conventions for a professional screenplay (sitcom, webisode, etc.) and can be produced as written.
10. General: The script involved the reader with a memorable story, intriguing characters, and solid overall writing.

Getting Scripts to Producers

There are many different screenwriting competitions; most don't promise to put winning scripts in producers' hands. A good number require a fee to enter and may not provide the author with any usable feedback. Some might offer coverage of the script for an additional fee. Studio readers and production companies generally don't offer any feedback to writers either, even for an additional fee. Some production companies and studios have an internal form their readers use that is similar to those outlined in the judge's form for a screenplay competition. Readers will evaluate these elements and then generate coverage that also speaks to whether this property is something that might interest producers and have profit potential for the studio or production group. Writers don't usually see this material. Some independent producers are particularly sensitive about the anticipated production budget required for a script and their readers will comment on things like potential expenses associated with travel, the number of locations, stunts, effects, pyrotechnics, cast sizes, and so on. Having a script rejected by a mainstream producer doesn't necessarily mean that the script was bad. It could mean that the producer doesn't have the resources or the disposition for this type of work.

Independent readers are people with a mainstream media resume who offer to sell authors coverage on their scripts. These readers may no longer be associated with a studio or production company and won't offer any direct access to producers. They are not agents. Script consultants and script doctors are independent readers who provide detailed suggestions for a script's improvement and offer this service to writers for a fee.

The idea that in order to become a movie, the spec script must find its way to a Hollywood producer is not the only way to reach an audience. Traditional commercial media industries have powerful infrastructures and devoted relationships that make it difficult for outsiders to have access. However, there is an independent market that exists outside the commercial studio system. Producers in this market might be actively looking for properties, though contacting an independent producer is also a challenge. The last few years have seen the emergence of online agencies claiming to be the magic door connecting writers to legitimate agencies, producers, and studio readers. These "agencies" generally charge writers a fee to list a logline and synopsis for the consideration of potential producers, but they are not agencies that work to actively promote writers. They simply welcome production companies to register with them in order to peruse a list of loglines. These agencies might also charge writers for the opportunity to see what types of properties production companies currently seek. Some of these producers are very specific about their interests. They might be seeking feature-length low-budget thriller scripts set on a cruise ship with a lesbian Latinx lead, a feature-length family drama inspired by a true story that reinforces faith-based values, an ultra-low-budget feature-length horror with a paraplegic male lead, or some other property with very specific criteria. It can be frustrating for writers when the specific story demands of indie producers never seem a comfortable match with the spec script they've written. The thinking is that these are likely student producers, extremely low-budget indie producers, or dentists based in Los Angles with the dream of producing a film in which their child, cousin, sibling, or significant other can have a starring role. Advice from reviewers of these online services is to steer clear of any that charge writers a fee for simply including their loglines in a list.

The old-fashioned and sometimes inconvenient and time-consuming method of cultivating friends and associations may be a better path to a producer. Who do you know? Who do they know? How many degrees away are you from a commercial industry gatekeeper or a scrappy indie producer? Do you know people who will help bankroll a production so you can direct your own script? Does your community have a theatrical group interested in making a film, TV pilot, or webisode? Do you have the energy for crowdfunding or writing grant applications? Each writer tends to find a unique path. One writer might happen to be at the right party at the right time, sharing a goofy experience about growing shiitake mushrooms in coffee grounds and the story manages to intrigue someone associated with a production group. Another writer might volunteer with the local film commission, meet people through that work, then grow associations with a production company. Another writer might decide to self-produce if the resources are available. Spike Lee produced and directed his script *She's Gotta Have It* (1986) with credit card funding.

Some writers move into the entertainment industry from other media groups such as advertising agencies or newsrooms. Others form creative friendships and future production groups while still in school. It is a very bad idea for media studies students to disregard the person sitting next to them in a production class. Though writers want a reliable method for getting scripts in the hands of producers, there isn't a consistent process that works for everyone in the same way. It doesn't really help to ask another writer about their particular route to a professional career and expect that their unique path will show you the way to yours. What worked for one writer may not work for others.

Back in 2006, Henry Jenkins observed that when creative people have access to distribution, alternative cultural economies also emerge. Amateur films sometimes become commercial successes. Grassroots experimentation even generated new production practices "such as the use of game engines as animation tools" (p. 132). Ideas bubbling up from amateurs catch on and make their way into commercial media, influencing both storytelling and production. Because we live in an attention economy, commercial entities will notice viral videos, and as Jenkins observes, the best of the amateurs or those who can garner public attention will often be recruited to serve mainstream commercial entertainment. Sometimes it's that quirky, brutally honest, outsider perspective that gets attention when everyone else is selling the same predictable patterns.

The good news is that there has always been a robust independent production community and independent production seemed to be clawing its way back to work in the spring of 2021. Some of these are recent graduates of media schools. Some are established groups with the experience of making many different kinds of commercial media products. Some are determined genre fans who enjoy making parodies or spinoffs of the products they love best. Networking at media festivals, volunteering for film commissions, offering services to a team on a 48 Hour Film Project are some of the many ways writers have cultivated friends in the production community and found indie producers for scripts.

Creative Self-Discovery

When we were children and drawing pictures together, my young neighbor Wade was more likely to "play" his picture than draw it. Wade's artistic processes absorbed him completely. His drawings tended to be his re-interpretations of vicious World War II battles that he had seen in movies such as *The Bridge Over the River Kwai* (1957), *The Guns of Navarone* (1961), or on television shows like *Combat* (ABC, 1962–67). He embellished the media battles he remembered with more terrifying and daring exploits of the soldiers and munitions scribbled on his paper. Wade muttered, howled, and vocalized sound effects while he drew. He shouted out commands to platoons of stick figure soldiers with rifles and grenades, lining them up in formation behind tanks and jeeps across the bottom of his paper. He would fill in his paper skies with fighter planes, crude outlines of Spitfires, and P-51 warplanes, making the engine sounds deep in his throat. Once the planes were in place, the attack came: crayon-embellished gunfire, graphite-launched missiles and bombs. Little dashes across the page represented bullets, dark bumpy ovals were the grenades. He accompanied missiles with droning, then explosion noises and screams when missiles hit his stick figure soldiers. The drawing was finished when the biggest bomb dropped and the furious scribbling of Wade's number two pencil scarred the page, covering and tearing it with an explosion of dense graphite, ravaging all he had previously drawn. When the paper was covered completely and the roar and spittle of his accompanying sound effects finally subsided, Wade sometimes finished his performance art by balling up the page and tossing it in the trash, all while humming the bugle call of "Taps."

Wade was his own audience, consumed audiovisually with his own internal story. Because I was unable to draw anything while Wade was sitting across the table, spewing gunfire at pencil point, Wade may have been trying to entertain me. But I don't think he cared to impress me or even remembered that I was in the room. I was an unnecessary audience. The only audience member that was important, the only person who needed to understand what was happening, was Wade. His art was all process with no finished product he cared to exhibit, no story he wanted to share with others. I can't remember ever seeing any of Wade's drawings proudly displayed on his mother's refrigerator.

There is nothing wrong with creative self-discovery, with writing a story entirely for yourself as the audience. One of the joys of creating stories is becoming immersed in the actions of imagined characters or imagined places in another time with events that happen exactly as you planned them. The creation of that first draft of a script should allow the author that kind of self-absorption. But for most of us the creative journey is both an expedition inward to encounter the characters and unearth their stories and then a voyage outward, offering those discoveries to an external audience.

A writer immersed in creative self-discovery with the first draft might decide that the next draft is the time to reconsider a popular professional recipe. If a table reading and workshop suggested structural problems in the story, revisiting the general recipes for three act, multistory, and nonlinear structures might be helpful. Sometimes recipes work. It is entirely possible to precisely follow Great Aunt Ethel's famous cornbread recipe and recreate it pretty closely. It takes the right amounts of a good quality cornmeal, flour, sugar, milk, eggs, sour cream, butter, and a sizzling hot skillet. But cornbread is not a script or a story. One writer's recipe is not a guarantee for success, no matter how many websites suggest that all a writer needs for a professional triumph is to have a specific type of character follow a particular outline in a restricted presentation style with familiar actions. Taking care that specific types of events happen on specific pages in a script is not a guarantee of story success.

Comparing the writing of stories to the baking of cornbread, it's pretty safe to say that creativity is a form of soul food. Denying creativity is starvation for both artists and their communities. When writers step outside commercial demands to ask if their stories are good for people, enlighten people, shine a light on something unexplored, blow away the smokescreen, or help audiences understand a stubborn perspective, then act of writing becomes a public service deserving of its First Amendment protections. If we use cornbread as a metaphor, it is possible to discover a palatable story following bits of a formula, just as enjoyable cornbread is a fairly predictable outcome of careful attention to the ingredients and the recipe. What's more difficult to achieve are Great Aunt Ethel's moments of transcendence, when she added creamed corn, minced jalapeno peppers, bits of bacon or ham, cranked the heat down, added five minutes to the cooking time, or otherwise deviated from the recipe. Moments of transcendence with cornbread follow from understanding flavor combinations, baking times, and palate tolerances. However, as good as it was, Great Aunt Ethel's cornbread didn't satisfy every appetite, but she didn't limit her creativity to cornbread. She could also fry chicken, stew okra, and bake a sweet potato casserole with a toasted marshmallow crust.

I can feel my judgmental friends from California shaking their heads over the health concerns of this metaphor. Those of us from the South have to grapple with the many toxic elements in our culture. Being awake to that toxicity isn't cancel culture, however. It means being aware of what's harmful, and then adapting, substituting, improving, finding that new edge, that deeper flavor, but keeping what reflects you as a creative person. This is what honest revision can do. And as with Great Aunt Ethel's fried chicken, the best stories take a fair amount of shortening.

Shortening a script is sometimes just what it needs.

The Abstract Truth

A script is an abstract thing. It is a conceptual, speculative creation, imagining conditions and personalities and the responses of these fictional characters to those actions and obstacles a writer invents for them. Some problems in first drafts come from the reality of this abstract quality.

Abstraction is useful. It allows people to generalize, letting us categorize ideas, events, and people. Abstractions include some details about reality but leave out others. The word "children" lets us categorize people based on the earlier stages of their lives. This is convenient. But abstraction can also make difficulties if writers are unaware that abstractions omit important details. Children are not all the same. Each child has unique characteristics and childhood has different stages of development. It isn't enough to create a protagonist who is a child. A writer needs to know and reveal what stage of childhood drives the protagonist's demands, what makes this child protagonist unique and reveal these qualities in the character's youthful dialogue and actions. The revision process is the time to add flesh to characters that might otherwise seem too skeletal or abstract.

Abstractions become dangerous when people substitute an indistinct concept for the reality it represents without realizing that this is what they've done. In the 1978 film *Superman*, Lois Lane asks Superman, "Why are you here? There must be a reason for you to be here." Superman replies, "Yes. I'm here to fight for truth, justice, and the America way." Stuck at a *high level of abstraction*, the practical consequences of Superman using his formidable powers to fight for "truth, justice, and the American way" are vague. Recognizing this, Lois scoffs and suggests that he will end up, "fighting every elected official in this country." Superman will need concrete examples of what the "American way" actually means before he can confidently fight to defend it. In the 1946 radio show, Superman used his powers to challenge a hate group, the Klan of the Fiery Cross, and its constricted definition of what it meant to be a "pure American" (Bowers, 2012). Superman needed to know that the hate group's tangible definition of a pure American excluded people of color and certain religious groups. Superman had to know which details he would dedicate his powers to defend. The highly abstract phrase, "Truth, justice, and the American way," needed a concrete definition.

Language and words are abstractions, but some words are more abstract than others. The word "truth" is a word at a high level of abstraction. Without facts or details to define it, different people can have different interpretations about what truth means, so that the word "truth" suggests vastly different things to different people. Some might visualize an image of Lady Justice, blindfolded, not influenced by prejudice or bribes as she balances the facts on her scales. Others might visualize a detective, examining clues to uncover the culprit in a murder case. Still others might visualize truth as a person who is vigilant to problems of social justice and the atrocities of contemporary life, recognizing that in our tainted world, the judges who serve on the courts of Lady Justice and make life-altering decisions for others are simply human beings who can be vulnerable to bias, ideology, and corruption. When people bring their own understanding to an abstract idea, abstractions like "truth" and "justice" can become emotional and subjective. Characters might be stuck at high levels of abstraction, but a script can't be. Narratives suffocate if stuck at one level of abstraction or *"dead level abstraction"* (Johnson, 1946, p. 270).

Authentic fiction, like life itself, will have characters who become confused by abstractions like "justice" or "honor," but it's important that writers understand what those abstractions mean within their own narratives. Characters caught at a high level of abstraction have allowed a vague concept to determine their actions. This might be an important territory for a writer to explore. The television series *Star Trek: Deep Space Nine* (1993–99) often considered the dilemmas of characters whose ideas seem stuck at high levels of abstraction until they are confronted with evidence that challenges their personal understanding. In the episode "Tacking into the Wind" (May 12, 1999), Federation Officer Lieutenant Worf must confront the romantic notions of his Klingon people that the highest possible honor for a Klingon warrior is to die in battle, sacrificing self for the greater glory of the Klingon empire. That abstract passion is sullied considerably with revelations that the Klingon leadership is corrupt and self-serving.

Stories caught at *low levels of abstraction* become sidetracked with too many unimportant details and never get to the point. Tangible descriptions help visualize the action but should not become prolonged or interminably detailed. Meticulous descriptions of locations and plodding, detailed accounts of character wardrobes are typical places where narratives get delayed. If a narrative is stuck at this lower level of abstraction, readers become overwhelmed or bored with an unending inventory of trivial specifics and can become impatient for the story to move forward. What some writers have not grasped is that this boredom includes violent actions, too. A script describing a prolonged fight between a superhero and his enemies that extends for many paragraphs, itemizing every blow the combatants aim at each other from every direction and meticulously repeating these actions with minor variations is stuck at a low level of abstraction. When writers attempt to keep audience attention with a constant, monotonous flow of graphically violent details, the repetition actually becomes tedious rather than terrifying or exciting. Writers need to balance high-level abstractions with concrete examples but stop when those details have served their purpose to the story and not become overly fixated on the specifics.

While the larger narrative should not get mired in minutiae, a script's characters might get fixated on details, usually to the annoyance of other characters. In the 1980 film *Ordinary People*, a middle-aged mother, Beth, has lost a favorite son in a boating accident, but denies her own bereavement and the grief of her husband and surviving son. She becomes fixated on the trivial details of maintaining a social appearance that reflects the ideal of a normal family. Irrelevant social niceties are Beth's cushion against the larger truth of her loss. Though interesting stories might have characters grappling with problems of dead-level abstraction, the script itself should never get stuck. Stories caught at a high level of abstraction have not defined their truth, their characters, or those abstract concepts that motivate what characters do in a tangible way. Stories caught at a low level of abstraction are cluttered with repetitive details.

The characters a writer creates, their actions, dialogue, and purpose are limited to the abstract magic of letters and words until production transforms these into a performance. Writers have to chase after those performances with the smells, sights, sounds, touch, and tastes to evoke that felt experience, while realizing that the final media experience is generally confined to sight and sound. When words on a page evoke the thrill of experience, they wield a kind of magic, though the writer's tools, letters, words, and grammar are abstract and logical. The abstraction that evokes and bonds to a potent lived experience can be powerful.

A Story's Perspective

Just as characters have a perspective, stories also have a perspective, which usually mirrors the point of view of its author. A script's perspective shows audiences how to consider the actions of characters, which characters to regard as important, and what their choices mean. Do you understand the position your story takes? The story's perspective becomes basic to the way audiences will interpret or judge its characters. From one story perspective, a character who blows up a prison and releases all the prisoners is a terrorist; from a different story's perspective, that same character might be considered a noble champion of freedom. The process of review and revision is the time to reflect on a story's perspective and if that perspective is clear or satisfying.

One example of different story perspectives on the same characters is the way two different films considered the Marvel Comic characters of Venom and Eddie Brock. Venom and Eddie Brock make their early film appearances in *Spider-Man 3* (2007), when a symbiote infects Peter Parker, bringing out Parker's dark, aggressive side and turning his Spider-Man costume black. Parker is eventually able to evict the symbiote from his body, but the creature discovers and attaches to his rival photographer, the vindictively jealous Eddie Brock. The bonding between Brock and the symbiote creates Venom, a powerful supervillain. However, in the 2018 film, *Venom*, the character of Eddie Brock is an honorable journalist investigating a research facility that conducts unethical and dangerous bioengineering experiments on alien creatures, who are unable to survive Earth's environment without a host body. The symbiote Venom bonds with Brock and, because of Brock's generous spirit, Venom develops an appreciation for Earth and humankind. Instead of a supervillain, Venom becomes a superhero, connecting with Brock to help protect the people of Earth from others of his species.

A problem with the character of Venom in the 2018 film is the character's sudden change from a dangerous alien symbiote on a mission to control Earth to a character that deeply appreciates the qualities of his human host and turns traitor to other symbiotes. The bonding with Brock creates a Jekyll and Hyde character blend of ruthless symbiote and hapless reporter that never seems authentic, even for a science fiction comedy. Because Venom declares that on his own planet, he is also a `loser` just like Brock, audiences are supposed to understand that there is a character perspective added to the creature's simple biological drive to eat and survive. Venom instantly absorbs American popular culture references and is ready with human quips and comebacks in bantering with Brock as the two unite to defend Earth from other invading symbiote creatures. Regardless of how alien, harmful, and determined the symbiote is, the movie suggests the creature is vulnerable to the innate superiority and charms of American culture and the protagonist who defends it. Venom is unable to exist without his host and the host culture he admires.

Spider-Man 3 tells audiences that Eddie Brock and Venom are villains. *Venom* tells audiences that Eddie Brock and Venom are a heroic team. Writers confused about their own perspectives toward ideas, events, and choices surfacing in their scripts may want to review the pesky questions from Chapter 1.

Story in the Larger Context

Some writers approach their projects with a mission in mind. They know who their audience is at the outset and what they want that particular audience to understand. Professional writers generally appreciate the mission they've been hired to fulfill, if it's to adapt a commercially vibrant existing property to the screen, create a new story for a particular production company, or design an adventure game to lure young children into learning a math lesson. Whatever the mission, with a clear purpose and a story outline, professional writers roll up the sleeves and get to it.

Writers working on that spec script may need or want to become absorbed in the inward journey first and finally arrive at that completed rough draft without a clear idea of who their audience will be and how they hope to involve that audience with a grand adventure and deeply felt message. For these authors, the first draft is about discovery, plunging into the reservoir of research, knowledge, and personal experience and lifting out the characters, images, and actions paddling around in there. It may not happen until the revision process that these writers begin to ask questions about their potential audience. Is this story just for me or will it be an offering to others? Who are these other people? Why will they be drawn to my story? What will my story mean for them? Will my story "sing to the choir" or do I want to attempt a connection to people whose perspectives are very different from mine? How will my story resonate with them? How can I lure these people into my narrative and help them appreciate a different opinion?

Social reality is an elaborately improvised drama that relies on the cooperation of many individual actors to understand and perform their roles according to the norms of that unpredictable floorshow that is our public life. Social rules, rituals, and routines shield citizens from brutal realities and inhibit their worst impulses. The virtuosos of history invented these institutions and their social rules. These are also fictions. We are all complicit in helping to construct, interpret, and maintain these fictions (Berger, 1976). For the larger social fiction to function, people must accept the basic principles of our collaborative public drama. These are the rules, rituals, and routines learned from family, friends, and institutions like school or church. These rules for life get displayed time and again in popular media stories and are fundamental to how audiences understand the world. As people collaborate on their larger, shared social dramas, some pretend that institutions and customs are eternal truths rather than human creations. Future leaders may tear these fictions apart and replace them with new fictions, different rules, other codes of conduct, and different values. Our larger social fiction belongs to those with the power to shape it.

Consider how power works in your story. Is it a function of force and brutality, a function of manipulating social codes, a function of economic wealth, or some combination of these? For example, power in *The Hunger Games* franchise is a function of force and brutality. Power in the film *Maid in Manhattan* (2002) is a function of wealth and the way characters understand and manipulate social cues. Power in a television crime series like *Law and Order* is a function of law and precedent.

Hegemony is a concept that explains how the ruling capitalist class, or the bourgeoisie, maintain their authority without resorting to the heavy hand of force (Gramsci, 1971; Ives, 2004). *Cultural hegemony* suggests that popular media stories often support ideological domination, where powerful groups have their worldview accepted without scrutiny as a universal truth. Popular media stories contribute to cultural hegemony by showing audiences what they should consider to be normal, deviant, important, beautiful, destructive, and valuable. For hegemony to work, citizens, institutional leaders, and media producers must agree that the intellectual and moral leadership of the ruling class and their dominant ideology is natural and right. Cultural hegemony insinuates that these dominant values are the truth and anyone refusing to recognize that truth is being unrealistic.

Just as native speakers of a language are oblivious to the grammar and form of their language, writers may also be unaware of their own bias. The values of the powerful appear in storytelling as the instinctive, unpolitical circumstances that everyone accepts as a natural, taken-for-granted, common sense understanding about the ways of the world. Ours is an inauthentic existence if our roles are played blindly, if we are oblivious to the flaws, ironies, biases, and hypocrisies of our humanly constructed social world. Part of being able to craft authentic fiction and alternate universes is being fully aware of the one in which you reside. The authentic story will avoid the unexamined morality of the herd.

The ancient Greek philosopher Diogenes (404–323 BC) believed society was an artificial smokescreen that trapped people in a deceptive dream world. Diogenes supposedly lived in an abandoned tub because a house was an unnecessary excess. He reduced his needs to a minimum, thinking this was a condition of freedom. Possessions created the soft prison that nurtures excess and dependency. Diogenes behaved like a dog, better to bark at the idiocies of humanity than join the oblivious human pack. Sometimes he even went so far as to bite or piss on people to awaken them to truth he wanted them to see (Shea, 2010). It isn't necessary to urinate in public or bite people when writers can snare an audience with creative storytelling that is observant, using narrative to reveal how characters respond to human challenges. The job of writers is to be alert to the stories of our larger cultural fiction and understand how their own stories function to help maintain that consensual cultural story or blow holes in it. To manage that, writers need to be awake to the world, to understand the perspective from which they see that world, and bring those observations to their writing.

References

Berger, P. L. (1976). "Society as Drama." In James E. Combs and Michael W. Mansfield, eds., *Drama in Life*, pp. 38–45. New York: Hastings House.

Bowers, Rick (2012). *Superman versus the Ku Klux Klan: The True Story of How the Iconic Superhero Battled the Men of Hate*. Prince Frederick, MD: Recorded Books.

Bordwell, D. (1989). *Making Meaning: Inference and Rhetoric in the Interpretation of Cinema: Inference and Rhetoric in the Interpretation of Cinema*. Cambridge, MA: Harvard University Press.

Collins, S. (1997). "Call It Father of 'Sling Blade': Video Rides Oscar's Coattails." *Los Angeles Times*. March 29, 1997.

Edwards, E. (2020). *Graphic Violence: Illustrated Theories about Violence, Popular Media, and Our Social Lives*. New York: Routledge.

Epstein, R., and Friedman, J. (Directors). (1996). *The Celluloid Closet*. Sony Pictures Classics.

Gramsci, A. (1971). *Selections from the Prison Notebooks*. London: Lawrence and Wishart.

Ives, P. (2004). *Language and Hegemony in Gramsci*. Ann Arbor, MI: Pluto Press.

Jenkins, H. (2006). *Convergence Culture: Where Old and New Media Collide*. New York: New York University Press.

Johnson, W. (1946). *People in Quandaries: The Semantics of Personal Adjustment*. New York: Harper & Row.

Johnson, W. (1975). "The Communication Process and General Semantics Principles." In W. Schramm, ed., *Mass Communication* (2nd ed.), pp. 301–15. Urbana: University of Illinois Press.

Nelson, L. (2017). "'Why We Voted for Donald Trump:' David Duke Explains the White Supremacist Charlottesville protests." *Vox.com*. Updated August 12, 2017.

Russo, V. (1981). *The Celluloid Closet*. New York: Harper & Row.

Shea, L. (2010). *The Cynic Enlightenment: Diogenes in the Salon* (Ser. Parallax). Baltimore, MD: Johns Hopkins University Press.

Superman. (1978). Dir. Richard Donner. Warner Bros.

INDEX

9 to 5 41

Abraham Lincoln: Vampire Hunter 94
abstraction 213–15
Academy of Television Arts and Sciences 2
Acronym 168–69
act 1 61–63
act 2 63–65
act 3 65–66
action 124, 128–35
   narrative description 124, 128, 131, 133, 162, 163
   Visualization 124, 128, 130, 144, 172, 173
actor's business 54
adaptation 10
ad-lib 172–73
Alias 74
Alien 72
Alien Abduction 97
Altered States 187
Alternative Scriptwriting: Rewriting the Hollywood Formula 80, 100
Altschull, Herbert 24
anima 44, 45, 56, 72
animation 7, 13, 211
animus 44, 45, 56, 64, 70, 72, 94
antagonist 6, 29, 45, 46, 55, 85, 115
antihero 30, 31, 32
archetypes 42, 43, 44
Aristotle 60
Arrival 82
Athena fixation 103, 198, 208
Authenticity 2
automated dialogue replacement 149

Baby Formula, The 95
Ballad of Little Jo, The 94
beat sheet 118

Being Human 86
Big Bang Theory, The 83
Big Lebowski, The 92
Billy Elliot 45
Birth of a Nation 180
Black Death 5
Black Lives Matter 203
Black Orpheus 12
Black Swan, The 186
BlacKkKlansman 180, 181, 182, 184, 201, 202, 203, 204, 206
Blair Witch Project, The 97
Blake, Michael 151, 156, 203
Blazing Saddles 191
Bohemian Rhapsody 19
branch targets 98
Breaking Bad 31, 45, 155
breaking the fourth wall 190–91
Bridge Over the River Kwai, The 212
Broken Flowers 89

Cabaret 185
Campbell, Joseph. *See* Hero's Journey
cancel culture 212
Casper 31
categorical thinking 40
Celluloid Closet 41
Chaplin, Charlie 150
character
   balanced 30
   character arc 37
   collective unconscious 43
   steadfast 39
Character Drives
   ego 23, 31, 48, 51, 52, 105, 113
   id 48, 51, 52, 56, 92, 105, 113, 114, 152
   superego 48, 51–53, 56
character goal 46

Children's Hour, The 41
children's journeys 73–75
cinéma vérité 95
classic stories 8
collective unconscious 42
Combat 211
comedy 22
Contagion 5
counter-storytelling 41
Cowboys and Aliens 94
Crash 86
Creativity 20
Cultural hegemony 218
Cursing 170–71
cutscenes 56, 147

Da 5 Bloods, 183
Dances with Wolves 151, 157, 203
Daniel, Frank 66
Dave 39
dead level abstraction 215
Death to 2020 96
Decameron 4
Dekalog 10
delayed link. *See* intelligent link
denouement 65
derivative story 23, 206
deus ex machina 62
deuteragonist, 57
Devil All the Time The 195
dialogue block 125, 149–73
dialogue on devices 171–73
diegetic 137
diogenes 219, 220
direct cinema 95
direct link 98
disenfranchised protagonists 92
Disney 6, 9, 33, 90
Dr. Seuss 3
dramatic contrast 79
dramatic irony 64
dramatic need 46
dream sequence 186

Edge of Tomorrow 82
ego 41, 48, 51
Elephant Man, The 53
Enola Holmes 191

Erin Brockovich 71
ET 31
exaggeration 22
Expository writing 131–32, 191, 222

fact 21
fairytales 8
false telegraphing 65
fantasy 4, 8, 16, 73, 75, 85, 94, 98, 186, 188
Fargo 41, 202
Fifth Element, The 177
film noir 7, 16
flashbacks 60, 77, 132, 186
Florida Project, The 90, 178
Flow charts 118
found footage 96, 97
four act structure 61
Freud, Sigmund 48

Galaxy Quest 193
Gallows, The 97
Game of Thrones, The 85
Gasligh 195
gaslighting 195
gender and Heroine's journey 72–73
gender fluidity 44
genre 6, 7, 8, 9, 10, 16, 19, 47, 59, 73, 93, 94, 95, 96, 98, 101, 103, 113, 114, 116, 117, 119, 156, 211
Gods Must be Crazy, The 95
Gone with the Wind 180
Good Girls 38
Gravity 176
Guardians of the Galaxy II 55
Guns of Navarone, The 211

Hallucinations 185–87
Handmaid's Tale, The 71
Harry Potter 55, 75
Heroine's Journey 69–72
Hero's Journey 67–69
Hidden Figures 41, 71
hierarchy of needs 46–47
historical 19, 23, 33, 34, 67, 93, 96, 108, 150, 153, 184, 189, 218
homophones 135
House of Cards 190–91
How to Build a Girl 186

INDEX

Hunger Games, The 75, 186, 217
Hyperbole 22

id-driven 48, 52, 56, 105, 113, 114, 152
ideology 24
If These Walls Could Talk 2, 93
Incredibles, The 171
In the Dark 53
Inside Out 31
interactive stories 97
intelligent link 98
intercut scene 189
inverted pyramid 78
Invisible Man, The 195

Journey to the Final Level 117
Jung, Carl 42

Keaton, Buster 150, 186
Kennedy, John F. 26
King's Speech, The 19
Kramer vs. Kramer 72, 73

La Vita è Bella. *See* Life is Good
Lady Bird 152
lampshading 193–95
Land of Skate 117
Lara Croft: Tomb Raider 72
Law and Order 85, 218
Law and Order: UK 85
lead. *See* lede
lede 77
Lee, Spike 183, 210
Legally Blonde 71
Levelland 117
Life Ahead, The 184
Life is Good 93
Lion King, The 33
Little Lame Prince 47
Little Miss Sunshine 47
Logline 6–13, 200

Maguire, Gregory 8
Maid in Manhattan 217
margins 125, 144
Martian, The 55
Mask 53
Maslow, Abraham 46–47

master scene format 124
meaning
    explicit meaning 74, 202, 204, 205, 206, 207
    implicit meaning 202
    referential meaning 201
    symptomatic meaning 204
Midsummer Night's Dream 190
Mighty Morphin Power Rangers 74
mistake 22
Miyazaki, Hayao 13
mockumentary 95, 96, 115
montage 183, 184, 185, 186, 189, 202
Mosquito Coast 21
Mrs. Doubtfire 45
Mulan 6, 7, 206
MVP: Most Vertical Primate 117
myths 8

Nanook of the North 95
Napoleon Dynamite 92
narrative description. *See* action
No Country for Old Men 32
Nomadland 91, 205
non-diegetic 137, 186, 191
non-player characters. *See* NPC
non-verbal 154
NPC or N-P-C 56

obstinate audience 203
Off set 137–38
One Flew Over the Cuckoo's Nest 52
on-the-nose 156
Ordinary People 215
Orpheus 10

Paranormal Activity 97
parentheticals 125, 137, 138, 142
Passive Voice 128
PC or P-C 97–98
persona 44
personal unconscious 42, 44
perspective 9, 26, 31, 34, 35, 36, 37, 38,
    39, 44, 45, 52, 54, 56, 82, 86, 91, 92,
    96, 99, 105, 140, 146, 151, 153, 156,
    174, 181, 192, 193, 207, 211, 213,
    216, 217, 219
Phoenix Forgotten 97
physical traits 53

INDEX

player character. *See* PC
plot 59
Pollock, Donald Ray 193
Potiche 41
Pride and Prejudice and Zombies 94
Prince and the Pauper 11, 40, 58, 223
Pronouns 133–34
protagonists 4, 19, 29–30, 47, 52–53, 55, 60, 69, 72, 75, 102
pseudo-documentary 95, 96, 97
Pulp Fiction 87, 88
Punctuation 162–69
Pursuit of Happyness 47

Queen's Gambit, The 183

random events 98
Rashomon 86
Rear Window 194
recapitulation 64, 98, 154
Red Violin, The 86
Regional phrases 160–62
Rocket Man 19

Scene Headings 125–28
science fiction 7, 16, 45, 82, 94, 177, 188, 194, 217
script competitions 208
scripting foreign languages 156–58
Sequence Structure 66
shadow 44, 45, 46, 56, 70, 199
Shape of Water, The 153, 184, 185
She's Gotta Have It 210
Sherlock Jr. 186
Shining, The 55
shooting script 124
Six Blind Men and an Elephant 36
Skate Kitchen 117
Skateboard Madness 117
Skateboard or Die 117
Skateboarding Revelations: The Skateboard Kid 117
slice-of-life 90
Sling Blade 160
slug 127
Slum Dog Millionaire 82
Smell of Us, The 117
Snow White and the Seven Dwarfs 9

Some Folks Call It a Sling Blade 198
soundbite 159
spec script 124
Spider Man: Far from Home 31
Spider Man: Homecoming 31
Spider-Man 31, 34, 216, 217
Spinal Tap 95
Stallworth, Ron 179, 180–83, 188, 201
Star Trek 45, 194
Star Trek: Deep Space Nine 45, 214
Star Wars 45
Star Wars Episode IV: A New Hope 154
Star Wars: The Force Awakens 46
Star Wars: The Last Jedi 46
Star Wars: The Rise of Skywalker 46
step outline 101–18
Stereotype. *See* Categorical Thinking
story 59
story goals 205
storyboard 13, 16, 138, 147
Structure 59, 66, 76, 79, 84, 88, 99, 101, 104, 114, 118, 209
subtext 140, 155, 182, 206
Superman 214
Swing Blade 198
Swiss Army Man 90
synopsis 118

taglines 7
telegraphing 62, 65, 98, 154, 156
Television scripts 143–46
Terminal, The 91
tertiary characters 57
Three Billboards Outside Ebbing, Missouri 89
ticking clock 62, 64, 69
Tin Drum, The 94
Tootsie 45
Toy Story 31, 206
Transitions 142
Transmedia storytelling 148
treatment 118 *See* synopsis
tritagonist 57
Turn: Washington's Spies 32
Twilight 75

United States vs. Billie Holiday, The 187
unmotivated protagonists 92–93

Venom 217
Vice 19
villain 32
Voice of God 192
voice over 95, 137–38, 180–82, 184, 191–92

Walk the Line 19
WALL-E 31

War Horse 31
Wicked 8
Wizard of Oz, The 8, 60, 62, 63, 64, 66, 67, 68, 73, 74
Wonder 53
Wonder Woman 72
workshop 199–203, 211

You 192

www.ingramcontent.com/pod-product-compliance
Lightning Source LLC
Chambersburg PA
CBHW021826300426
44114CB00009BA/334